The EI Advantage

PUTTING EMOTIONAL INTELLIGENCE INTO PRACTICE

The EI Advantage

PUTTING EMOTIONAL INTELLIGENCE INTO PRACTICE

Patricia McBride

Susan Maitland

The McGraw-Hill Companies

London Burr Ridge IL New York St Louis San Francisco Auckland Bogotá
Caracas Lisbon Madrid Mexico Milan Montreal New Delhi Panama Paris
San Juan São Paulo Singapore Sydney Tokyo Toronto

Published by
McGraw-Hill Professional
Shoppenhangers Road, Maidenhead, Berkshire SL6 2QL
Telephone: 44 (0) 1628 502 500
Fax: 44 (0) 1628 770 224
Website: www.mcgraw-hill.co.uk

British Library Cataloguing in Publication Data
A catalogue record for this book is available from the British Library

Library of Congress Cataloging in Publication Data
The Library of Congress data for this book has been applied for/is available from the Library of Congress

Sponsoring Editor: Elizabeth Robinson
Editorial Assistant: Sarah Wilks
Production Editorial Manager: Penny Grose
Desk Editor: Alastair Lindsay

Produced for McGraw-Hill by Steven Gardiner Ltd, Cambridge
Text and cover design by Senate Design Ltd
Printed and bound in Great Britain by Bell and Bain Ltd, Glasgow

McGraw-Hill

*A Division of The **McGraw·Hill** Companies*

McGraw-Hill books are available at special quantity discounts. Please contact the Corporate Sales Executive at the above address.

ISBN 0 07 709850 1

Patricia's Dedication

This book is dedicated to my partner Rick, who is a wonderfully emotionally intelligent man. Thanks also to him for allowing me to use some of his (disguised) true life stories from his less emotionally intelligent days!

Susan's Dedication

To my family

The authors are grateful to Frances Johnstone for the cartoons

Contents

Introduction 1

Chapter 1   How to use this workbook 5
Chapter 2   The emotional intelligence advantage 9
   ■ What is emotional intelligence? 9
   ■ What are the advantages of emotional intelligence? 12
   ■ What are the disadvantages of not being emotionally
      intelligent? 17
   ■ What are emotions for? 17
   ■ Where do emotions come from? 18
   ■ Habitual behaviour patterns 22
   ■ Why do we block emotions? 23
   ■ What happens when we block emotions? 24
   ■ Are emotional responses universal? 26
   ■ Rules for life 26

SECTION ONE
Personal competence – how we understand and manage ourselves 29
   ■ Definitions of emotions 32
   ■ The three steps to emotional intelligence 33
   ■ Sharing – appropriate self-disclosure 35
   ■ Other forms of support 37
   ■ Identifying benefits 37
   ■ Recording progress 38
Chapter 3   Personal competence advantage 1 Self-awareness 39
   Activity 1 Identifying emotions 39
   Activity 2 Recognizing emotions 41
   Activity 3 Re-stimulation 41
   Activity 4 History revisited 42

                                Activity 5 Positivity log 43

                                Activity 6 Your SWOT analysis 44

                                Activity 7 Treat yourself well 45

Chapter 4   Personal competence advantage 2 Self-confidence 46

                                Activity 1 Identifying parent messages 48

                                Activity 2 Monitoring self-talk 50

                                Activity 3 Goal setting 53

                                Activity 4 Role modelling 54

                                Activity 5 Visualizing confident behaviour 55

                                Activity 6 Advertising yourself 57

Chapter 5   Personal competence advantage 3 Integrity 59

                                Activity 1 Your values 61

                                Activity 2 Integrity scale 63

                                Activity 3 Activity log 64

                                Activity 4 Walking the talk 65

Chapter 6   Personal competence advantage 4 Taking responsibility 67

                                Activity 1 My readiness to accept responsibility 68

                                Activity 2 'Shoulds' into 'coulds' and 'musts' into 'wills' 69

Chapter 7   Personal competence advantage 5 Positive beliefs 71

                                Activity 1 Identifying negative beliefs 72

                                Activity 2 Using visualization to conquer fears 74

                                Activity 3 Positive affirmations 74

Chapter 8   Personal competence advantage 6 Dealing with negative emotions 76

                                Activity 1   Using physical reactions to recognize negative emotions 76

                                Activity 2   Recognizing negative emotions by their outcome 77

                                Activity 3   Changing a negative mood 78

                                Activity 4   Say goodbye to bitterness 80

                                Activity 5   Banishing martyrdom 83

                                Activity 6   Acknowledging your anger 84

                                Activity 7   Overcoming anger 86

                                Activity 8   The two-second pause 87

                                Activity 9   Stop sulking 87

                                Activity 10 Overcoming excessive guilt 89

                                Activity 11 Pushing guilt aside 91

                                Activity 12 Stop worrying 92

                                Activity 13 Allocate worry time 92

                                Activity 14 Beat worry by skill building 92

Activity 15   Using visualization to beat worry 93
Activity 16   Self-questioning 93

SECTION TWO
Relationship competence – how we understand and manage our relationships with others 95

Chapter 9   Relationship competence advantage 1 Empathy skills 100
Activity 1   Your empathy level 101
Activity 2   Your emotional empathy 104
Activity 3   Responding with empathy 105
Activity 4   Seeing another's perspective 107
Activity 5   Loss and bereavement 109
Activity 6   Empathy and body language 113
Activity 7   Reflecting feelings 113
Activity 8   Recognising feeling messages from others 115

Chapter 10   Relationship competence advantage 2 Effective listening 116
Activity 1   Barriers to effective listening 117
Activity 2   Recognizing prejudice 119
Activity 3   Overcoming prejudice 121
Activity 4   Listening to the opposite sex 122
Activity 5   Overcoming distractions 124
Activity 6   Active listening skills 125
Activity 7   Separating viewpoints 126
Activity 8   Rewording skills 127
Activity 9   Summarizing 129
Activity 10   Checking progress 130

Chapter 11   Relationship competence advantage 3 Questioning skills 132
Activity 1   Identifying question types 136
Activity 2   Designing effective questions 137
Activity 3   Practising question types 139
Activity 4   Conversations overheard 139

Chapter 12   Relationship competence advantage 4 Rapport skills 140
Activity 1   Making small talk 144
Activity 2   Discovering values 145
Activity 3   Matching body language 146
Activity 4   Using matching to calm down others 147
Activity 5   Checking assumptions 148
Activity 6   Observing a role model 149
Activity 7   Asking for forgiveness 149

Chapter 13   Relationship competence advantage 5 Control and trust 151
              Activity 1 Stop being controlling 152
              Activity 2 Coping with a controlling partner 154
              Activity 3 Start trusting others 156
Chapter 14   Relationship competence advantage 6 Assertiveness 157
              Activity 1   Assertiveness rating 157
              Activity 2   Asking for what we want 163
              Activity 3   Assertiveness scale 164
              Activity 4   Your unmet needs 166
              Activity 5   Broken record technique 167
              Activity 6   Understanding body language 168
              Activity 7   Your body language 172
              Activity 8   Responding to criticism confidently 172
              Activity 9   Assertive statements for use in receiving criticism 174
              Activity 10 Assertive statements for use in giving criticism 176
              Activity 11 Using choice 179
              Activity 12 Assertive letter 180
              Activity 13 Saying no 182
Chapter 15   Relationship competence advantage 7 Conflict management 185
              Activity 1 Negotiation skills 187
              Activity 2 Conflict skills practice 189
              Activity 3 Accepting responsibility 189
              Activity 4 Own your feelings 190
              Activity 5 Summary exercise 192

SECTION THREE

Leadership competence – how to be an inspiring leader 195

              ■ Six leadership styles 198
              ■ Seven characteristics of emotionally intelligent leaders 198
              ■ Your leadership style questionnaire 200
Chapter 16   Leadership competence advantage 1 Authoritative leadership
              style 202
              Activity 1 Defining the vision 202
              Activity 2 Inspiring others 203
              Activity 3 Increasing creativity and flexibility 206
              Activity 4 Develop your own creativity, flexibility and risk-taking
                          skills 209
              Activity 5 Managing change 210
              Activity 6 Establishing standards 212

Chapter 17   Leadership competence advantage 2 Affiliative leadership style 214
              Activity 1 Positive feedback 215
              Activity 2 Strokes and motivation 215
              Activity 3 Strokes and knowledge of staff 217
              Activity 4 Praise and acknowledgement 218
              Activity 5 Motivation: pleasure and pain 219

Chapter 18   Leadership competence advantage 3 Coercive leadership style 221
              Activity 1 Bullying 221
              Activity 2 Developing a no-blame culture 224
              Activity 3 Encouraging feedback in the workplace 227
              Activity 4 Words that wind people up! 228
              Activity 5 Learning from feedback 229
              Activity 6 Being an inclusive leader 232

Chapter 19   Leadership competence advantage 4 Pace-setting leadership
              style 235
              Activity 1 Feedback for improved quality 235
              Activity 2 Relaxation techniques 239
              Activity 3 Words that wound, sounds that soothe 240

Chapter 20   Leadership competence advantage 5 Democratic leadership
              style 241
              Activity 1 Effective decision-making 242
              Activity 2 Clear boundaries 243
              Activity 3 Asserting your leadership 245
              Activity 4 Delegation 246
              Activity 5 Dealing with difficult people 249
              Activity 6 How to get people to listen to you 252

Chapter 21   Leadership competence advantage 6 Coaching leadership style 254
              Activity 1 Coaching practical skills 254
              Activity 2 Coaching EI skills 257
              What kind of leader are you now? 259

SECTION FOUR
Future competence – understanding and managing continuous personal development 261

              Activity 1 Emotional intelligence achievement record 264
              Activity 2 Emotional intelligence wheel 265
Chapter 22   Future competence advantage 1 Lifestyle appraisal 267
              Activity 1 Relationship balance 267
              Activity 2 Life goals 269

            Activity 3 Wants and not wants 270
            Activity 4 SMART goals 272
            Activity 5 Future goals 273
            Activity 6 Personal aspirations 274
            Activity 7 Work /life balance 275
Chapter 23 Future competence advantage 2 Motivation 277
            Activity 1 Positive motivation 279
            Activity 2 Personal motivators 280
            Activity 3 Personal demotivators 281
            Techniques to get you up and running 283
Chapter 24 Future competence advantage 3 Inner dialogue 285
            Activity 1 Improving inner dialogue 285
Chapter 25 Future competence advantage 4 Visualization 287
            Activity 1 Self-energize 288
            Activity 2 The magic wand 288
            Future competence consolidation questionnaire 290
Chapter 26 Future competence advantage 5 Networking 292
            Activity 1 Current networks 292
            Activity 2 Range of networks 293
            Activity 3 Networking grid 295
            Activity 4 Networking advantages 295
Chapter 27 Future competence advantage 6 Career development 297
            Activity 1 Personal commitment 297
            Activity 2 Identify personal learning and development needs 298
            Activity 3 Career development pathway 299
            Activity 4 Celebrating success 301

Recommended reading 303
Answers to activities 306
Index 307
The EI Advantage workshops 310

Introduction

Common interests typically bring people together and create the foundation for relationships to develop; the idea for this workbook was conceived in precisely that way. Though we originally met through our work within the field of management development, we very quickly became aware of certain shared interests. We found the concept of emotional intelligence particularly intriguing, as it seemed to encompass a set of skills which we had seen in individuals working within cohesive and successful organizations and, equally, were absent in less well-functioning organizations. A profile of these skills would usually indicate high levels of:

- self awareness
- emotional control
- integrity
- initiative
- influencing skills
- flexibility
- assertiveness.

You can see that the abilities identified in this list are transferable between the home, the community and the workplace. It was essentially our interest in this overlap between the 'personal' and the 'professional' that became the subject of many discussions and out of which eventually came the idea for this workbook. This is the Emotional Intelligence Advantage!

Emotional Intelligence – so what's new?

Emotional intelligence currently has a very high profile. There are many reasons for this, some straightforward, others more complex. In the workplace for example, there have been significant organizational changes for many businesses. The uncertainty of global market changes and the need for flatter organizations has brought about a reassessment of existing practices. The benefits of recognizing their 'people' element is becoming more obvious to employers.

Here are some examples of encouraging signs that this notion is becoming more widely acknowledged within the work place:

> *The BBC is* the creativity of its staff. Without them we are nothing. Our people truly are our business.
>
> (Greg Dyke, Director General [designate]
> BBC, IPD Annual Report 1998/99)

> *Emotional Intelligence testing carried out on a group of SME owner-managers . . . showed clearly that owner-managers with low emotional intelligence held back their companies' growth by trying to hold on to total control . . . . Managers who let their people take responsibility and did not hold on to control had high scores on consideration for others, tolerance and sociability. They were also much less stressed than the other owner-managers – and they had profitable, booming companies.*
>
> (Buckholdt Associates, 18 January 2000)

> *After supervisors in a manufacturing plant received training in emotional competencies such as how to listen better and help employees resolve problems on their own, lost-time accidents were reduced by 50 per cent, formal grievances were reduced from an average of 15 per year to 3 per year, and the plant exceeded productivity goals by $250,000.*
>
> (Pesuric & Byham, 1996)

> *In another manufacturing plant where supervisors received similar training, production increased 17 per cent. There was no such increase in production for a group of matched supervisors who were not trained.*
>
> (Porras & Anderson, 1981)

On a wider front, many countries now have a number of common social problems, for example football violence, road rage, drug and alcohol abuse. It might be said that people are no longer prepared to control their impulses, but increasingly demand instant gratification. The common ground here, however, is emotion. This is not to say that emotions make us less effective – quite the reverse. Feelings provide energy, insight and a basis for almost every decision we make. It is 'emotional well-being' that is the key and, like physical well-being, it has to be self-developed.

Because of our work, we were sensitive to the powerful impact that emotional intelligence strategies could have upon organizations, though it seemed to us that there was little available by way of practical and accessible methods of application. There are many excellent reference books but, it seemed to us, a lack of anything in a user-friendly format. For example, those of us who have read Daniel Goleman's publications will no doubt have found them fascinating. As the author credited with popularizing emotional intelligence, Goleman's ground-breaking academic version forms the underpinning framework but is probably not the easiest book to use for personal self-development. We wanted to adapt the principles of emotional intelligence into a self-development toolkit which would appeal equally to individuals, as well as to whole organizations. For us this meant emphasizing the *emotional* part of emotional intelligence.

Soft skills for tough times

The emotionally intelligent person has a competitive advantage in today's world and this will increasingly become the benchmark for the 'normal' or average individual. Many changes in our world are forcing people to re-assess the notion that the expression of emotions should be avoided. It is in fact, not the avoidance of emotions which we should be focusing upon, but the recognition of them, and from where they originate. For example, most of us have been brought up to be 'good girls' or 'good boys', with cultural assumptions about what equates to the average 'good' person.

All of us, the 'good' and the 'bad', are socialized into particular methods of conforming and will revert to tried and tested strategies within our personal and our professional lives. This grounding carries through into adulthood and brings about the assumption that 'good' boys and girls grow up to be desirable employees. The real power behind emotional intelligence lies in being able to identify and recognize where your responses are coming from and to use them positively. You will find out more about this later in 'What is Emotional Intelligence?'

In today's rapidly changing world, however, people trying to act like 'good' five-year-olds do not adapt or cope as well as people who have a more emotionally intelligent approach. For example, 'good' children feel blocked against acting in selfish ways and struggle with making their own needs heard because they fear being seen as 'bad' persons. They can't handle criticism or constructive feedback because of their low self-esteem. They are more emotionally fragile and react to unfair developments like victims and martyrs. How many of these behaviours do you recognise in yourself:

- belittling others' success
- 'forgetting' to say please or thank you
- sulking
- apologizing for something you know is not your fault
- bearing grudges
- shouting
- hitting out.

If you are being honest, you will have reacted in all these ways on a number of occasions. Let's consider for a moment some alternative responses:

When faced with	An emotionally intelligent person would:
The painful end to a long term relationship	Acknowledge the range of emotions which will be experienced but focus on the positive aspects; relationship breakdown is distressing but can also bring about exciting changes
A persistently grumpy colleague	Try to establish the possible reasons for this ill-tempered behaviour – being so miserable can't be much fun
A colleague's unearned' or 'undeserved' promotion	Congratulate them, being secure in your own sense of self-worth
A neighbour's loud music played late at night	Telephone and calmly request the volume to be turned down

As authors, it is our interest in the way that the 'personal' impacts upon and influences the 'professional' that caused us to write this workbook. We are all constantly exposed to this behavioural 'overlap' within our working environment and all therefore need the skills to recognize our own triggers. We hope that this workbook will provide you with the necessary framework to achieve this. There are no magic wands included but by working through this book you will increase your EI dramatically.

You might at this point just want to be aware of a possible side-effect to raising your emotional intelligence levels: you may develop a tendency to 'analyse' friends and family to a degree that could make them uncomfortable! You may even feel that you have less in common with your existing group of friends or that you don't 'fit' so well with them. This is entirely natural and you should see this as part of your emotional intelligence development. Through time, it is quite likely that the people around you will see your behaviour as a positive model and begin to reflect back similar responses.

We hope that your journey to becoming more emotionally intelligent will be challenging, stimulating, worthwhile . . . and fun! Enjoy it!

It is better to swallow words than to have to eat them later.

(F. D. Roosevelt)

Chapter 1

How to use this workbook

Since you are reading this book you may already be familiar with the concept of emotional intelligence. Or perhaps you have noticed that the terms 'Emotional Intelligence', 'EI' (Emotional Intelligence), or 'EQ' (Emotional Quotient), are very topical, and you'd like to find out more. We hope that whatever your level of prior knowledge or interest, you will feel comfortable with the practical approach of this workbook.

It is probably useful to draw your attention to the way we will use the terms 'Emotional Intelligence', or 'EI' at random throughout the book. We see these as interchangeable, and will use them in this way. Full definitions of these and any other keywords will be set out at the appropriate points in each section.

Maybe you have chosen to work through the book alone, or perhaps with a friend or a 'buddy'. You may or may not be familiar with the term 'buddy' – it is certainly one which you will come across frequently throughout this workbook. Here we use the term 'buddy' to mean anyone who will help you through this programme. It could be someone who is also interested in gaining the EI Advantage, so that you will be working through together, giving each other support. This is the method by which you will gain most value from the workbook; having another's perspective is very helpful and encouraging. Alternatively your buddy might be a work colleague who has agreed to be your mentor while you work through the book, or a close friend whose opinions you value.

Or, perhaps, you are happy and confident to work through independently. That is also fine. The main issue is that you should feel that you are gaining as much as you can from the activities and exercises you'll come across.

Maybe you may have registered for The EI Advantage Workshops, more of which you will find at the end of the book. But, whatever the route, your goal, and the outcome we want you to achieve is the Emotional Intelligence Advantage.

Let's look at what you can expect to find in this workbook:

- activities
- case studies
- check lists
- inspirational anecdotes
- flow charts
- quotes
- questionnaires
- recommended reading.

After Chapter 2, which explains what emotional intelligence is, the book is in four sections, each one covering key components of emotional intelligence skills. Section One looks at Personal Competence and how we manage ourselves. In Section Two we move on to Relationship Competence and consider, for example, ways in which we listen to and influence others. Section Three deals with Leadership Competence and offers ideas on how to motivate and inspire. Finally, in Section Four, Future Competence reviews the enormous benefits that emotional intelligence skills can bring to planning your short and long term goals.

This is a workbook and as such is designed to be used interactively. We believe that most people develop their skills by practical methods and therefore we have included a wide range of activities. You may want to improvise on some of these: go ahead. This book should guide rather than instruct you.

We've talked a little already about working with a 'buddy'. If you have not already done so, then you might want to consider finding a friend or colleague to work through this book with you. This person needs to be someone you will feel comfortable disclosing personal information about yourself to. You may find some activities quite challenging and the temptation could be to skip these parts. Look carefully at these: perhaps you want to avoid them because you need them most. If you have a buddy to work with you are more likely to complete the whole book and thereby gain much better value from your time and money!

Either instead of, or in addition to, your buddy, you could consider finding a mentor at work. Again, this should be someone you trust as you may, at some point, be disclosing personal or sensitive information about yourself. If the idea of a mentor appeals, look around your workplace. Look for people you respect and admire. Try approaching one of them and talk to them about becoming your mentor. It is more than likely that they will agree to support you – most people are happy to help, but you need to do the asking!

You could find it helpful to attend some stand-alone training courses while you work through this book. There are various topics that are very relevant to emotional intelligence. For example, courses on Assertiveness, Interpersonal Communication or Team Building would all provide useful underpinning knowledge. Ask around – personal testimony is usually the best recommendation for training. Look at the course programmes, check what the tutor will cover and be clear about what your expectations from the course are.

Whichever route you are taking now, it is worth remembering that the development of emotional intelligence is a continuous process. This is not a manual which can be looked at and absorbed in a day. You will need to practise and reinforce these skills, but you will find that, like learning to drive, once you have acquired the know-how, you will automatically use emotionally intelligent responses in all sorts of situations.

And talking of learning to drive, do you remember how that felt? Learning, be it how to drive or how to become more emotionally intelligent, follows a distinct pattern. Knowing the pattern helps you to feel at ease if you make a mistake, as we all do. There are four stages to learning:

Stage 1 Unconscious incompetence

This is when you don't know how to do something but you are either unaware or unconcerned about it. If we use the driving analogy, it was most likely that before you started driving lessons you were unaware of how much you didn't know.

Stage 2 Consciously incompetent

This is when we begin to learn something new and realize it's harder than we thought. We can feel stupid because we can't do things first time. When driving, this is when the driving instructor says 'Take the next right' and we panic.

Stage 3 Consciously competent

This is when we are getting a skill on board but still have to think how to do it. The driving instructor says 'Turn right' and you think to yourself: 'Indicate, look over shoulder, check mirror, change gear.' You can do it, but you have to concentrate.

Stage 4 Unconsciously competent

This is when we have become so skilled that we don't even think about what we're doing. Ever got to work and realized you don't remember the journey at all? That's unconscious competence.

The reality is that even people who are pretty skilled at emotional intelligence and who usually operate at Stage 4, will occasionally find themselves thrown back into Stage 3. That's fine, that's life. No one gets it right all the time. Becoming emotionally intelligent is a journey, ever more enjoyable as we travel the road.

Everyone can benefit from improving their emotional intelligence – whether they know it or not! Some people just need a tune-up, others a complete overhaul. If you approach this workbook with a genuine wish to have a richer, more contented life, then the activities and case studies contained here should guide you on your way. Good luck!

In twenty years time it will be the things which you did not do that you will regret; not the things you did do!

Chapter 2

The Emotional Intelligence Advantage

What is emotional intelligence?

If you're reading this workbook, there's a good chance that you've heard about emotional intelligence and know at least a little of what it's about. In a nutshell it is:

The ability to recognize that we have emotions, name them, and control them enough to enable us to choose how to behave.

Having emotional intelligence is wonderful. It won't provide you with a trouble-free life – nothing can do that. But it will equip you with the tools to proactively make choices in all areas of your life, and that's a great way to live.

The EI supermarket

Fran Johnstone

So let's look at the types of qualities you might expect to find in someone who is emotionally intelligent. They would:

- be in touch with their emotions
- be able to control their emotions sufficiently to have the best possible communication with others
- be able to express their emotions appropriately
- deal with conflict appropriately
- have good 'boundaries'
- have integrity and be trusted by others
- be flexible in their approach to life and other people
- cope with change effectively
- feel confident
- have realistic awareness of their strengths and weaknesses
- give constructive feedback to others
- accept feedback appropriately
- learn from their mistakes.

But let's go back to our definition. This simple sentence encompasses a whole host of abilities. First of all we must be able to *recognize that we have an emotion*.

Have you ever found yourself opening your mouth and putting your foot it in before you even knew you intended to speak? Have you ever found yourself responding defensively when someone was trying to give you helpful advice? Have you ever found yourself eating fattening food when you weren't even hungry? If these types of situations sound familiar to you, you've been emotionally hijacked. Most of us have. Probably all of us have. And several times.

> **PATRICIA'S EMOTIONAL HIJACK**
> As well as being an author I run courses on management and communication skills. Recently there was a man on one of my courses who looked just like an ex-boyfriend. The ex-boyfriend was a very sexy, lively person and it took all my will not to flirt with the man on the course, he was very attractive and my eyes kept being drawn towards him. On one occasion, just briefly, I failed and flashed him a flirty look. Luckily, he seemed not to notice. Thank goodness I realised what was happening or I could have acted very unprofessionally!

So first of all we have to recognize that the emotion exists *before we take action*. Secondly, it helps if we can *name the emotion*. Most of us recognize when we feel love or fury, but recognizing more subtle emotions is a challenge for many. After all, there are said to be over a thousand words in the English language that describe emotions. Do you, for example, always recognize when you feel jealous, contented, apprehensive, bullied, or embarrassed? By naming the emotion we feel we can bring our conscious mind to bear on the third part of our definition. We can use the thinking part of our brain, the cognitive side, to choose how to respond to the emotion and the situation.

Controlling behaviour enough to choose how we behave, rather than have our emotions control us, is really empowering. We never need to kick ourselves for behaving badly or failing to take necessary steps ever again. We have personal control over our behaviour. We still feel emotions; we can still feel loving, irritated, amused, joyful, angry, threatened, guilty, aroused, bemused and so on. Interestingly though, as we become more emotionally intelligent we will certainly have more positive and less negative feelings. This is because by behaving in an emotionally intelligent way, we deal with situations more appropriately and our lives are improved.

Emotional intelligence is made up of three types of intelligence:

- *abstract intelligence* is the type of intelligence that is judged in traditional IQ tests. The ability to think things through in our minds, using our cognitive abilities – to calculate, to rationalize, to evaluate.
- *concrete intelligence* is the ability to perform concrete tasks that require physical skills. Skilled sports people or craft workers would be examples of people with high concrete intelligence.
- *social intelligence* is the ability to empathize with others, to communicate effectively.

Whilst some people have high skill levels in all three areas it is certainly possible to have very different levels of ability in each. For example, one can find children who are too young for their abstract intelligence to be fully formed but who are well able to empathize with others. You can also find brilliant academics who are barely socially competent. You can find people with learning difficulties who may have high concrete intelligence. For example some learning-disabled autistic children have excellent ability to draw from memory fine detail of buildings they have seen. These same children also have very low social intelligence inasmuch as they don't appear to recognize people as being any more significant than other features in their everyday life.

This workbook does not specifically aim to increase your IQ, but the work needed to increase your emotional intelligence automatically stretches your abstract intelligence. This is because you will think more widely, broaden your horizons and take on other people's points of view as well as your own.

Measuring any sort of intelligence is intrinsically difficult. The people who design the tests inevitably do so from the standpoint of their own culture and what they believe intelligence to be about. For example, IQ tests were originally devised by the US forces to test the suitability of personnel to fight in war. These tests, and those of a similar type, test abstract intelligence valued by Western academics. Who is to say that this type of intelligence is more valuable than the intelligence used by an aborigine negotiating the desert in Australia? Neither is better than the other – they are just different. Sadly, in Western culture judgements are made as to the value of different abstract intelligences.

Likewise, measuring emotional intelligence is fraught with problems. There are many such tests available but the results should be treated with care. One feature of poor emotional intelligence is the inability to see ourselves clearly. It follows then that someone with poor insight into their own behaviour is unlikely to complete a questionnaire accurately.

> *Pay attention. You never know what disguise your next teacher will be wearing.*
>
> (Anon)

What are the advantages of emotional intelligence?

As we've already seen, being emotionally intelligent means that you are able to control your emotions to widen your repertoire of coping skills. Let's look at a few of the specific advantages that EI brings.

Improved relationships

Whether we are talking about working with colleagues, friendships or romantic relationships, emotional intelligence is vitally important. Without the ability to empathize, to keep calm in the face of another person's needs and wants, to be flexible enough to sustain a relationship, things can go badly wrong.

Improved communication with others

When we act with emotional intelligence we improve our communication with others because we develop a whole set of skills and strategies that allow for more meaningful communications.

Better empathy skills

Empathy is a core EI skill in communication. Without the ability to feel how the other person might be feeling, we are unlikely to have a close relationship or influence others effectively. They will always feel that we don't really understand them – and they'll be right.

Acting with integrity

Integrity is another core EI ability. It means being integrated; behaving in a way that is consistent with our core beliefs; being true to ourselves and honest with others. Integrity is a central theme of this workbook.

Respect from others

Because you act with emotional intelligence and integrity other people will respect and trust you. They know that you are flexible, honest, empathetic and straightforward in your dealings.

Improved career prospects

All managers want to employ someone who is emotionally intelligent. They won't necessary call it that though. They'll say they're looking for someone with:

- good communication skills
- ability to work as part of a team
- creativity
- flexibility
- ability to work independently and proactively.

Clued-up managers know that they can train people in technical skills much more quickly than they can train them in emotional intelligence.

Manage change more confidently

People with low EI often find change difficult. They don't feel confident enough in themselves to bend and adapt with the wind of change. This means they often turn their face against change, denying the need for it and eventually lose out as progress happens around them. Instead of embracing change and growing with it, they change only when forced to, and then reluctantly and with poor grace.

Fewer power games at work and home

Have you ever worked somewhere where people 'played games'? Most of us have experienced workplace politics and home confrontations, and know how time consuming, energy sapping and distressing they can be. Here are just a few of the games you might have experienced. Later in the workbook we provide exercises to help you to avoid this game playing.

- *'If it weren't for you . . .'*. This player blames the other person for their lack of success in a given area. 'If it weren't for you I'd be happy.' 'If it weren't for you I'd be a manager by now.'
- *'Yes, but . . .'* . This player asks for advice but rarely takes it. There's always a 'good' reason why your suggestions won't work.
- *'Got you now!'*. People who don't give you enough information to enable you to complete a task well play this. The pay-off for them is that they can feel superior when they see you fail.
- *'Victim, persecutor, rescuer'* – a common game with three or more players. In this game one person is victimized by the persecutor. The rescuer then steps in to sort out the situation. Commonly played at home as well as at work. At home it's often mother who rescues the children who are being persecuted by father. A dangerous game in any arena because the roles often swop around with alarming speed and the rescuer becomes the victim.

Many of these games are about avoiding responsibility – emotionally intelligent people always accept responsibility for their own actions.

> *We cannot become what we need to be by remaining what we are.*
>
> (Anon)

Feeling confident, positive and at peace with yourself

The wonderful thing about being emotionally intelligent is that it increases your confidence, enabling you to take a positive view of life and be at peace with yourself. Why? Well, imagine your life when you don't have to:

- kick yourself for saying the wrong thing
- feel bad because you avoided a difficult situation you should have dealt with

- feel guilty about acting without integrity
- worry excessively
- continually notice other people's failings
- getting in a muddle with situations because your boundaries are unclear.

Sound good? Emotional intelligence won't promise you a stress-free life or guarantee that everything will go smoothly for you. It will give you the personality and skills to deal with situations in the best possible way as they arise.

Reduced stress levels

Feeling confident and emotionally intelligent won't eliminate stress – life isn't like that. It will reduce it though, enabling you prioritize, take an objective as well as subjective view of situations and give you a range of coping skills.

Increased creativity

Poor emotional intelligence means that we get stuck in habitual ways of behaving and this reduces creativity. In this context we take creativity to mean the ability to look at situations from a variety of perspectives and consider a wide range of possible solutions. Emotional intelligence allows us to do this and also to take our own emotional viewpoint into consideration.

Learning from mistakes

For many people, mistakes they make over and over again are 'just me'. They don't realize that they can learn from them and thus avoid making the same mistakes in future. One of the reasons we continue to make the same mistakes is because we don't complete what is known as the learning cycle (Figure 2.1).

FIGURE 2.1

The learning cycle (adapted from David Kolb's model) (*Source*: Kolb, D. A. (1984) *Experiential Learning*, reprinted by permission of Pearson Education Inc., Upper Saddle River, NJ 07458

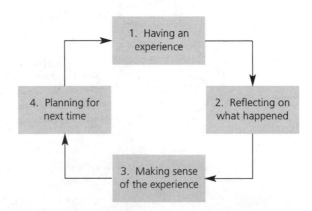

Let's demonstrate how this model works using a common experience – having the same kind of disagreement with the same person several times.

In stage one, we have an experience – let's say we have a disagreement with old Barney yet again. You can see that some people never get past this stage – they keep having the same argument again and again.

By moving on to stage two they could reflect on the situation. Did you approach Barney in the same way? Did you take offence where none was intended? Did you choose the right time for the discussion?

In stage three you weigh up all the arguments and reach a conclusion. Stage four is where you plan how to tackle Barney next time.

We've looked at what happens to people who only use stage one. Other people might prefer stage two. They like to reflect on experiences so much that they never move through the cycle to actually do anything different, or sometimes even anything at all!

People who like stage three will enjoy theories and models but again, may not turn them into reality.

Those who feel most comfortable with stage four are very pragmatic and want to know whether something will work in practice. This could mean that they rush into the first thing that works without reflecting on whether something else would work better.

With the emotional intelligence you will gain through this workbook, you can ensure that you benefit from each learning experience you have.

Learning experience

Fran Johnstone

What are the disadvantages of not being emotionally intelligent?

The short answer is that the disadvantages are the opposite of the advantages already spelt out. It's worth spending a minute though looking at how other people see someone who lacks emotional intelligence. Of course, this lack shows itself in different ways in different people. In fact, the same person may be quite 'adult' in some areas of their life and quite emotionally childish in others.

Some of the things that people might say about someone who lacks emotional intelligence are:

- 'You never know where you are with him, he changes with the wind'
- 'She's always acting like a-two year-old'
- 'He's a bully'
- 'It's no good asking her, she couldn't make a decision to save her life'
- 'He's completely inflexible'
- 'Twenty years' experience? More like one year used twenty times!'
- 'I daren't ask her to do that, she couldn't say "no" even if it really inconvenienced her'
- 'He never takes responsibility for his own actions'
- 'It must be nice being perfect!'
- 'I wish my manager would sort this out, but he doesn't do conflict.'

Much, much nicer to be someone people like, trust and respect.

What are emotions for?

> *Emotion* – *a moving of the feelings; agitation of the mind; any of various phenomena of the mind, such as anger, joy, fear, or sorrow, associated with physical symptoms; feelings as distinguished from cognition or will.*
>
> (Chambers Dictionary, 1995)

Probably emotions were originally for two main purposes. First, for procreation, to ensure the continuation of humankind. Powerful feelings of attraction may lead to conception and powerful feelings of love to protection of infants.

Second, feelings are necessary for safety. Without instinctive reactions to danger and the consequent fight, freeze or flight responses, humans would not have stood much chance against other animals and the elements.

Emotions don't just give us these *psychological* advantages though, they also provide the necessary *physiological* changes to carry them through. So with sexual attraction, human bodies prepare themselves in a number of different ways for intercourse. Similarly, when danger is sensed increased blood flow to the muscles allows us to run away or fight more effectively.

Now, of course, whilst these basic emotions are still vitally important, it is a necessity of everyday life to be in tune with subtler emotions and their effects.

Where do emotions come from?

Sometimes we can be stunned with our swift emotional response to a situation and find ourselves wondering, 'where did *that* come from?' There are many answers to the question of where emotions come from and perhaps the simplest way is to divide the answer into two – the physiological and the psychological.

Physiologically we can say that the part of the brain called the amygdala is the centre of emotion. The brain has two amygdala, one on each side. These are essential if we are to experience emotions. Research has shown that humans whose amygdala has been damaged lack emotion, as do animals whose amygdala have been surgically removed.

The more 'rational', analytical part of the brain, the neocortex, can be hijacked by the amygdala when the stimulus is very powerful. Using our definition of emotional intelligence, we would recognize an emotion, analyse it and decide how to act. With emotional hijacking the neocortex is effectively bypassed and we act impulsively and sometimes unwisely.

People born with fully functioning brains inherit an ability to feel emotions. As we have seen, emotions are essential to physical as well as psychological well-being. However, the extent to which we feel any emotion varies tremendously with the individual. We could call this the psychological foundation to emotions.

Childhood experiences play a huge part in our ability to experience emotions. For example, in some families feelings are openly displayed and discussed whilst in others they are well controlled and never acknowledged.

Our brain constantly stores memories and those events which were very powerful emotionally or which were repeated many times will be very dominant in our amygdala. So it could be that we remember very little about periods in our lives when things chugged along with few changes. However, once momentous events take place they are firmly stored in the amygdala.

The earlier in life a meaningful memory is laid down, the more powerful hold it will have throughout life. In fact, research suggests that dramatic events probably change the make-up of the brain.

This analogy might help you understand what happens. If you take a route to a particular destination just once and then want to take it again some time later you will probably have to look it up again. You will certainly have to search your brain for which way to go. However, once you have taken the same route many times it is as if your car finds its own way.

We have all experienced the situation where we set off on a journey and realize that instead of going towards our destination, we are unconsciously heading towards some very familiar place – our workplace, for example. It is as if our brains have been bypassed and our muscles are driving the car for us.

A similar thing happens to the emotional networks in our brain. When an event occurs a chemical pathway is laid down in our brain. If the same thing happens over and over again, or the event is very powerful, the pathway gets thicker and thicker. When triggered by a stimulus that reminds us of the original event (even unconsciously), we react in the old, well-rehearsed way even though it may not be the best way to respond. Our emotions, like our car, have gone onto automatic pilot.

Psychologically then, emotions come from events in our lives. Or do they? It's not quite that simple, unfortunately. After all, lots of people may have faced the same situation yet have reacted differently. Sticking with the driving analogy, some people barely notice bad drivers whilst others instantly experience road rage. So our emotions will be made up of our inherent abilities plus the combination of events we face throughout life and what we have made of them.

We have already seen that emotions affect our behaviour. Most of us can point to bits of our behaviour we could well do without. Whilst it makes sense to work towards changing this behaviour, don't be hard on yourself for past 'mistakes'. One way of looking at it is that we made a decision at some earlier point in our life that this behaviour was the best we could do at the time. In this sense the decisions were quite wise when you were two or four or five or whatever. Now, of course, the behaviour might be quite inappropriate, but it is not until you undertake some personal development work such as in this workbook that you can begin to change it.

Let's look at some examples of 'wise' early decisions. By the way, some 'wise' decisions may have happened when you were so young that you can't remember them.

Experience	Behaviour decision
Father responds more affectionately to Jane when she accidentally behaves in a 'girly' way	Jane learns to always act in a very feminine way
Tony has a role model of a tough talking father	Tony emulates his father to gain his approval
Maya is ignored except when she is naughty	Maya decides to be naughty to get attention
Kate only gets attention she she is good	Kate decides always to be a good girl
Sally regularly hears her mother and her mother's friends talk about men who have affairs	Sally learns that men are untrustworthy
Chris only gets attention when his parents want something from him	Chris decides that people who give him attention are after something
When Toby's father is drunk and he spots Toby looking at him, he shouts, 'Who do you think you're looking at?' and lashes out	Toby learns to avoid eye contact with others
Gail and her siblings are given the clear message that children should be seen and not heard	Gail and her siblings decide to say little
A common saying in Dan's family is 'Look before you leap'	Dan learns not to take risks
Nick's mother is unpredictable in her approach and Nick never knows whether he might get a hug or a smack	Nicl learns to be suspicious about other people's intentions
Mandy's father has an explosive temper and her mother tiptoes around him, constantly trying to keep the peace	Mandy learns to submerge her own needs and avoid conflict at all costs
James is told, 'Those that ask don't get, and those that don't ask don't want'	James learns never to ask for anything
A common saying in Pasha's house is, 'If something's worth doing, it's worth doing well'	Pasha becomes a perfectionist

Margaret is a sickly child and is teased for being poor at sport at school	Margaret learns to despise sport
Darren's mother and father are clearly nervous of meeting his teachers and other professionals	Darren learns that professional people are more important than his parents and are to be respected. He begins to 'learn his place'
Mark comes from a big family where if you didn't grab something quickly it was gone	Mark learns to take what he wants without consideration for others
Ann gets little affection from her parents, and spends her time with her dog who is always affectionate	Ann becomes a fierce campaigner for animal rights but has no close friends
Her uncle who shows her much affection sexually abuses Tara	Tara becomes very promiscuous early in life as she has learned this is how to get affection

As Bryn Collins says in her book *Emotional Unavailability*, 'What begins as a protective device becomes a destructive habit . . . .'

It's easy to get into blaming parents for poor parenting skills and it's true that a minority of parents knowingly mistreat their children. The majority, though, just parent their children in the way they were parented. Why would they do otherwise unless they become self-reflective, learn some psychology or attend parenting classes? If you are a parent you have probably occasionally heard your parents' words coming out of your mouth when you speak to your children. Most parents have, and many have kicked themselves having sworn they'd never do exactly that!

Bryn Collins aptly points out that many baby-boomers were brought up by people whose parents were raised by people who were Victorians. This was when children were expected to be seen and not heard. Emotions were considered a sign of great weakness and discouraged. The 'stiff upper lip' was seen as a great virtue.

But this rigid way of teaching people how to parent didn't stop in the Victorian era. In the 1930s psychologist John B. Watson wrote a book called *The Psychological Care of Infant and Child*. It was to have a widespread effect on beliefs about child care. Watson believed in rigid codes of behaviour, and wouldn't consider the emotional side of human behaviour. In one chapter of his book entitled 'Too much mother love' he warned his readers, 'When you are tempted to pet your child, remember that mother love is a dangerous instrument. An instrument which may inflict a never-healing wound, a wound which may make infants unhappy, adolescence a nightmare, an instrument which may wreck your adult son or daughter's vocational future and their chances for marital happiness . . . . Never hug or kiss them, never let them sit in your lap. If you must, kiss them once on the forehead when they say goodnight. Shake hands with them in the morning.' (Watson is described as having a ne'er-do-well father whom he hated all his life and a devoutly religious mother. One has to wonder how much this upbringing influenced his views.)

Other advice on parenting from experts at the same time was also pretty damaging. 'Never praise your child or he'll get a big head' was one such piece of advice. Another was that thumb-sucking must be stopped at all costs. If putting mittens on the child's hands or dabbing unpleasant tasting lotions on the offending thumbs didn't work, parents were advised to tie the baby's wrists to the sides of the cots.

It was not until the 1950s that the much gentler teachings of Dr Spock taught parents that emotions should be considered and that children need love from both mother and father (involving fathers in this way was a revolutionary idea at the time).

Habitual behaviour patterns

As you work through the activities in this book, you will become more consciously aware of your own habitual ways of behaving. You may find that memories of the root of the behaviour come back and it will be helpful if they do. But don't worry if this doesn't happen. You can continue to work towards changing emotions and behaviour even if you can't remember earlier events.

The examples of early life decisions have tended to concentrate on family life, but it's worth considering that this is not the only influence on us. Other external influences that affect our feelings include our:

- gender
- class
- race
- age
- colour
- ability/disability level
- position in our family
- education
- religion
- income
- size
- geographical location.

Later life experiences can also affect our emotions and feelings of self-worth. Being in a damaging relationship, for example, can pretty quickly turn a confident person into someone with poor self esteem. Being bullied at work can have the same effect.

Why do we block emotions?

REAL LIFE STORY – PATRICIA WRITES:
'I was recently on holiday in a foreign country when I noticed a woman walking along with her two sons. They stopped and she badly twisted the ear of the younger son, aged about five. He whimpered and walked on. She then turned her attention to the older boy, aged about seven. Almost pulling his ear off she gave him a good talking to, speaking directly into his ear. As we waited at the same bus stop the younger boy was still rubbing his ear and whimpering. His mother's response was to hit him in the face with the side of her fist. The older boy had already learned his lesson though. He stood like a stone despite the fact that his ear must have been very painful. He'd already learned to block emotions. Poor lads.'

We have already acknowledged that some people are readily in touch with their emotions whilst others are not. Some people may be emotionally illiterate because feelings were never acknowledged in their family. The role models they saw day after day taught them to deny or remain in ignorance of their emotions.

Other people block emotions because they had very bad childhood experiences. Children, like those described above, who are constantly subjected to distressing events often tune down their emotions as a way of coping, of getting through the bad times. It's a good protection mechanism at the time. They mentally turn away from what is going on, telling themselves that it doesn't matter. This is an example of a sensible decision in early life that needs to be revisited.

These abuses do not have to be physical. Emotional abuses that can lead to blocked emotions include:

- ignoring the child
- constantly telling the child to her face that she is worthless
- telling other people in front of the child that he is worthless
- never giving praise
- giving punishments that are very extreme in relation to the 'offence'
- telling the child that harsh punishment is 'for your own good'
- being emotionally unavailable to the child – giving insincere attention.

Sadly when we block negative emotions so powerfully we can accidentally block the ability to feel positive emotions also. This means that we become an adult with little awareness of our emotional inner life. We fail to feel the benefits of love, hope, optimism, joy, and humour. What we notice in the emotional land-scape, if we notice much at all, is dull and colourless.

Emotional landscape is a useful metaphor for thinking about what we notice in the world, both emotionally and otherwise. The world offers us far too much data in terms of visual, auditory, odour and emotional input for us to be able to take it all in. So we select what we notice. Mostly this selection is unconscious.

Here's a way to understand this. Imagine you are a cartographer called upon to make a map of London. Before you put pen to paper you have to ask the purpose of the map. A tourist map would be very different from an ordnance survey map or a road map. Cartographers have to know what features to select from the landscape before they set to work, otherwise they would have to draw a map as big as the town. In the same way we constantly select features from our own landscape to notice. Much of this is done unconsciously.

Have you noticed sounds around you until you read this sentence? Now they've been bought to your attention you will become consciously aware of them (or their absence) for a while. What about that feeling in your left foot? How hungry are you?

Once your attention is focused you notice what was always there. In our every-day lives we generally focus on much more important issues than the examples above – although some people prefer to focus on the trivial and ignore the important. Generally though we consider a range of topics such as politics, our beliefs about people, religion and a whole host of major and minor issues, including our emotional state. The Personal Competence section of this book is especially strong on helping you to identify your emotional state and landscape.

We don't see things as they are, we see them as we are.

(Anais Nin)

What happens when we block emotions?

We have already seen that blocked negative emotions can lead to blocked positive emotions. However, blocked emotions have an uncomfortable way of popping out all over the place. Think of it like trying to squeeze a partially inflated balloon between your fingers. As fast as you squash one bit, another bit pops out.

What this means is that we find ourselves responding in an emotionally illiterate way to particular events. These responses are often rooted in child-hood and we behave as if we were still that age. Here is another example of emotional hijacking:

PATRICIA'S HIJACKING

Recently I was on holiday in Vancouver and my partner and I decided to hire bicycles from a hire shop in the city centre and ride to and around a big park. I hadn't ridden a bike for ages and my bike is an old sit-up-and-beg version. Imagine my horror when I was handed a state-of-the-art mountain bike. We got outside the shop and I tried to get on. The seat was too high, the handlebars were too low and I nearly had to fracture my wrists to use the brakes. Traffic roared by (on the wrong side of the road of course) and I found myself instantly in four-year-old mode. 'I don't want to do this!' I said, getting off quickly. (My partner tells me my bottom lip was trembling.) 'I won't do it'!' And all before I'd even considered whether the handlebars, seat etc. could be shifted to suit me.

Patricia's mountain bike experience is an example of regressing to four-year-old behaviour. Can you identify with any of the following examples?

- Reverting to childlike behaviour when with our parents. Some people find themselves slotting into behaving like a good boy or girl. Others find themselves behaving like a rebellious teenager. It is often not until our parents are very elderly and roles become reversed that this pattern changes.

- People experiencing mid-life crisis often revert to adolescent behaviour. We've all heard of people who leave their partners for someone much younger. Along the way they buy sports cars, get their ear pierced, drink more than they should, and generally act is if they were eighteen.

- People who are frustrated often revert to child-like behaviour, crying, shouting or stamping their feet.

Of course no one admits they're behaving like a two-year-old, a teenager, or whatever. We're much cleverer than that. We find all sorts of ways to justify our behaviour and *none of it is our fault* (according to us). Just listen to the guests on shows such as Oprah or Jerry Springer. You'll be stunned at how little responsibility they take for their own actions.

Sometimes people block out their negative feelings about others only to have them pop out in 'innocent' hurtful remarks. Sometimes they block out negative feelings about themselves by bluster and cockiness.

Success is not spontaneous combustion. You have to set yourself on fire.

(Anon)

Are emotional responses universal?

Whilst it is certainly true that people worldwide feel emotions, it is also true that the type of emotional response varies from person to person and culture to culture. In some countries, for example, the following behaviours would be regarded with disgust or mistrust:

■ showing the soles of your feet

■ using a handkerchief and then putting it in your pocket

■ a woman wearing clothes that expose her shoulders and arms

■ a woman putting out her hand first to shake hands with a man

■ a woman looking a man in the eye.

In most countries these behaviours would be of no particular significance, whilst in others they offend. In the same way, behaviour that delights or appals one person may be unremarkable to another. This again suggests that behaviour, whilst biologically based, is culturally influenced.

Rules for life

Before you embark on your voyage of discovery working through the activities in the remainder of this workbook you might enjoy these 'Rules for Life' we came across. Number 10 will make you smile.

1. You will receive a body. You may like it or hate it, but it will be yours for the entire period this time around.

2. You will learn lessons. You are enrolled in a full-time informal school called life. Each day in this school you will have the opportunity to learn lessons. You may like the lessons or think them irrelevant and stupid.

3. There are no mistakes, only lessons. Growth is a process of trial and error experimentation. The 'failed' experiments are as much a part of the process as the experiment that ultimately 'works'.

4. A lesson is repeated until it is learned. A lesson will be presented to you in various forms until you have learned it. When you have learned it, you can then go on to the next lesson.

5. Learning lessons does not end. There is no part of life that does not contain its lessons. If you are alive, there are lessons to be learned.

6. 'There' is no better than 'here'. When your 'there' has become a 'here', you will simply obtain another 'there' that will, again, look better than 'here'.

7. Others are merely mirrors of you. You cannot love or hate something about another person unless it reflects to you something you love or hate about yourself.

8. What you make of life is up to you. You have the tools and resources you need. What you do with them is up to you. The choice is yours.

9. Your answers lie inside you. The answer to life's questions lies inside you. All you need do is look, listen and trust.

10. You will forget all this.

(Anonymous)
Reproduced with kind permission of John Seymour Associates Ltd,
NLP Consulting & Training 0117 955 7827

Personal competence
How we understand and manage ourselves

Personal competence in emotional intelligence is important because it enables us to:

- recognize and accurately label our emotions
- control our emotions appropriately
- choose how to react
- increase our confidence in our ability to act appropriately in any situation
- use different aspects of our personality for maximum flexibility.

This section contains information and exercises on:

- self-awareness
- developing self confidence
- emotional control
- understanding your values
- integrity
- belief systems
- accepting responsibility
- seeing yourself as others see you.

Personal competence is the foundation for all other emotional intelligence competences. To achieve personal competence you must be self aware, aware of your emotions and able to control them. This gives you the widest possible choice of behaviour styles; a clear winner when it comes to communication and confidence. Personal competence is about using a wide range of abilities, for example being able to use both the logical and emotional parts of our brain.

Another way of looking at this would be to say that we use both the male and female parts of our personality. Traditionally these would be:

Male	*Female*
■ logical	■ intuitive
■ goal follower	■ instinctive
■ self focused	■ other focused
■ good spatial abilities	■ good verbal abilities

By calling on all these aspects of ourselves we are more likely to engage in the three types of intelligence mentioned in the previous section – concrete, abstract and social intelligence. In terms of working towards increased personal competence, we can say that our concrete intelligence will allow us to identify situations where we would like to improve our emotional intelligence. Our abstract intelligence allows us to reflect on the past and imagine a different future. Our social intelligence allows us to work with a buddy to enlarge our knowledge of ourselves through their help and support.

Activities in this section help you to develop all these abilities. First though, let's take another look at emotions.

Definitions of emotions

It is useful to consider that emotions are on two levels. There are the big four emotions that we all recognize such as anger, joy, sadness and fear. However, there are usually other emotions we feel before we reach these stronger emotions. Knowing these can be helpful because simply naming the big emotions doesn't always help us to know what to do to put things right (or in the case of joy, keep doing it right). Naming the emotions that led to anger, joy, depression or fear provides that information.

Here are some possible emotions that might lead to ANGER:

- irritation
- annoyance
- animosity
- bitterness
- frustration
- exasperation
- upset
- resentment
- defeat
- displeasure
- stress
- hostility.

You can see that the actions needed to overcome bitterness, which may have been locked inside us for years, are different from those needed to overcome exasperation at something that's happening right now.

Here are some emotions that may lead to JOY:

- pleasure
- delight
- bliss
- gladness
- happiness
- satisfaction
- tranquillity
- gratification
- amusement
- rapture
- merriment.

Likewise, action needed to continue to feel tranquil is quite different from action needed to feel merriment.

And some emotions that may lead to DEPRESSION:

- sadness
- misery
- gloom
- dejection
- remorse
- unhappiness
- anguish
- grief
- distress
- despondency
- regret
- melancholy.

Action needed to overcome grief is different from action needed to overcome regret.

And finally some emotions that may lead to FEAR:

- nervousness
- dread
- terror
- worry
- apprehension
- fright
- trepidation
- consternation
- dismay
- alarm
- uneasiness
- anxiety.

And action needed to overcome nervousness is different to action needed to overcome alarm.

Activities in this section of the workbook will help you to develop the skills of differentiating between these second-level emotions. This fine tuning will help you with step one to personal competence.

The three steps to personal competence

STEP 1   *Recognizing that we have an emotion*

The first step to personal competence is just recognizing that we have an emotion. Sounds simple, but as we saw in the last chapter, many people have learned to blot out emotions, to deny even to themselves that they have them. But everyone has emotions, however deeply buried. The exercises in this section will help you to recognize that you have emotions by bringing them to your conscious awareness.

A good friend tells you that she has landed a wonderful new job. More money, a company car and lots of travel.

You find yourself gritting your teeth and forcing yourself to say the right things.

Unexpected reaction to a friend's good news

Fran Johnstone

STEP 2   *Being able to label the emotion*

If you have become skilled at ignoring your emotions it may take some practice until you can accurately label the emotion you feel. However, once you are able to do this, you can bring logic into play to help you to analyse why you feel the way you do and what steps you can appropriately take. Remember, you should listen to your emotions – they're often a useful guide to how to behave. However, emotions sometimes lead us into unwise behaviour and this is when the emotional control is especially needed.

Because you are becoming more emotionally literate you realise that are not happy about your friend's success. Asking yourself why, you realise that she has achieved something you want. You correctly identify the emotion as jealousy.

STEP 3   *Controlling the emotion so that you can choose how to behave*

When you label your emotions, you can often identify logically why you have them. This presents you with an opportunity to work out alternative ways of thinking and behaving for yourself. Negative emotion, Activity 3 on mood change (p. 78) will be particularly helpful for getting those emotions under control.

From there, instead of feeling powerless and unhappy in the face of your friend's 'good fortune', you can work out how you can improve your job prospects. This means that you claim personal power for yourself over how you control this aspect of your future.

Accepting that you can make choices in your life about your behaviour and the steps you take is tremendously empowering. It stops you feeling like a victim and leaves you feeling positive and strong about the future.

A TRUE STORY – JACK'S LOSS OF VOICE
Jack met Lisel on holiday in Holland and they fell head over heels in love. It was a long-distance relationship, but luckily Jack could afford to go to Holland occasionally and better still, Lisel worked for an airline and got frequent free tickets. This meant that they met most weekends. Although at first everything

was magical, over a period of time Jack realized that he was getting dissatisfied with the relationship because Lisel could be very overwhelming. A great talker and organizer, she would pack their weekends with activities and not give him time to breathe. His needs were rarely taken into account.

Over a period of a couple of years Jack fell out of love and after much soul-searching decided to end the relationship. He kept putting off giving Lisel the bad news all weekend. Eventually, he realized that he'd have to say something on the way to the airport. Getting into the car, he found he couldn't speak, he had lost his voice completely. It would have to wait until next time, he thought.

Two weekends later Lisel visited again. All weekend he tried to find the right words. He thought it through logically and calmly, after all he was an intelligent, reflective sort of person. Sunday evening came and they set off to the airport together. It happened again – his voice went completely, so the words remained unspoken. When he got home a friend phoned and he answered the phone speaking normally quite without thinking.

When the call finished Jack sat and thought, realizing that this couldn't be a coincidence. He hadn't been aware that the unpleasant thing he had to say was affecting him emotionally, but now he realized that he was just awash with emotions. Fear at Lisel's anticipated strong response. Guilt at finishing the relationship. Sadness that it hadn't worked out. Worry about finding another person to love. Enough to make anyone lose their voice.

Have *you* ever behaved in a way that's surprised you?

Sharing – appropriate self-disclosure

This section gives you a range of activities to improve your personal competence. Some you can do alone, some are best done with someone else. To maximize your learning, we would recommend that you share as much of your learning as you can with at least one person you trust. A reminder: be aware of the exercises you shy away from doing. They could just be the ones that would help you most . . . .

Sharing your learning helps you to develop a truer picture than you could ever gain on your own. After all, how are we to know if our perception of how others see us is accurate? With the help of a trusted friend or partner you can get a much clearer picture. And talking of pictures here is a useful way of seeing personal development.

Johari's window is a useful way of looking at the benefits of self-disclosure, and by working with someone else on the activities in this workbook you will inevitably be disclosing information about yourself. When we disclose more

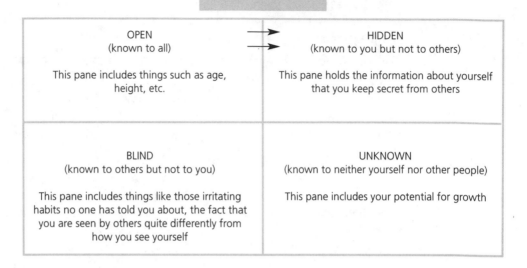

from our hidden area, others are more likely to give us feedback from the blind area. This mutual disclosure takes us into the unknown area and unlocks our potential for growth.

There are many advantages of appropriate self-disclosure. When we disclose appropriate information about ourselves we encourage others to do the same and this deepens the relationship. This is known as the norm of reciprocity. I tell you something and you reciprocate by telling me something in return. Self-disclosure can also help because when someone accepts who you are when you tell them something private about yourself, it validates you as a person and increases your feelings of self-worth.

A word about appropriateness. What is appropriate to say to one person in a given situation may be quite inappropriate in another situation. Here are some general guidelines showing typical relationships and the things one might disclose in that relationship:

Relationship	Appropriate information to disclose
Domestic partner	Pretty much anything assuming the relationship is healthy and non-abusive
Close friend	Fairly detailed information about yourself, information about yourself in relationships with others if this does not breech confidentiality
Friend	Information in less depth about yourself and your life
Acquaintance	General information about your life, little depth of conversation
Stranger	General topics such as the weather, travel, etc.

If you disclose too much information too soon, you might alarm the other person. You can test the water by disclosing a small piece of information and then, by watching their verbal and non-verbal response to what you say, adjust your level. Hopefully, if you are working through this workshop with a trusted friend you will quickly find yourself able to disclose a high level of information.

Other forms of support

Sometimes undertaking personal development work such as that in this workbook raises difficult issues from the past. Even valued friends may not have the skills to help you if this is the case. If this situation arises for you, do consider seeking the advice of an appropriate counsellor.

Identifying benefits

Before you move on to the activities in the remainder of this section you may like to reflect on the benefits for you of becoming more emotionally intelligent.

Benefits for you	Benefits for your organization	Benefits for those close to you

Recording progress

This workbook provides many opportunities for you to record your learning as you increase your emotional wisdom. You may also like a notebook so that you can record additional progress. Below is a 'learning log' based on the four steps to emotional intelligence. You may like to photocopy it and record your learning over a period so that you can give yourself a regular pat on the back. There is no need to write reams, just brief notes to remind you of progress. Remember, you can learn just as much from what you handle badly as what you do well. It's all about reflecting on what happened and asking yourself what you would do differently in future.

LEARNING LOG

Date ....

What happened? (brief details)

What pre-existing assumptions did I have before the situation happened?

How did the assumptions affect my approach to the situation?

How did I feel during the incident?

How did I behave during the incident?

Did my feelings overtake my behaviour? If not, what steps did I take to control my feelings?

What have I learned for the future?

Chapter 3
Personal competence advantage 1
Identifying emotions

When you are self-aware you are alive to your feelings and how they affect your thoughts and behaviour. You can assess, with reasonable accuracy, your strengths and weaknesses, and feel confident about your ability to deal with situations.

People with high self-awareness act in an assertive, adult way, consciously being aware of their behaviour and the effect it has on themselves and others. They can 'stand outside themselves' and watch themselves so that they can adjust their behaviour to achieve the best outcome.

Self-awareness activity 1 – identifying emotions

If you find it difficult to identify your emotions, the methods below will help you develop this skill.

Practise becoming aware of feelings in your body. Do you ever have a sinking feeling in your stomach or experience an 'adrenalin high'? Emotions always have an effect on our body. Sometimes this effect is so subtle we hardly notice it, sometimes it is so strong it forces itself into our consciousness. Here are some examples that you may have experienced.

- When you have a near miss when driving you get hot and your skin prickles
- When you are embarrassed you often laugh
- When you feel shame you often get hot
- When you see someone you fancy or something that interests you your pupils get larger
- When you are frustrated you may laugh, get warm, move uncomfortably
- When there is danger to your self-image, you may feel light fear or embarrassment accompanied by laughter and/or cold sweat
- When you are in physical danger you may shake, tremble, have cold sweats, have active kidneys

■ When you lose people or things close to you, you may cry or sob
■ When you are bored you may laugh, scratch, become reluctant to talk or talk quickly and non-repetitively.

Look at the following situations. If you have ever been in any of them identify the emotion you felt at the time. Also identify any bodily reactions. It is easier to do this if you take yourself mentally back to the time in question. Here are the names of some emotions to prompt you – please add to this any that you think of:

■ happy	■ sad	■ embarrassed	■ angry
■ furious	■ thoughtful	■ supportive	■ irritated
■ incensed	■ enraged	■ sensitive	■ loving
■ kind	■ empathetic	■ enlightened	■ sympathetic
■ tender	■ devoted	■ engrossed	■ solicitous
■ concerned	■ apprehensive	■ introspective	■ anxious
■ restless	■ nervous	■ enchanted	■ worried
■ guilty	■ troubled	■ hopeful	■ friendly
■ compassionate	■ good-hearted	■ flirtatious	■ cheerful
■ contented	■ delighted	■ sexy	■ blissful
■ gladdened	■ pensive	■ attractive	■ reflective
■ tormented	■ harassed	■ unattractive	■ bewildered
■ dazed	■ confused	■ charismatic	■ astonished
■ blameworthy	■ culpable	■ bored	■ dutiful.

Situation	*Emotion/physical reaction*
1. Your boss fails to say 'good morning' to you yet again	
2. You don't get the job you really wanted	
3. It is half an hour before your appraisal interview	
4. You have a near miss in your car	
5. Someone you care for is very late home	
6. Your favourite football team wins an important match	
7. You smile at someone attractive across the room and they smile back winningly	
8. You realize you haven't phoned your elderly parent for a long time	

9. You put your foot in it
10. Your partner walks into the bedroom
     with a twinkle in his/her eye
11. You fall over in the street
12. You are unfairly criticized.

Self-awareness activity 2 – recognizing emotions

1. On five occasions every day for next week, stop and check how you are feeling about what is going on. Be aware of any clues that your body is giving you. It's helpful to find a prompt to remind you to check your feelings. You could consider checking your emotions: on the hour, every time the phone rings, each time the boss walks towards your desk, or as you walk in the door after work.

2. Reflect on how your emotions are affecting your behaviour at the time.

3. Consider whether your behaviour is appropriate or could usefully be changed.

4. Try a new behaviour if necessary.

Self-awareness activity 3 – re-stimulation

Re-stimulation is a term used when feelings about an earlier event become superimposed on a current event. Here is a true story to demonstrate re-stimulation.

DEBORAH'S STORY

In her 40s Deborah visited an historic tourist house in America. As she walked round the house she listened to an audio tape of the life of early settlers who had lived in the house. As was not unusual in those days, the first family to live in the house had lost three children in early infancy. Listening to this story had an immense impact on Deborah. She burst into tears and had to leave.

On reflection she realized that any talk of dying babies affected her more strongly than it appeared to affect others. Her own children were healthy and happy so she had no worries there. She thought back further in her life and remembered that her mother had had two children who died, one when Deborah was 2 and one when she was 17. She vividly remembered the latter death although had no conscious memory of the former. In those days no help in the form of counselling was offered and the emotional effects of the deaths were never dealt with. By the time her mother returned home from the maternity hospital all the baby equipment had been cleared away and the baby was never mentioned.

Deborah hadn't until that time consciously linked the early events with her strong reactions. Now she realised she had some old feelings that had been submerged at the time in order to cope. However, the feelings 'broke through' when re-stimulated by hearing about similar events happening to others.

Do you have any stronger-than-usual feelings in response to particular events? If so, you might like to reflect back to any similar situations earlier in your life. If you can't remember any, it could be because the event happened when you were so young you cannot remember it. Is there anyone who would remember you as a small child whom you could discuss this with?

Self-awareness activity 4 – history revisited

Reflect on an experience from earlier in your life that had a big emotional impact. Consider how this experience may still be affecting your feelings and/or behaviour today. You might like to discuss this with someone you trust. The following space is for you to make notes.

Experience	*Continuing effects*

There are many ways in which you can work to overcome the impact of these experiences. Talking about them to a counsellor or wise friend helps. Very powerful also is visualizing the scene but changing the picture to something more pleasant. For more information on this have a look at p. 55 Activity 5 – Visualizing confident behaviour.

Self-awareness activity 5 – positivity log

In the previous section we saw that we notice what we consciously or unconsciously choose to see around us. Like cartographers, we select from the environment what to put on our own world maps. If you have a tendency to notice the negative in your environment this activity is for you.

STEP 1   Buy yourself a really nice notebook, one you'll enjoy writing in and owning.

STEP 2   Each day write in your notebook five good things you've noticed that day. They don't have to be big things – the sun is shining, Sandy wore a nice sweater to work, my bus was on time. Also write five things you're pleased you've achieved that day. Again, they don't have to be big things – you called that difficult person, you finished the filing/ironing, you gave yourself some exercise by walking up the stairs instead of using the lift.

STEP 3   Review your positivity log occasionally, it will give you a lift. It's especially useful to re-read it when you're feeling a bit down.

Write in your log every day for a month and then review the process. The activity will force you to focus your attention differently, positively. If you feel you need to improve further, continue writing in your log for another month or two. You may also like to add any inspiring quotations you come across. Here's one of my favourites:

> *The grass isn't always greenest on the other side of the fence. It's greenest where it's watered. Go home and get out your watering can.*
>
> (Anon)

By changing our focus we can turn our negativity cycle into something much more positive.

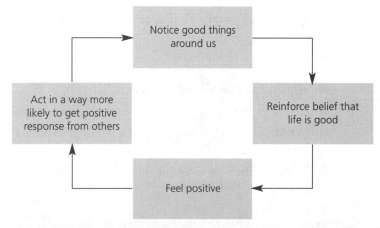

FIGURE 3.1

Self-awareness activity 6 – your SWOT analysis

Working on your own, make a SWOT analysis of your **S**trengths and **W**eaknesses, **O**pportunities and **T**hreats. You might like to consider social, concrete skills and emotional intelligence skills.

Strengths	*Weaknesses*
(What I am good at)	(What I'd like to improve)

Opportunities	*Threats*
(To develop my abilities)	(What might stop me improving and how I'll overcome it)

Copy this page and ask one or more people you trust to complete the SWOT analysis on you. When you have received the SWOTs from other people ask yourself:

- How close was my analysis to other people's?
- If it was very different what does this say of my self-perception?
- What does it say about my behaviour if people see me differently from the way I see myself?
- What behaviour changes would I need to make to be seen as the person I imagine myself to be?

Self-awareness activity 7 – treat yourself well

1. Spend a few minutes reflecting on how you would like to be treated by others. Would you like others to treat you with kindness? consideration? respect? compassion? allowing you to learn from mistakes rather than blasting you for them?

2. Next, reflect on how your life would be if you treated yourself in the way you would like others to treat you.

3. Plan how to change your treatment of yourself. Be kind to yourself. Buy yourself some flowers. Give yourself time to relax. Turn away those judgemental thoughts and replace them with memories of your strengths. Plan to develop any skills you'd like to improve with a positive 'can do' attitude instead of giving yourself a hard time about what you can't do.

4. Do this consistently and you'll find that not only do you treat yourself better, but other people will too. People who have a low opinion of themselves often find themselves treated as they expect to be.

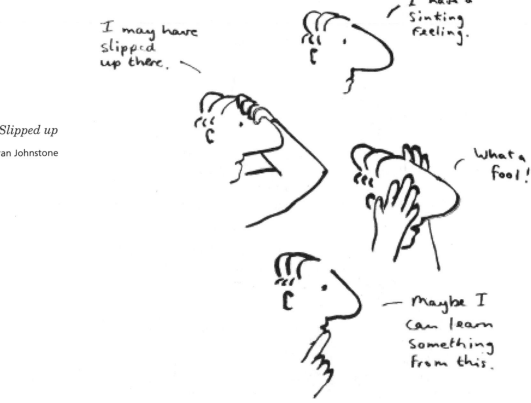

Slipped up

Fran Johnstone

Chapter 4

Personal competence advantage 2 Self-confidence

Self-confidence is crucial to our ability to deal with a whole range of situations. Without it we find ourselves acting and reacting in a way we regret. For example, we may blush, stutter, get angry and defensive, talk too much, talk too little, undersell ourselves or even get depressed.

There are a many reasons for poor self-confidence and many, but not all, come from childhood experiences. A major cause is that as a child we receive negative messages about ourselves from important people in our lives. Psychologists call these 'parent messages' and although they might come from parents, they also come from other relatives, neighbours, teachers, in fact anyone who you, as a child, think has a valid opinion. Of course, their opinion is not necessarily valid, all of these people are capable of being insensitive or just plain mean. But as a child we know no better and accept their judgements of ourselves as reality. For the rest of this section when we talk about 'parents' please include in this all the influential people mentioned above.

Many parents criticize their children because their children are imperfect (know any perfect children?). Sadly their view of the perfect child may be very distorted. It may be that you should be clean, quiet and well-behaved at all times. It may be that you should meet their every need. It may be that you should excel in everything you do. Their own unrealistic expectations lead them to find you failing and to pass on the message to you that you are a failure.

But even more realistic parents can unwittingly damage self-esteem by the words they use when criticizing. For example, some parents criticize the child rather than the behaviour (usually because this is the way they were criticized). Here are some examples:

Criticism of person	Criticism of behaviour
'You're a slob'	'Your bedroom's untidy'
'You'll never amount to anything'	'Your exam results were disappointing'
'You're clumsy'	'You dropped the glass'
'You're stupid!'	'You're not listening to my explanation'
'You're a pain in the neck'	'You don't do everything you're told first time.'

You can see that the examples on the left are likely to be much more damaging than the ones on the right, because they talk about the person rather than the behaviour.

And parents don't even have to say anything to pass on these messages, they can give them non-verbally. A sigh when you come downstairs looking a bit untidy. Giving you the cold shoulder when you haven't washed up as requested. Pushing you away when you cry. These and many other silent actions give you messages as loudly and clearly as if they'd been shouted.

If we receive these parent messages often enough they become hard-wired into our memory and we accept them as reality. When you're an adult you may know that logically they're untrue but you never accept this at an emotional level.

Our family's common phrases or sayings can also affect us. They tell us a lot about people's belief systems. Some common ones are:

- 'It'll all come out in the wash'
- 'It'll all be the same in a hundred years'
- 'Life is what you make it'
- 'A bird in the hand is worth two in the bush'
- 'Look before you leap'
- 'All men are bastards'
- 'Women are all the same'
- 'The early bird catches the worm'
- 'Better safe than sorry'
- 'If a job's worth doing, it's worth doing well'.

Which expressions 'feel right' to you and which of these, or others, do you use? Think through the implications of these for your belief systems and the stresses that may follow.

For example, if a common saying for you is 'A bird in the hand is worth two in the bush', you'll probably have a cautious attitude to life. If you believe that 'It'll all come out in the wash' you probably have a more relaxed attitude to problems.

Sometimes our confidence is knocked later in life. A relationship break-up, a bully at work, losing your job, bereavement, ill health, and many other reasons can leave us feeling drained and unhappy.

Poor confidence perpetuates a downward spiral. We lack confidence so we don't act as we'd like to; not acting as we'd like reduces our self confidence. From this low point it feels as if we have no control over changing our emotional state. Luckily there are several techniques you can use to improve your self-confidence. It takes a while, but even while you're working on it you feel better because you're taking action instead of feeling helpless.

> **CASE STUDY – DARREN'S INTERVIEW**
>
> Darren knew he was good at his job. He was a careful and accurate worker, yet flexible enough to get through the mountain of work on his desk every day. When promotion beckoned in the shape of a job one level up Darren decided to go for it. Unfortunately he lacked confidence in interviews. Because of this he kept putting it to the back of his mind instead of preparing for the big day.
>
> At the interview he failed to shine, and didn't let the interview panel know the full extent of his abilities. He didn't get the job. One of his colleagues got it even though he wasn't as experienced as Darren. He was better at interviews though.
>
> What Darren overlooked was that being good at interviews is simply a skill, so it can therefore be learnt.

Nothing is a waste of time if you use the experience wisely

(Auguste Rodin)

Self-confidence activity 1 – identifying parent messages

We recommend that you undertake this exercise with a supportive partner or colleague because it may arouse strong emotions. Work at your own pace, doing just as much as feel able to each time. You may want to repeat some steps several times.

Parent messages affect the conversations that we have with ourselves all day long. This inner dialogue is the subject of the next activity but for now let's look at what parent messages you may have heard as a child and who they may have come from.

STEP 1

Think about things that were commonly said to you as a child. Probably some were positive ('That's a good girl', 'What a strong boy') whilst others were negative. Remember, some messages come in the form of 'sayings' such as 'If a job's worth doing, it's worth doing well', 'Look before you leap', etc.

Also ask yourself why they were said and what the circumstances were.

What was said	Circumstances

STEP 2   Now ask yourself, 'Who gave me these messages?' If you can't remember, imagine the words with 'You' in front of them. So for example you might hear someone saying 'You're ugly' or 'You're a wicked, wicked child', 'You're gorgeous.' This may prompt your memory.

STEP 3   This will begin to work on these messages at a cognitive (thinking) level. Ask yourself, 'If this person were giving their opinion about someone else, how valid would I consider their opinion to be?'

STEP 4   This step will work at a more feeling level. Imagine yourself talking to that person. Play around with the picture in your mind. Make sure that in your mind's eye you are an adult (rather than the child at the age when the messages were given). If you would feel more comfortable, imagine yourself much bigger than the other person. Now have a conversation with the person telling them that you forgive them for the things they said and that you reject their opinion of you. From now on your own opinion is what is important. (If you find the forgiveness difficult, activities on p. 80 will help)

STEP 5   Repeat Step 4 as often as necessary until you reject their opinion of you at both a logical and emotional level.

Self-confidence activity 2 – monitoring self-talk

All day long we have conversations with ourselves in our heads. We mentally rehearse conversations, tell ourselves off, encourage ourselves, make decisions and much more beside. For some people this inner dialogue is a source of strength, whilst to others it is demoralizing. Which of these sound familiar to you?

Positive self-talk

- 'Now, let's see, what's the best way to do that?'
- 'That's brilliant, I finished that task on time'
- 'Oh well, I'll get through this lot somehow'
- 'Hmm, I look okay in this.'

Negative inner dialogue

- 'It's hopeless, I'll never finish this on time'
- 'No one ever helps me'
- 'Why does no one ever listen to me?'
- 'Does my bum look big in this?'

People with positive inner dialogue are able to see the difficulties in life but, even if they have negative thoughts, soon seek ways to turn the situation around.

Signs of negative self-talk are:

- feeling like a victim
- using 'universal' words like anyone, no-one, everyone, never, always
- excessive worry
- blaming other people for everything
- not feeling in control of your life
- excessive guilt
- telling yourself off
- dwelling excessively on old hurts.

Check your self-talk rating several times a day by stopping in the middle of your thoughts and reviewing them. Are they generally positive or negative?

Congratulate yourself on your positive thoughts. If you realize you have negative thoughts, particularly recurring ones, write them in the space below and then write a more empowering positive thought you will replace it with in future. There are some examples to help you get going.

Negative thought	Positive thought
'I'm hopeless, I'm always running late'	'I'm occasionally late, I will prioritize my work carefully in future'
'Everyone hates me'	'It's true that there are one or two people I don't get on with at work, but I have a good circle of friends'
'I look awful'	'Losing a few pounds would be good, but I have lovely hair, sparkling eyes and a happy smile' .

Positive self talk

Fran Johnstone

Self-confidence activity 3 – goal setting

Do not follow where the path may lead. Go instead where there is no path and leave a trail.

(Ralph Waldo Emerson)

Most people say that they would like to be more confident but don't know how to go about it. The goal feels too vague and overwhelming and you wouldn't really know when you'd achieved it. It may be a long time before you can really say to yourself, 'I am a really confident person!' (even confident people have areas about which they feel unsure). Vague goals fail to give you that moment of satisfaction when you can pat yourself on the back and say, 'Done it!'

The trick is to identify specific areas where you lack confidence and then work towards improving them. Below are some situations that may be familiar to you. How confident would you feel in each of them? Give yourself a score from 1 = very unconfident to 10 = very confident.

Situation	Score
Walking late into a meeting when it has already started	
Telling a joke in front of a group	
Trying an unfamiliar dance in public	
Giving a presentation	
Giving negative feedback to your boss	
Disagreeing with someone else's point of view	
Standing up for yourself when you are unfairly criticized	
Doing role play when attending a course	
Speaking to an autocratic medical consultant	
Asking for help	

How did you get on? Any situations where you score less than 7 would be areas to concentrate on improving.

By breaking down your big goal into smaller goals, you can work towards something that feels very achievable. And it helps to write yourself goals in such a way that they pass the 'pat yourself on the back' test. The best way to do this is to write goals in a SMART way. SMART is a mnemonic for:

Specific
Measurable
Achievable
Results-oriented
Time-bound

Here are some examples of vague goals rewritten to pass the pat on the back test. To reach goals you often have to undertake planning or develop other skills. Alongside each goal are typical steps you may have to take to reach the goal.

Vague goal	SMART goals	Steps to reach the goal
I'd like to be better in meetings	For the next three meetings I will say one thing, then for the next three I'll say two things	Before each meeting I will read the agenda and work out what I want to say
I wish I could tell my boss how her disorganization irritates me	Within one month I will ask my boss to give me work in good time to get it completed	I will read an assertion training book and practise saying this with a friend
Help, I've got to give a presentation at the interview for that job	At the interview I will give a comprehensive and polished presentation	I'll go on a presentation skills course and practice until I'm word perfect
I always feel nervous when speaking to the consultant	When I go to the hospital I will ask the consultant questions confidently	I will write down my questions before going to the hospital and practice asking them with a friend

In the following boxes make a list of three areas where you would like to feel more confident. You may not be able to identify them all immediately, but over the next couple of weeks notice every time you feel uncomfortable in a situation. This is your clue that your confidence needs improving. Write yourself a SMART goal for each area and then work out a step-by-step plan to achieving confidence in that sphere. It is a good idea to start with a relatively easy goal. The boost you get from achieving it will motivate you to work towards more difficult goals. Achieve one goal this week!

SMART goal	Steps to achieve the goal

When you set your goals give them an even better start by spending a moment or two visualizing yourself achieving them. See, hear and really feel yourself achieving your goal. Do this several times a day, it will increase both your confidence and skill levels.

Self-confidence activity 4 – role modelling

Often when we lack confidence we admire others who can do things we'd like to do. Strangely though, we rarely think to model ourselves on them. By watching someone who has a particular skill, whether it's painting, handling conflict or anything else, we can learn how to improve our own skills. Remember that you may learn by simply observing the person in action. On the other hand, you might like to ask them to explain the secret of their success to you.

Try this step by step approach to learning from your role model:

STEP 1   Identify someone who has the skills and/or personal qualities you would like for yourself.

STEP 2   Select five of those skills and qualities.

STEP 3   Prioritize them in terms of what you most want to achieve.

STEP 4   Work out a plan for achieving your goal using the SMART goal method outlined above.

STEP 5   Get support for yourself from people you trust.

STEP 6   Work towards your first goal.

STEP 7   Congratulate and reward yourself when you achieve your goal.

STEP 8   Move on to your next improvement area.

Skilled person	Skill to be modelled	Action needed

Once you have studied your role model in action you can draw on their experience even when they're not present. If you are stuck wondering how to behave in a given situation, ask yourself 'How would . . . (role model) act here?' – and act in that way. It works by unblocking your creativity and allowing you to use skills and abilities you already have in a flexible way. This is called acting 'as if'. You act as if you were your role model.

Self-confidence activity 5 – visualizing confident behaviour

As we saw in Chapter 2 of this book, whenever we experience something we lay down a chemical pathway in our brain. If something happens often enough or has enough impact, the pathway becomes very thick and when stimulated by any reminder of the original event we react in a predictable way. Deborah's story on p. 41 is an example of this.

One of the interesting things about the brain is that, in one way, it cannot tell the difference between us actually experiencing something and visualizing it. This means that if we visualize ourselves responding to a situation enough times we will naturally behave that way when the stimulus presents itself. Sports people have used this method for many years to improve their performance.

Creative visualization of this sort can have a powerful impact on how we feel about situations and respond to them. When you want a visualization to have more impact on you:

1. Visualise your desired goal as clearly and colourfully as you can.

2. Make the picture even bigger and brighter.

3. Get 'into' the picture as closely as you can.

4. Allow yourself to engage as many of the senses as possible – sound, smell, touch, as well as vision.

5. Adjust the picture until you are really happy with the result.

6. Hold that picture for a few seconds.

7. Allow yourself to feel the wonderful satisfaction of behaving in the positive way.

Practise the positive visualization several times a day in the lead up to the event. It only takes a couple of minutes and you'll be delighted with the results.

TRUE LIFE STORY – JENNY'S PHOBIA
Jenny grew up in a country where the education system was very different from that in her home country. As a result, when Jenny reached the age of five her parents decided to have her educated at home. A private teacher was appointed and was left in charge of Jenny while her parents were at work all day. The teacher was foul-tempered and if Jenny 'misbehaved' she tied her to the chair. She also hit her sharply across the shoulders every time she made a mistake with her letters.

Jenny was far too frightened to tell anyone about this and the treatment continued for some time. Gradually Jenny developed a phobia about having to write with a pen or pencil. This lasted until she saw a therapist at the age of thirty-four. She was fine with a typewriter or PC, but couldn't put pen to paper without feeling physically sick.

With the help of a therapist Jenny used visualization to cure her phobia. Going through a series of stages she visualized the damaging scene several times gradually taking out the awful ingredients and replacing them with more positive pictures. Eventually the picture was one of her teacher being pleasant and herself enjoying learning. Naturally Jenny still knew what actually happened but the picture in her mind was changed.

When the therapist gave Jenny a pen and paper she sat down and calmly wrote a letter. She has had no problems with writing since.

As this true story above demonstrates, this creative visualization is very powerful also for changing how you 'see' a damaging earlier event. By the way Jenny saw a therapist skilled in Neuro-Linguistic Programming (NLP). If this is of interest to you, you can locate a therapist through the Association of Neuro-Linguistic Programming, at PO Box 10, Porthmadog, LL48 6ZB Wales. Their web site is www.anlp.org.

If you have undertaken Self-Awareness Activity 5, you may already have identified damaging events in your life. Using the techniques outlined before Jenny's story, you can work on changing your emotional response to old hurts. This complements traditional counselling very effectively.

Self-confidence activity 6 – advertising yourself

Most people are far too modest about their own abilities and positive qualities. They'll put themselves down many times rather than praise their own achievements. This activity is a way to get you thinking about your positive attributes. This is a particularly good exercise to do with a trusted friend or colleague.

We all have many roles in life – parent, partner, worker, club member, and so on. Spend some time making an advertisement for yourself in one or more of these roles. The advertisement can be in the form of a poem, prose, a painting, or a collage of magazine pictures. It doesn't matter how you do it – think of yourself as a worthwhile product that will interest others.

As a prompt you might like to consider the following areas: skills, abilities, interests, personality, physical characteristics, emotional maturity, reliability.

My Advertisement

*Make a poster
advertising
something you
do well*

Fran Johnstone

Chapter 5

Personal competence advantage 3 Integrity

We all like to think that we have integrity and that our actions support that belief. But what exactly is integrity? It's a word that is used freely but vaguely. A useful way to think of it is to remember that the word comes from integration – making something whole. A person who has integrity is mature with a set of honourable beliefs on which they base their actions.

So integrity is about being integrated. Being honest and having beliefs and consistently acting in a way that supports your beliefs. Sounds like you, doesn't it? Maya would say that she acts with integrity too:

CASE STUDY – MAYA'S DAY

It was just an average Tuesday morning at work. Maya was a customer services agent for a big retail chain, a busy and sometimes tough role. At present she was also looking after Tom, a 16-year-old on a month's work experience, teaching him about the job and the business.

She looked at her watch. Ten past nine and Tom wasn't here yet, even though they started at 8.45. Still, she'd told him not to worry too much about time-keeping and often let him go home half an hour early.

When he arrived a couple of minutes later she smiled a welcome even though a little bit of her was feeling irritated by his lateness. When he'd made himself a cup of coffee she began the planned coaching session, teaching him how to cope with a particular sort of complaint. She knew that the best way to learn this type of skill was by doing a role play but Tom hated them and she didn't much like them herself so she let it go. They just talked through the sort of situations that might arise.

While Tom looked through the post Maya phoned a friend to confirm their lunch date. Jane was always chatty and before she knew it Maya realized that half an hour had gone by. Quickly making excuses and feeling guilty, she finished the conversation and turned to her work.

It was an exhausting morning – there had been a faulty batch of goods in several stores and she was still picking up the flack. In between dealing with customers she heard Tom taking a few calls. He wasn't handling things very well but she didn't like to say anything, after all he was only a lad and he was doing his best.

Maya went to lunch. She met Jane as arranged and they settled down to a snack and more talk. Before she realized it Maya was late for work. 'Sod them', she thought, 'I work hard enough, they'll have to wait a few more minutes.' Eventually she got back twenty minutes late. Her boss called her in . . . .

Maya is clearly not a bad person, probably even a good person. Unfortunately, her unclear values lead her to behave in a way that is less than helpful to herself, her customers, her company and Tom. So what went wrong and what were the effects?

Integrity issue	Effects
Allowing Tom to be late	Does not teach him appropriate work ethic, might affect his career success
Not saying something about his lateness	Being dishonest to herself. Again, not teaching him work ethic
Avoiding role play	Ineffective teaching – bad for Tom, the company and the customers
Long phone call	Damages reputation, 'steals' company time
Not correcting Tom's work	Failing again to train him properly, customers get a poor deal, company reputation is damaged
Long lunch	'Stealing' company time again

Having integrity is about:

- being clear about your own values
- being open about your values to others
- behaving in a way that supports your values.

When we deal with someone who consistently shows integrity we feel comfortable around them. They are reliable, honest, honourable, and open. They can deal with difficult situations in a way that does not damage others. It's not always easy though. Sometimes having integrity means that we have to tackle difficult issues we'd rather avoid. But combining integrity with emotional intelligence, empathy and assertion skills is a winning combination.

There is nothing more frightening than ignorance in action.

(Goethe)

Integrity activity 1 – your values

This step-by-step activity will help you to identify your values and work out how to live a life consistent with those values.

STEP 1 Working alone or with your buddy use the following grid to identify what is important to you. There are some prompt words to help you.

At work	*Relationships*
(Prompt words: job satisfaction, development, good salary, advancement)	(Prompt words: happy family, trust, time for friends)
For yourself	*For society*
(Prompt words: integrity, kindness, intelligence, health, low stress level)	(Prompt words: peace, environment, tolerance, good for all, freedom)

STEP 2   When you have identified your values, prioritize them into Essential (E) and Desirable (D). It would be helpful also to note where values conflict. For example, job advancement might conflict with more time for family.

Value	E	D	Conflicts with

STEP 3   Now ask yourself, am I living those values that are essential to me? If not, what can I do to make this happen?

Value	Action needed

STEP 4   Now consider your values that conflict. Conflicting values usually leave us feeling guilty, sad or angry. Unfortunately, there is never time to do everything we would like to do and we have to accept the need to prioritize and make some compromises. In the space below make a note of your conflicting values and how you will resolve the conflict to make the situation as comfortable as possible for yourself and for relevant people.

Conflicting values	Resolution

Integrity activity 2 – integrity scale

How high is your integrity level? Consider the pairs of statements below. Put a cross on the dotted line between each pair of statements to indicate where you think your *behaviour* lies in respect of that area. So, for example, if you often or regularly fail to do things you have committed yourself to, to put a cross on the right of the dotted line.

Integrity scale		
I am as good as my word	....	I often fail to do things I say I will do
I am straightforward in my dealings with others	....	I often have hidden agendas when dealing with others
I take responsibility for my actions	....	I try to off-load blame when something goes wrong
I am discreet	....	I enjoy a good gossip
I am consistent in my approach	....	I vary my approach, sometimes unintentionally

I maintain confidentiality	....	I sometimes tell unauthorized people confidential information
I am willing to tackle difficult issues	....	I avoid dealing with difficult issues
I talk about people in a positive way	....	I frequently run people down
I tell people assertively if I am unhappy about something they've done	....	If someone does something I don't like, I don't say so though I may complain about them to others

When you have worked through all the pairs of statements look at the results. Are there areas where you would like to be able to move your cross more to the left? If so, what will you do to achieve that goal? Make some notes in the space below:

Integrity goal	What I'll do to achieve it	Resources needed

Integrity activity 3 – activity log

At the end of each day reflect back on your behaviour in relation to your integrity. Ask yourself:

- Have I acted in a way that respects other people?
- Have I acted in a way that respects myself?
- Have I been honest in my dealings throughout the day?

- Have I spoken positively to and about people?
- If I have had to say difficult things to people have I done so in a constructive and empowering way?
- Have I dealt with difficult issues rather than avoiding them?

You may like to use the learning log on p. 38 to record your findings.

Integrity activity 4 – walking the talk

In your day-to-day life continually work on the following areas:

Being trustworthy

When you say you will do something, do it or explain to the person why this was not possible. If you realize you have forgotten to do something, let the person know as soon as possible and apologize for your error. If you slip up, forgive yourself and ask yourself what you can learn from the experience.

Being honest to your beliefs as long as you damage no one

Ask yourself what you believe, whether in big issues such as politics, relationships, etc. or small issues such as timekeeping. Live to your beliefs. If others have different beliefs which are damaging, find a constructive assertive way of discussing it with them.

Respecting confidentiality

When someone tells you a secret, keep it.

Sharing your feelings

Be willing to let people know who you are and how you feel about things. If your feelings towards someone are negative, have respect for their feelings if you decide to confront them about an issue. Tackle difficult issues in an assertive, empowering way. Section II on Relationship Competence (Chapter 14 on Assertiveness) will provide advice for this situation.

Treating people equally

Examine your prejudices, most people have some. It may be that you are prejudiced against people with a different skin colour, or people who have body piercing, or people with different politics to yourself. Prejudice comes in many disguises. Make sure that your treatment of people is fair and equal.

TRUE LIFE STORY

Several test readers have been kind enough to comment on this book as it has been written. After reading the section on Integrity, one wrote:

'I can illustrate how reading the book so far has made me think differently . . . I met on Friday someone I hadn't seen for years, she's a friend of a friend. There has always been something about this woman that I felt uncomfortable with, but I couldn't put my finger on what it was. When I read this section, I realized almost immediately that it was her personal integrity. She boasts a lot, in an off-hand and casual way, about how much she wrings out of her employer in expenses and how they accept her word about things and are easily hood-winked. She really thought we would be impressed by her cleverness at pulling these mean little deceptions off. Her employer has just funded an expensive operation – she took this absolutely for granted as her due.

She routinely asks – expects even – that friends and colleagues will collaborate with her in these deceptions. She lies about her age, for example, in job applications and cannot imagine why her referees should object. Before reading the book, I had only a feeling of uneasiness about her. Now at least I know where that comes from!'

Chapter 6
Personal competence advantage 4
Taking responsibility

People who are good at making excuses are rarely good at anything else.
(Anon)

A sure sign that someone is not emotionally intelligent is if they are unwilling to take responsibility for their own actions. People who fail to take responsibility say things like:

- 'I only had the affair because he kept chasing me.' (As if they couldn't say 'no'.)

- 'I know I shouldn't go out with such an unsuitable person but I can't help myself.' (Well, if you're not in charge of your mind, who is?)

- 'It's just fate, there's nothing I can do about it.' (Some people believe in fate, and sometimes things do just happen. However, there's nearly always action we can take in a situation.)

- 'I owe so much money. Those credit card companies make it too easy to get into debt.' (As if the credit card companies held a gun to their head and made them spend the money.)

- 'It's your fault I forgot to do that. You didn't remind me.' (As if the person can't take responsibility for remembering things themselves.)

- 'I wish they wouldn't bring cream cakes into work, how can I lose weight with cakes around all the time?' (As if the person has no power to say 'no'.)

- 'I can't go to my child's school play that day, my favourite programme is on then.' (As if they have no responsibility as a good parent to act in the child's best interests.)

- 'I know I'm aggressive sometimes, I was treated badly as a child.' (As if you have no responsibility to find ways to overcome earlier experiences.)

- 'I can't control my child's temper tantrums. That's just the way she is.' (As if parents have no need to explore ways to encourage good behaviour in their child.)

Failing to take responsibility for yourself has many consequences. It is a way of being disempowered, of making yourself feel and appear helpless. If you are not responsible for your own actions, the implication is that someone else is. Often this someone else is unspecified; a nameless 'they' who forces us to action or inaction. Do you want to be seen as that helpless? No. Much better to realize that you can make the decision to act in a positive, emotionally intelligent way.

Further, other people will see that you are not taking responsibility. They will see you as weak, lazy or incompetent.

By taking responsibility for your actions you grow; you develop competencies, you respect yourself more, you feel more confident about the future. Others also see you as a more valued person.

Naturally, this avoidance of responsibility is not necessary conscious. We often pretty much believe the excuses we offer others and ourselves. For example, we justify cheating our employer out of working hours by telling ourselves that we work hard when we're there (as if that's not normal in the working environment).

These activities will allow you to identify when you are avoiding responsibility and help you to develop the vital skill of accepting it.

Taking responsibility activity 1 – my readiness to accept responsibility

To test your willingness to take responsibility read the following statements. If the statement sounds more like your behaviour than not, answer 'yes' to the statement. Otherwise, answer 'no'.

Statement	Yes/No
I avoid taking responsibility for being late by making up a story	
I avoid taking responsibility for being unkind to others saying that they ask for it or it's for their own good	
I avoid taking responsibility for having 'extra-marital' affairs by blaming on the other person, my spouse, my sex drive or some other reason	
I avoid taking responsibility for nurturing my child by saying that he or she is 'trouble', 'just born that way', or similar	
I avoid taking responsibility for taking 'illegal' sick days off work by saying things like 'Well, they owe me!'	

I avoid taking responsibility for being impatient by saying that I don't suffer fools gladly.

I avoid taking responsibility for having forgotten something by saying that I wasn't told when I could have found out.

I avoid taking responsibility for hurting another person's feelings by being more concerned about my own needs.

For each statement you marked with 'yes' write your thoughts on:

- Why do I avoid taking responsibility in this way?
- What are the consequences of behaving in this way for myself? For others?
- What behaviour would be more helpful?

This would be a very useful activity to work on with your buddy.

Taking responsibility activity 2 – 'shoulds' into 'coulds' and 'musts' into 'wills'

One way to recognize when we are avoiding responsibility is simply to listen to what we say to ourselves or others. Whenever we say 'I should . . .' or 'I ought to . . .' or 'I must . . .' it is as if we are giving the responsibility for that action to someone else. Common shoulds, oughts and musts are: I should/must lose weight, stop smoking, stick to my new year resolutions, get up earlier, go to bed earlier, learn a new language, get on better with my partner, spend more time with my children, etc., etc., etc. The list is endless. Naturally, we are all inclined to say this occasionally, but some people use this thinking a lot. They are the ones who don't accept that they actually COULD do these things. It may take some planning, some time, some work, some effort, but they can be done. So, does this sound like you? This activity will help.

STEP 1   Below write a list of all the things that you tell yourself you should do.

'I should ....'

'I should ....'

'I should ....'

'I should ....,'

'I should ....,'

'I should ....,'

STEP 2   Go through the list and cross out the word 'should' and replace it with the word 'could'.

STEP 3   Now look at the list again. You now have an action list. Work out what you need to do to achieve each of these goals. If you find this difficult look at p. 52 where there is advice on how to write SMART goals.

If you suddenly find resistance in yourself, ask yourself if it's a goal you really want. If it is, but there is still resistance, ask yourself if the goal conflicts with another goal. We can't have everything we want in life, life's not like that. You can't, for example, spend more time with your partner AND more time developing your career AND learning a new language if your time is already heavily committed. In this case you will have to decide your priorities. There is advice on how to do this in the Future Competence section of this workbook.

Sometimes, too, you realize that the goal just isn't that important, in which case you may just decide not to go for it. In this case there will still be a good outcome – you will have stopped giving yourself a hard time over that feeling that you 'should' be doing something!

When you have decided your goals write them here:

'I will...,'

'I will...,'

'I will...,'

'I will...,'

'I will...,'

'I will...,'

It's funny, but the harder I work, the luckier I get.

(Anon)

Chapter 7
Personal competence advantage 5
Positive belief

Having a positive belief system means that we tend to adopt a 'can-do' attitude towards life. This doesn't mean being unrealistic, believing that we can achieve anything. It merely means assuming that most things are possible, even though they may take a long while or a lot of work.

Sadly, some people have beliefs which are anything but positive. Negative beliefs are bad for our self-confidence and cause us to put limits around what we believe to be possible. This is far from a 'can do' attitude. More of a 'must do' or even a 'must I?' attitude.

The sorts of beliefs that lead us to think that we 'must' do this or 'should' do that really do limit our lives. These beliefs then influence our behaviour, often unconsciously.

Overcoming limiting beliefs is a huge step towards realizing the choices you have in your life and becoming more emotionally intelligent. Limiting beliefs restrict your choices in life. You believe that you're no good at maths and this influences your job choices. You believe you're no good at sports so you become increasingly unfit instead of finding a fitness regime that you enjoy. You believe you're useless at the job because you never get everything done in one day, so you burn out instead of organizing yourself or taking a more realistic approach.

Changing beliefs is possible and enjoyable once you develop a strategy. Suppose that you have a belief that you are no good at maths. You probably fight shy of any tasks involving maths and put yourself down when you talk about it.

One strategy would be:

Step	Examples
Decide what aspect of maths you'd like to conquer. Make the goal realistic and achievable. Give yourself a timescale	1. Feel confident helping your children with their homework within the next three months? 2. Balancing the team budget accurately by the middle of the financial year? 3. Keeping your cheque account in credit with immediate effect?
Write down the steps needed to achieve your goal	1. Ask the teacher what maths your children will be learning in the coming year. Ask what books you could read to get you up to date, or attend an evening class 2. Attend a course to learn budgeting skills 3. Learn to analyse your regular outgoings and faithfully keep a record of other expenditure
Motivate yourself to action	1. Visualize yourself having accomplished these goals 2. Decide on a reward for yourself
Check progress	1. Decide on a timescale for progress review 2. Check to establish success and plan for any future action to further develop skills

Another strategy that can be used alone or in conjunction with the one above is to visualize yourself behaving in the way the new belief would allow and have a positive affirmation to say to yourself as you visualize. Later in this chapter you will learn how to write positive affirmations.

Positive belief activity 1 – identifying negative beliefs

Reflect back over the past few days and remember the times when you have stopped yourself doing things because you believed you couldn't. Some further examples might be:

- 'I can't run for that bus, I'm too unfit'
- 'I can't learn to use that new software package, I'm hopeless'
- 'I can't find a new partner, I'm too old/fat/thin/ugly'
- 'I can't say 'no' to my boss, because he'll be really angry'
- 'I can't tell my friend I'm unhappy about her behaviour because she won't like me any more'
- 'I can't ask my boss what she thinks about my performance, I might not like what I hear'
- 'I can't lose 10 lbs, I'm just built this way.'

In the following box, write down on the left your limiting belief. In the centre box write down a more useful belief. Then in the right-hand box write down the steps you will take to make the more useful belief come true. There is a worked example to help you.

Limiting belief	More helpful belief	Steps to achieve more helpful belief
'I can't ask my boss what she thinks about my performance, I might not like what I hear'	'With proper feedback I could work towards improving my skills and getting that promotion I want'	'I will attend an assertion training course and learn how to ask for feedback'

Remember what your mother told you – there's no such word as 'can't!

Beliefs and fear

In fact these limiting beliefs are based on *fear*. Fear that we won't achieve and strangely sometimes fear that we will achieve. Remember, success means change whilst retaining the *status quo* can feel safe and familiar. Sometimes, too, we believe that we don't deserve to succeed or that something awful will happen if we do.

So much fear is based on irrational beliefs that have little basis in reality. This leads us to worry unnecessarily and cause ourselves enormous stress. Even if the fear has some reality base, worrying about it is a useless and emotionally draining action. Take whatever steps you can to ensure that things go well in future and then move on. After all, if you're not in control of your brain, who is?

Fear can be useful, if it's within normal bounds. Actors frequently say that the adrenaline that stage fright gives enables them to perform better. And fear of actual dangers such as traffic or heights can lead us to make safe and informed decisions.

> *One way to avoid conflict is to say nothing, do nothing and be nothing.*
>
> (Anon)

Positive belief activity 2 – using visualisation to conquer fears

One way to overcome fear is suggested by Todd Siller in his book *Think Like a Genius* (Bantam Press, 1977). Visualize your fears and place them in a sphere – the 'Sphere of Fears'. Know that the sphere is airtight and that the fears can't get out, although it is within your power to put more in if necessary.

You can actually make a physical representation of this if you prefer, by using a container and putting pictures or other symbols of your fears inside. Seal the container well and put aside the fears.

Either way, your fears are now contained and you can act like to scientist, watching them objectively. You can acknowledge their existence without letting them hamper your life. You are safe from their effect.

Positive belief activity 3 – positive affirmations

Positive affirmations, like visualizations, focus your mind on what you want to achieve. They are statements outlining what we want to happen and they are written in a very particular way to encourage us to think positively about what we want to achieve.

To write your own positive affirmations follow these steps:

1. Decide what you want to achieve.
2. Write your goal in the present tense ('I am . . .', 'I can . . .', rather than 'I want to . . .' or 'I will . . .').

3. Write positively with an encouraging word or two ('I *enjoy* having balanced books at the end of each month').

4. Write as if you have already achieved your goal.

Some examples would be:

■ 'I enjoy speaking out in meetings with colleagues.'
■ 'I easily deal with Mrs Brown.'
■ 'I confidently and comfortably present information during case reviews.'
■ 'I have fun learning new skills.'

Identify a belief you would like to change. Write yourself a positive affirmation. Write it down somewhere where you will see it regularly (on your computer screensave or a piece of card propped on your desk for example). Develop an appealing visualization to accompany the affirmation. Four times a day spend a minute or two visualizing your new behaviour and saying the affirmation to yourself.

> *Mental maps of the world shape beliefs and subsequent actions. You have the power to make your beliefs positive and empowering*

(McBrideism)

Chapter 8

Personal competence advantage 6 Dealing with negative emotion

The term negative emotion covers a wide range of feelings: jealousy, anger, sulking, guilt, worry and fear are just a few of the big ones. You may well be able to identify many more. Everyone feels negative emotions at some time, but it's true that some people have more negative than positive feelings and this is a pretty uncomfortable way to live your life. This section will give you the know how either to change or use constructively those negative emotions and make your life happier in the process.

Dealing with negative emotion activity 1 – using physical reactions to recognize negative emotions

Sometimes we don't know we have a negative reaction to something until after we have responded. For example, it is very common for people who never say 'no' to others to say 'yes' before they were even aware that they wanted to say no.

One way to recognize your emotional response is to follow these steps:

STEP 1   When someone asks you a question or makes a statement, give yourself a pause – the two-second pause. Count to yourself 'one thousand, two thousand', and while you do that check out your bodily sensations.

STEP 2   When you register a physical sensation ask yourself what this means. For example, a sinking feeling in the stomach usually means dread or at least unhappiness. A surge of adrenalin in the chest usually means excitement. Little or no response probably means that you have no strong feelings about the topic.

STEP 3   Use your knowledge of your physical responses to help you to decide how to respond to the person or the situation. It is highly recommended that you do this in conjunction with the activity that follows.

Dealing with negative emotion activity 2 – recognizing negative emotions by their outcome

Sometimes what feels like a positive emotion and response can lead to negative consequences. This true story demonstrates this beautifully:

JIM started off the office party well enough, after all he was the departmental manager so he was determined to set a good example. But after the first couple of drinks Jim thought, 'To hell with it, it's Christmas, I'm going to enjoy myself!'. Seven drinks later Jim had reached the stage of performing his favourite party trick, previously saved only for away-from-work events. He dropped his trousers and set fire to his pubic hair.

Hard to have credibility after that one . . . .

By the way, alcohol works by inhibiting your inhibitors so there's some truth in the old saying that when we're drunk we do what we really want to do. And if we all went around doing what we want all the time there would be mayhem. How many people would you have kissed or killed by now if there were no consequences?

But it's not only alcohol that causes us to make bad judgements. We can get carried along with peer pressure. Have you ever got carried along with the excitement of a crowd at a concert or match? This is an example of peer pressure, although of course there are many others.

Third, you can make bad judgements because you are in a negative pattern where short-term gain overcomes good sense. Have you ever:

- fallen in love with the same type of wrong person over and over again?
- used your credit card knowing that it will get you in more debt than you can afford?
- knowingly driven too fast for the road conditions?
- taken on really interesting work even though you know you're already overstretched?

At the time, your immediate excitement and good feelings lead you to ignore the longer-term consequences of your actions.

To prevent yourself from making this mistake use the two-second pause in Activity 1 of this chapter above, saying 'One thousand, two thousand' before responding. If you recognize a buzz of excitement (any of the examples above would give you that), stop and ask yourself, 'What will be the longer-term consequences of going along with this excitement?' Do some future pacing (imagining yourself at a time in the future). Imagine yourself opening up the credit-card bill, or being treated badly by the new lover, or crashing the car or getting stressed through taking on too much work. This should help you to slow down and reach a more reasoned decision.

Reflect back to two situations when you have made what appeared to be a good decision at the time, but which later turned out to be quite the opposite. For each situation answer the following questions:

Situation 1 ....

What were your feelings at the moment the situation arose?

What were your thoughts?

Did you think ahead to the longer-term consequences of your actions?   Yes/No

What can you learn from the situation to help you make a more balanced decision in future?

Situation 2 ....

What were your feelings at the moment the situation arose?

What were your thoughts?

Did you think ahead to the longer-term consequences of your actions? Yes/No

What can you learn from the situation to help you make a more balanced decision in future?

Dealing with negative emotion activity 3 – changing a negative mood

There are many ways to change a negative mood, after all, if you're not in control of your mind, who is?

Future pace

If your mood is caused by a specific incident ask yourself: 'How will I feel about this in two year's time?' Often as not, you'll realize that it will be of no consequence at all. Probably, you won't even remember it.

If you know you'll feel okay about this in time, why wait?

(McBrideism)

Visualization

There are a number of different visualizations you can do to change your mood. Select the one that best fits your need:

- Imagine the person who is causing you grief dressed as a clown and about 5 cm high.
- Visualize the situation resolved to your satisfaction.
- If you need to keep calm, visualize a beautiful piece of scenery with gently rippling water. As you visualize it, say to yourself 'calm' and allow the tension in your body to melt away.
- Visualize a time when something really funny happened.

Remember a joke

Remind yourself of a funny joke or story you know.

Catastrophize the event

When facing a difficult situation ask yourself 'Will this situation kill me?', 'Will it leave me maimed?' This will help you to see the situation in perspective.

> *When making a difficult decision, ask yourself, 'What's the worst that can happen?'*
>
> (McBrideism)

Change your body language

A bad mood means bad body language. Rectify this and immediately change how you feel by standing or sitting with your weight evenly balanced on your feet or bottom. Imagine a string pulling you up from the top of your head. This brings your eyes looking straight ahead, your back comfortably straight and shoulders relaxed. You'll instantly feel more in charge . . . .

Take a brisk walk

Walking raises your endorphin levels and gives you a greater feeling of well-being.

Eat sensibly

Ensure that you are eating food that keeps you balanced. Eating high-sugar food means that your energy level rises and falls quickly, making your mood fluctuate unnecessarily.

Jump!

Imagine the mood you want to be in is situated just in front of you. Take a deep breath and as you jump forward take on that great feeling! (You may prefer to do this one in private . . . .)

Dealing with negative emotion activity 4 – say goodbye to bitterness

We have all come across people who are still bitter towards their boss, their parents or their ex, many years after the event. The bitterness stays with them, corroding their spirit and preventing them from enjoying their current and future life.

When people do something that hurts us badly, it's understandable that we go on holding a grudge. These grudges and bitterness can last years, sometimes even after the 'offending person' has died.

Living constantly among painful memories damages us, gets in the way of other relationships and prevents us from living our lives to the full. Learning to forgive helps you because usually the person being most hurt by your continued bitterness is yourself.

So, take responsibility for changing what can be changed and forgive the other person for any damaging behaviour towards you. Forgiveness allows you to move forward to a happier future. The other person doesn't even have to know that you've forgiven them. Indeed the other person may be out of your life or even dead, but forgiving them is for YOU – to enable you to focus on the future instead of the past.

Of course, forgiveness is easier said than done. However, you can work on it as you would any other behaviour or attitude change. Reflect on the difficult situation and remember that the 'damaging person' undoubtedly had problems of their own. These can be immediate – they're feeling stressed and under pressure, or longer-term – they are themselves damaged by early life experiences.

1. Ask yourself whether you had any responsibility in the situation. Was it really all the other person's fault?

2. Act as if they had a positive intent for you even if you don't believe this to be true – it's better than feeling bitter and a victim.

- Your boss is consistently unfair towards you? Maybe their positive intent could be to encourage you to find a better place to work or learn coping skills.

- Your partner is unfaithful? Maybe their positive intent could be to develop a closer relationship with you or for you to both move on to more fulfilling relationships.

- Someone criticizes your work? Maybe their positive intent could be to give you an opportunity to reflect on your work and decide if any aspects could be improved. Alternatively, pat yourself on the back when you decide that you're doing pretty well and the criticism was unfounded.

- You were abused by your parents? Maybe their positive intent was to improve your behaviour or make you a stronger person.

By acting as if the person had positive intent towards you, you take control of the situation and move forwards towards a more positive future.

The forgiveness letter

You might also like to write a letter to the person who hurt you expressing your feelings. You don't have to post the letter, in fact burning it when it's written is a powerful way of destroying the feelings that it transmits. You can write the letter in whatever way seems most powerful for you, but if you are stuck for a format you may like to use the one below.

Dear……………………...................………   Date……………………………

I am writing this letter to share my feelings about an old hurt between us and to express my forgiveness.

When you………………………………………………………………………………

it affected our relationship by …………………………………………………………

and I felt …………………………………………………………………………………

and reacted by …………………………………………………………………………

I feel sad that you …………………………………………………………………………

and that I...

and I regret that ....

I forgive you for the old hurt and perhaps ....

Here is an example:

Dear Mum,

I am writing this letter to share my feelings about an old hurt between us and to express my forgiveness for the past.

When you constantly criticized me as a child it affected our relationship by making me want to withdraw from you and I felt very hurt and unhappy. As you know I reacted by being a 'difficult' child and teenager.

I feel sad that you were never able to see that I had some good points and that I have a lot to offer. I very much regret that I was not able to offer my love and affection to you for fear of rejection.

I forgive you for the old hurt and perhaps we can talk about this soon. If we can't, let's just be a little kinder to each other and perhaps we can get closer even now.

Love,

PAUSE FOR THOUGHT

Two monks were walking by a river. Both had taken a vow of silence. They had also taken a vow of chastity and were forbidden to speak to or touch women. As they walked along they came to a young woman standing by the banks of the river. She wanted to wade across but the water was too deep for her. She pleaded for help.

The older monk put down his belongings and carried the girl across the river. When he got back to his side of the bank the two monks continued on their way.

When they stopped three hours later the younger monk could contain himself no longer. Breaking his vow of silence he asked, 'Do you think you should have carried that girl across the river? What about our vow of chastity?'

The older monk said simply, 'I put her down three hours ago my son.'

Dealing with negative emotion activity 5 – banishing martyrdom

If I blame you, in effect I have empowered you. I have given my power to your weakness. Then I can create evidence that supports my perception that you are the problem.

(Stephen Covey, Principal, Centred Leadership)

A game favoured by some people is martyrdom. We tend to think that martyrs love to be hard done to – they are perpetual victims, even if they don't acknowledge it to themselves. Sadly, martyrs really do think that life is hard for them and by their thinking make it so.

Whilst it is certainly true that life is unkind to us all at times, martyrs have a belief system that life does it to them; that they don't control their lives in any way. And if they try to improve things fate will stop their best efforts.

Martyrdom is an unconscious game designed to meet unacknowledged needs. These needs can be varied and would be likely to include love, recognition and support.

So, are you a martyr? Look at the statements below and if you think the statement is more true for you than untrue, tick the 'yes' column. If it is more untrue than true, tick the 'no' column.

Statement	Yes	No
1. Life is harder for me that for most people		
2. Our lives are controlled by fate		
3. I have little control over what happens in my life		
4. Other people seem to persecute me		
5. People often seem to misunderstand me		
6. My genetic inheritance determines what I can achieve in life		
7. Other people seem to have more friends than I do		
8. When I try to help people they don't appreciate it as much as they should		
9. People often don't listen to me when I'm telling them how difficult my life is		
10. None of this is my fault		

Answered 'yes' to more than three statements? Time to throw away the sack-cloth and ashes, and get a life. One that *you* plan and *you* put into action.

Martyrs are often pleasant, helpful people who may nonetheless hold enormous amounts of anger within themselves. Early life experiences have taught martyrs that nothing they try works and they believe that is still true. And it's frustrating to believe that nothing you try works while you see others around you being successful.

Think back over the last week or two and answer the following questions:

- When have you felt like a martyr?
- What happened and who was involved?
- Are you more likely to feel like a martyr in particular situations or with particular people?
- If so, what are the belief systems that invoke that response in you?
- What was the pay-off for you for your martyred behaviour?
- What was the cost?
- What would the situations have been like if you hadn't played the martyr?
- How would the outcome have been different?
- What steps can you take to avoid being a martyr again?
- What beliefs would you have to change?

Make notes in the box below.

Martyrdom review

Dealing with negative emotion activity 6 – acknowledging your anger

Many aspects of emotionally illiterate behaviour stem from anger. Sometimes this anger is direct and focused on the person who caused it, but sometimes we don't feel safe to do this and we unconsciously redirect the anger. We can, for example, project our anger onto something else.

REAL LIFE CASE STUDY

Ken, a man in his mid fifties, is known for blowing his top at regular intervals. He never gets angry directly with people, he gets angry about things instead. These things include a wasp in the room, a traffic jam, a bad driver, a dirty plate in a restaurant, the list is varied and endless. When he blows his top he is almost beside himself with rage and although his words are about the wasp or traffic jam, people in the room feel the anger is directed at them.

The real probability though is that Ken has been harbouring anger since his childhood. His mother was mentally ill and eventually committed suicide when Ken was 8. Ken's father was very British and stiff upper lip. His older brother was his father's favourite. Whilst his father was charming, he was superficial with his affections. Ken's grief at his mother's death was never dealt with. However, when you're 8 who do you get angry with in this situation? Ken had been bought up to believe that his mother was 'ill' and he didn't really understand how or why she had died. It's difficult to be angry with an ill mother. Ken felt too intimidated to be angry with his father. Instead his anger turned inward. Anger turned inward frequently leads to depression.

It is likely that Ken was slightly depressed all his life and that the only time he really got in touch with his feelings was in these angry outbursts. Even then, the real source of the anger was not recognized.

So anger can be directed at its source, at ourselves in the form of depression or projected onto someone or something else.

Anger takes many forms: blaming, sarcasm, shouting, backbiting, destructive criticism, bullying, prejudice and selfishness are just some examples.

This activity may help you to get in touch more directly with sources of your anger. The activity is in two parts. First of all, complete these sentences with the first thing that comes into your head:

'I get angry when I ....

....,'

'I get angry when others ....

....,'

'I sulk about ....

....,'

'I get really frustrated about ....

....,'

'I can be selfish when ....

....,'

'The thing I hate most about myself is...

....,'

'I am sarcastic when..

....,'

'I gossip about..

....,'

'I hurt people by...

....,'

When you have completed these sentences talk through what you have written with your buddy. If you think that some of what you have written relates to a much earlier time in your life, you may like to find someone from your past who would discuss these matters with you. You may also like to consider seeing a counsellor to help you work through these feelings.

Dealing with negative Emotion activity 7 – overcoming anger

Sometimes we get so angry we would just love to blast the other person to bits. Whilst it's often appropriate to express your anger assertively (more on this in the Relationship Competence section), giving in and expressing the full force of our fury is rarely a good idea. We could ruin a relationship or a business deal, for example. Also, the person we are angry with may not be available to speak to – they may even be dead. This activity allows you to express your anger in a constructive rather than a destructive way. It may feel silly at first, but believe me, you'll feel better afterwards.

STEP 1   Find a quiet room where you won't be disturbed. Take the phone off the hook. Place two chairs facing each other, one for you and one where you are going to imagine the other person is sitting. Put a big cushion or pillow on the other person's chair.

STEP 2   Now sit in your chair and tell the other person exactly what you think of them or what they have done (okay, I know they're not there – you have to imagine that they are). If you feel really angry and want to express it physically, go and give the cushion a good beating.

STEP 3   Nurture yourself. Knowing that you won't deal with the situation in this way in real life, make yourself a cup of coffee and relax. It is quite common to feel shaky after an activity like this, so give yourself time to recover before doing anything else.

Dealing with negative emotion activity 8 – the two-second pause

> *If you are patient in one moment of anger, you will escape a hundred days of sorrow.*
>
> (Chinese proverb)

When we are angry we tend to act first and think later. This activity, which should be done EVERY TIME we are angry with someone, gives you a chance to engage the brain BEFORE opening the mouth.

First you need to learn the physical and psychological clues that you are becoming angry. The earlier in the process you can recognize this the better. Different people have different physical responses but common ones are: buzzing in the ears, knot in the stomach, throbbing head, or tense shoulders. This reaction is your clue to STOP and count to yourself. Count for two seconds – actually say to yourself 'ONE THOUSAND, TWO THOUSAND' and as you do so relax your body. You will now find yourself much better placed to react in an assertive, appropriate way

Dealing with negative emotion activity 9 – stop sulking!

When running courses I often ask people if they sulk and at least half of every group put up their hands. These are people working at all levels, admin workers, catering staff, and every status of manager, everyone. Considering that sulking is behaviour generally associated with children it's surprising that so many people are willing to admit to it.

So what is sulking all about? Well, we tend to sulk when we're not getting our own way. It's a form of indirect aggression. Our attempts to get what we want haven't worked so we try sulking. Of course, perhaps as children sulking did work. Our parents couldn't stand it any more and gave in to us. By doing this they reinforced in us the belief that this behaviour is effective. As adults, though, this probably isn't the case.

So as adults we continue with this emotionally illiterate behaviour even though it rarely works. Often we have not asked directly for what we want, resorting to dropping hints instead. We may not have even asked for what we want at all – we may have got into the mind-reading trap, when we assume that others can read our minds. This thinking goes something like:

- 'If he really loved me, he'd just know what I want.'
- 'My boss knows my computer is old, I mentioned it once three months ago but she hasn't done anything about it!'
- 'The kids know I'm busy, they should do the washing up without me having to ask.'

I don't know any mind readers, do you?

It's amazing that this behaviour from childhood continues into adulthood even though it's usually unsuccessful. More constructive ways of asking for what you want are included in the Assertiveness chapter of the Relationship Competence section of this workbook. But here we'll look at how to change your emotional state so that you can prepare yourself for making requests.

Reflect back to the last time you sulked and make notes on the following questions:

What was your unmet need that led you to sulk?

Was the need fair and realistic taking into account all the circumstances?

Who was not meeting your need?

Looking at the situation from the other person's point of view, why do you think they were failing to meet your need?

Had you asked directly for what you wanted?

What emotionally intelligent steps could you take in future to ensure you have a better chance of getting your needs met?

It is worth considering that sometimes we ask for things at a poorly chosen time. For example, we might ask for attention in the middle of our partner's favourite television programme. Or we might want to buy something when our bank balance is already in the red. In these cases we need to learn to curb our need for immediate gratification and take a longer-term view. Often just going off and concentrating on something else for fifteen minutes is enough to take away the urgent need for action NOW.

Sometimes, however, we are just dealing with someone who is so self-focused that they will never be willing to meet our needs unless they coincide with their own. If you truly believe this to be the case it's worth reflecting that in any situation you ultimately only have three choices.

Three choices

Choice 1: Change yourself. This means changing how you feel about the situation. With less important issues you may be able to say to yourself, 'This really isn't important, I'm going to stop worrying about it.'
Some examples of this type of behaviour are:

- your partner leaves the toilet seat up or down (whichever you don't like)
- your children have untidy bedrooms
- your boss frequently forgets to update you on her movements.

If the relationships are generally working well, it's probably not worth getting upset about these small 'offences'. Be aware though that they are sometimes a symptom of underlying problems.

Choice 2: Change the situation. You may be able to do this by asking for what you want, behaving differently yourself, or making other adjustments appropriate to the situation.

Choice 3: Get out! If you have a boss or partner who is completely unreasonable and utterly unwilling to consider any point of view other than their own, you're probably better off leaving. Often a hard choice, but it can save a lot of anguish in the long term. It would probably help to talk to a wise friend or counsellor if you are thinking of taking this action.

Dealing with negative emotion activity 10 – overcoming excessive guilt

Excessive guilt is a debilitating emotion. It sits on our shoulders dragging us down and lowering our self-esteem. Appropriate guilt has some value though:

without it we could create mayhem. Knowing that we'd feel guilty if we behaved in a certain way is a good behaviour controller. Sadly, the guilt is not always appropriate because we feel guilty about the most insignificant things that others wouldn't give a second thought. Some people say they feel guilt about just about everything.

The guilty person's self-talk is very negative: 'I really should visit my mother', 'I really shouldn't moan about my colleague', 'I should spend more time with my children', 'I mustn't ask for anything for myself when there are so many needy people in the world' – the list is endless.

Again, this is often our parent messages dictating our emotions. Perhaps your 'parents' told you by word or deed that you were in the wrong all the time. If so, it is easy to grow up feeling guilty about all manner of things, some of them insignificant.

Unfortunately, feeling guilty doesn't necessarily change our behaviour. You may feel guilty about not visiting your elderly relative, but does this make you visit more often? It may, but it may not. You may feel guilty about regularly arriving late for work, but does this make you more punctual? It may, but it may not.

Behind the guilt there is always a fear, yet the fear is not always strong enough to spur us to action. By identifying the fear we may be able to use our cognitive brain to help us feel better. Activities using an emotional brain follow this one.

Here are some examples of things people commonly feel guilty about, the fears behind them and possible steps to alleviate them. Add your own to the list and discuss them with your buddy. These steps are very practical. If guilt is a really severe issue for you, you might like to consider seeing a counsellor who will help you to work through the history of your problem.

Guilt feeling	Fear	Action
'I should visit my Mother more'	She'll be angry with me for not visiting	1. Visit 2. Phone instead 3. Write a letter 4. Discuss with her why I don't enjoy visiting
'I didn't get the job I went for'	I must be stupid	1. Prepare more thoroughly for the next interview 2. Improve my skills 3. Seek career counselling

'I don't spend enough time with my children'	They are neglected and will grow up unhappy	Explore ways to spend more time with them, such as: 1. Working shorter hours 2. Doing less housework 3. Cutting out other non-essential time-consumers

If you're not in control of your mind, who is?

(Wayne Dyer, *Your Erroneous Zones*)

So, take a long hard look at your guilt feelings. Take remedial action for those things that can be fixed (and are worth fixing) and work at diminishing the guilty feelings for these and the others.

Dealing with negative emotion activity 11 – pushing guilt aside

Guilt is a powerful emotion but by taking control of your mind you can lessen the feelings to a comfortable level. Try this. Each time you feel guilty about something, sit down and calmly ask yourself what remedial action you could take. If there is anything, do it.

Now, when the feelings come back acknowledge that they are there but direct your mind to think of something else. Yes, the guilt will push back in, but by constantly pushing it away and getting on with something else, you reduce its impact. And don't feel guilty about feeling guilty!

Dealing with negative emotion activity 12 – stop worrying!

Worry, the other side of the coin, can be just as powerful. We can waste so much time worrying about the future that we never enjoy the present. Worry is simply negative thinking about the future. We focus on bad things that might happen instead of looking forward to the good things that could just as easily happen.

Worrying can lead to a self-fulfilling prophecy. Here's an example. Jane and Eve have been close friends for years. Both single, they've always hoped for the right relationship but neither had achieved their wish. Unexpectedly Eve finds Mr Right and Jane worries that Eve won't have time for her any more. She begins to interpret everything Jane says as a rejection and responds inappropriately.

Instead of openly discussing her fears and finding ways in which they can still see each other, she becomes sulky and demanding. Eve feels torn – her new partner is wonderful company but she wants to give Jane attention too. Unfortunately time with Jane is hardly fun; she's too moody and unpredictable. Eventually Eve does what Jane predicted – she drops the friendship. Jane 'caused' her friend to 'behave badly' towards her.

Here are some tips for overcoming worry. Make a list of all the things that could happen. Catastrophize them. Go completely over the top. What's the worst that can happen at the meeting you're dreading? Will the boss leap up and kill you? Will you fall out of the window? Will the tea and biscuits poison you? Of course not. Probably the things you worry about won't happen either, although if you focus on them, they're more likely to. Learn to laugh at your worries.

Dealing with negative emotion activity 13 – allocate worry time

If you're a worrier, it can overwhelm your day. Instead, give yourself ten minutes a day to worry, then stop and give your mind to more productive matters.

Dealing with negative emotion activity 14 – beat worry by skill building

Often our worries are about not being good enough at something. You can beat a lot of this worry by planning for your future. Plan for the situations that worry you. If you worry about a presentation you have to give, plan it carefully and mentally and physically rehearse until you're word perfect. If you worry about criticizing someone, do a role play with a trusted friend until you're happy you can say it just right. If you're worried you won't get a promotion, talk to your boss about how you can develop the skills needed.

Worrying is passive, while taking action leaves you feeling more positive and in control.

Dealing with negative emotion activity 15 – using visualization to beat worry

This very effective way of overcoming worry works on your emotional brain by literally allowing you see things to differently. You may need to practise the visualizations several times before they reduce the immediate emotional impact of worry.

Visualization 1

Sit somewhere quiet and close your eyes. Get a mental picture of whatever is worrying you. If it is difficult to visualize imagine a gloomy rain cloud with the name of the worry written on it. Next visualize a huge box, big enough to contain the worry. Now place the worry in it. Put the lid on the box and seal the box tightly with string and tape. Now place the box outside the door knowing that you can pick it up again or leave it as you decide.

Visualization 2

Get a mental picture of whatever is worrying you. Put a frame round the picture – it is now a photograph. Shrink the picture until it is quite small. Now imagine a distant wall. Put the picture on it. It's there in the distance but you can't really make out the detail. If you ever need to refer to it, you know where to find it, otherwise leave it where it is.

Dealing with negative emotion activity 16 – self-questioning

Are you a worryguts? Do you expend a lot of emotional energy worrying about the future? Help is at hand!

Worry is a form of fear. It is fear of something that you anticipate happening in the future. Sometimes this event is something you know will definitely happen, while other times it is something you think *might* perhaps happen. Either way, you allow worry about it to gnaw away at your consciousness, undermining your confidence and reducing your feeling of self-determination. Facing worries head on allows you to take practical steps to avoid whatever it is you fear. Combining this with the visualization technique in Activity 2 above is a powerful way to overcome worries.

Reflect back over the last few days to two situations where you have been worried. For each event ask yourself: 'What am I afraid of?'

	Situation 1	Situation 2
What is the worst thing that could happen in this situation?		
Is this fear rational?		
What steps could I take/have taken to reduce the uncomfortable feelings before they started?		
What steps could I take to ensure that I feel more comfortable in future?		

As you reflect on these and other situations you may see a pattern emerging. Ask yourself whether your worries tend to focus on particular things – people, career, travel, being alone, finances? If so, these are areas where you can take practical steps to help you at the logical, thinking level. Using visualization as well will get the new approach through to a feeling level also.

Worrying is like riding a rocking horse. It gives you something to do but it doesn't get you anywhere.

Relationship competence
How we understand and manage our relationships with others

We live in an increasingly global world. In our workplace and in our social lives we have contact with a wider and more diverse group of people. As a key component of emotional intelligence, relationship competence gives us huge advantages here because, within this global context, those with the ability to relate positively to others will flourish and excel. This applies not only within the workplace but also on a more personal level, and includes the ways in which we interact with others at work, as well as how we maintain friendships. In this section you will find a variety of ways to help you achieve the underpinning range of emotional competencies needed for effective relationships.

To appreciate just how much emotional intelligence can improve relationships may involve a shift of perception. We all know people who simply have a natural ability to relate well with others. These people make it look so effortless; others listen to them and they are attentive back. Simple! And yet as we all know, maintaining good relationships is far from simple. What these emotionally intelligent individuals are displaying will include the characteristics of empathy, motivation and mutual respect. Typically these people are good to be around, sometimes inspirational and always supportive. Here's where the shift of perception might come in: these are not simply skills which you either do or don't have – they are skills which can be, and are, learned and developed. It's a straightforward cop-out to say 'I can't be like that'. You can. It depends how much you want it and how closely you are prepared to look at the way you currently interact with others. As you extend your interpersonal skills through the exercises in this section you will move further towards gaining the emotional intelligence advantage!

The rules for work are changing, we're being judged by a new yardstick; not just how smart we are, or our expertise, but also how well we handle ourselves and each other.

(Daniel Goleman)

This section contains information and exercises on:

- empathy
- listening skills
- rapport skills
- influencing skills
- control and trust
- assertiveness/boundaries
- conflict management.

Relationship competence builds directly upon the skills identified under the previous section on Personal Competencies. Given that you now have an understanding of where your own emotions are coming from, you can begin to consider:

■ that other people have a similar range of emotions
■ that other people may not react in the same way as you to similar situations
■ how to be sensitive/able to identify what those emotions are
■ making the appropriate responses to others' emotional outbursts
■ taking responsibility for your own actions.

Working collaboratively with others can be difficult. There may be a common goal but each individual brings a personal agenda, values and past experiences. If you want to be part of a successful team you need to understand these factors and be prepared to work with and around them, not against them. For example, in difficult situations in the workplace, managers have their level of organizational authority to use as a last resort. They are at liberty to insist things are done 'their way' because of their seniority. The principles of effective team working however, rule out this option and therefore good interpersonal skills are the key to achieving results.

> We define ourselves by our relationships, so when it is time to change and grow, it is changing those relationships that is both the challenge and the sustenance.
>
> (Josh Freedman, *EQ Today*, Winter 1999)

Relationship competence also refers to your ability to create and sustain long-term networks of friends and colleagues. These will be the people with whom you share your hopes, aims and fears. Do you relate to them in an honest way? Can you accept help from them when you need it? Do you offer unconditional support in return? Sustaining a good relationship with someone takes effort. Neglect them and they either vanish or withdraw emotionally. Look at the questions below and reflect on your findings or discuss them with your buddy or mentor.

	Yes	No
I have not contacted one of my friends for several weeks		
I 'lose' my friends		
I know little about the private life of the people I work with		
I often forget people's birthdays and fail to send a card or buy a present		
I remember to ask people how they are if they were poorly the last time I saw them		
I don't give compliments easily		

Now let's look more closely at the range of skills inherent to relationship competence, beginning with the most significant: empathy.

Chapter 9
Relationship competence advantage 1 Empathy skills

Empathy: the power of entering into another's personality and imaginatively experiencing his or her experiences

(Chambers Dictionary, 1995)

Empathy is arguably the basic building block for positive relationships. It is the ability to recognize and respond to other people's fears, concerns and feelings. It is sometimes expressed as knowing what it feels like to walk a mile in the other person's shoes. It motivates us to achieve outcomes that not only make us feel good, but those that make others feel good also. It is understanding the other person's point of view, not making assumptions about the person or the situation, but withholding judgement. We cannot 'know' how another person feels but in order to make a real connection with them we need to be able to appreciate their perspective. The skill of empathy then could perhaps be best described as an ability to reflect back to another person the emotions they are expressing so that they feel heard and understood.

What goes wrong when we fail to be empathetic?

- People become resentful of us because we can appear insensitive
- Communication becomes more difficult generally
- We fail to consider how people with diverse backgrounds think and feel
- We jump to conclusions
- We give poor or no feedback
- We give poor or no praise
- We fail to anticipate others' needs
- Resentment occurs.

On the other hand when we are empathetic we:

■ have strong bonds with other people

■ communicate more clearly

■ are more reasoned because even if we don't like something the other person does or says, we understand their viewpoint

■ have compassion

■ forgive others for their transgressions.

Goleman, in *Working with Emotional Intelligence* describes empathy as our 'social radar'. He highlights the essence of empathy as being able to pick up another's feelings without them having uttered a word. In order to do this, it is really important to be attuned to body language clues. In the workplace this can be a huge advantage. This is the environment where people often do not verbalize their true feelings but where missing the non-verbal signs, such as lack of eye contact or tone of voice, can have a huge negative impact. You will find more detail on body language later in this section under Assertiveness (p. 168).

We begin to learn the basic skills of empathy at a very early age and it is something we 'learn'. Usually, people who are poor at picking up other's feelings come from relatively isolated social backgrounds or have parents who have not demonstrated empathy. Alternatively, they may have been brought up with overly accommodating parenting where consideration for others has not been registered as a value. Try the activity below to gauge your current empathy level.

Empathy skills activity 1 – your empathy level

Use the checklist below to help you identify where your empathy skills are high and any areas where you might need to improve. Read through the list and for each area decide whether you feel you:

■ are competent and use this skill effectively

■ sometimes use this skill but are aware that you could improve it

■ seldom or never apply this skill.

Skill	Low competence	Some competence	Competent
Sensitive to others' feelings			
Enquire how people are feeling			
Acknowledge people's feelings			
Tackle conflict or anger			
Tolerate silences			
Are aware of your own body language			
Invite others to express their feelings			
Are comfortable with closeness/ affection			
Help others express their feelings			
Pick up others' body language			
Feel comfortable when people express strong feelings			

So, how did you score? Are there areas in which you feel competent? If so, congratulate yourself on your emotional wisdom in that area. Have you picked out any areas for development? Exercises like the one above and those which follow should help to raise your level of empathy self-awareness. As in all things, your self-awareness level is critical to further improvement.

EMPATHY CASE STUDY – TRUE LIFE
Philip and Wendy took their 8-year-old daughter, Holly, to a holographic exhibition. Philip was busy looking at the pictures but Holly was complaining that she couldn't see the effects. Philip was impatient, 'Of course you can, just look!' At that moment Wendy walked over and simply picked up Holly so that she was the right height to see the hologram. Philip's lack of empathy was so all-embracing that he hadn't even thought that Holly was too short to see the exhibit properly.

Gender and empathy

This is probably a good point to mention the influence of gender on empathy skills. There is a popular view that women are intuitively more empathetic than men and, of course, there are some cases where this true. As with all assumptions, though, you should be wary of confusing fact with generalization!

Research has shown that women are better than men at picking up others' feelings from tone of voice and facial expression. However, research also shows that when body language clues are subtler, men are better able to detect the true feelings. As it is common within many cultures for women to display 'softer' interpersonal skills than men, why would men excel at picking out these less obvious non-verbal clues?

The answer to this question could be found by looking more closely at personal motivation, specifically within the workplace. What is interesting about this research finding is that it is often in a business environment that individuals try to control their 'emotional leakage'. It is quite possible, therefore, that men perceive this form of empathy as more useful to them; they are motivated to use it. For example, when negotiating in business, a great deal of effort is usually made by all participants to conceal feelings or emotions. Anyone skilled at reading emotional leakage in this type of situation could gain tangible business advantages. Perhaps then, when there is a perceived practical advantage in using empathy skills, men are just as motivated as women to use them. If this is the case, then clearly it throws all sorts of issues into the equation. Where does men's perceived lack of motivation to use softer empathy skills come from? That is quite possibly the subject of a research project, but in the meantime, something for us all to consider and be aware of.

Recognising empathy

In general, researchers and theorists agree there are two basic types of empathy: cognitive empathy and emotional empathy. There are many terms used to describe these two types of empathy, and identifying which is which can be difficult. Essentially it is the difference between simply taking the perspective of another person (cognitive empathy) as opposed to having an emotional response similar to the other person (emotional empathy). In emotional intelligence terms we would be more likely to use cognitive empathy. To illustrate this, let's look at Sam's example of emotional empathy:

SAM'S STORY

Sam worked in a multi-ethnic environment where everyone was comfortable with each other. Whilst away on a residential training course Sam and some colleagues visited a pub one evening. It became clear quite soon that there were some people in the pub who were unhappy with the ethnic mix of Sam's group. Before too long some very unpleasant racist remarks were made towards one of the women, which Sam could see had made her very angry. Anger flared up in Sam, with feelings of indignation and resentment towards the person who had made the slur. In doing so, he was mirroring the feelings he could see in his friend. Things escalated and got out of control very quickly and the group were lucky to get back to their hotel in one piece.

So, looking at Sam's experience we can see that he clearly empathized with his friend, feeling her anger and objection. By reacting to those feelings, however, he fell into an 'empathy hijack' situation and placed the group in physical danger. An emotionally intelligent response might have been to acknowledge the way that his friend felt, confirm that he too was offended and suggest trying another pub.

Empathy skills activity 2 – your emotional empathy

Can you think of a time when you responded like Sam? Jot something down in the following box and come back to it when you feel ready to review how you might have made an emotionally intelligent response. If you're not sure, try talking it through with someone you trust.

My empathy hijack situation	An emotionally intelligent alternative

Empathy skills activity 3 – responding with empathy

Think of an empathic response to each of the following statements. Use the space to write down what you consider to be an emotionally intelligent reaction. You could try this exercise with your buddy if you have one, or you may just want to try it out yourself. Remember, your response should reflect your understanding of the feelings behind the statement.

Some empathetic responses could include:

■ 'you must have been worrying about this for ages'
■ 'this has been a really difficult time for you'
■ 'it was hard for you to tell me this'
■ 'I can see that you are feeling upset'.

You have been unavoidably delayed for an important meeting. A colleague greets you at the door to the meeting with: 'Do you know what time it is? You should have been here ages ago!'

Your response:

A person in your team who has the reputation of being a bit of a 'moaner' tells you: 'I am finding my workload too heavy and need some assistance with it.'

Your response:

You take a telephone call from someone working in your department, though you do not know them very well. They are calling to let you know that: 'I'm sorry I won't be coming into work today, my father died last night.'

Your response:

At the end of what has been a tense Monday morning meeting you ask your boss to clarify an instruction you've not fully understood. S/he responds with: 'Do you never listen? I've gone over that twice now and I'm not about to do it again.'

Your response:

Here is a true story of what happened to someone when their manager was not empathetic.

SHIRLEY'S EXPERIENCE

Shirley had worked in an administrative role for the same organization for over ten years. She had good relationships with everyone and whilst she occasionally made thoughtless mistakes, her loyalty and willingness to help anyone meant that these were overlooked. This began to change, however, with the appointment of a new manager. Diane was young, ambitious and eager to make her mark in her first managerial role.

A number of procedural changes were introduced before Diane began looking more closely at what each individual in the department was involved with. She soon became aware that Shirley was not as focused as other members of the team and resolved to deal with this issue.

A team meeting was called during which Diane announced that an external trainer was to be brought in to tutor the team on a particular range of duties. It was obvious to everyone that these tasks made up Shirley's job description. As far as Shirley was concerned, Diane was publicly drawing attention to the fact that Shirley was not competent to demonstrate her duties to the team.

The meeting ended and Diane quietly congratulated herself on having made good progress in dealing with what she perceived as Shirley's lack of performance.

The following day, having spent a sleepless night, Shirley confronted Diane asking why Diane was dissatisfied with her work. During what became a very emotional exchange, Shirley's sense of self-worth and confidence took a complete dip and she again spent another sleepless night worrying about her ability to do her job.

Diane, too, soon began to wonder if her tactic had been ill-advised as Shirley's confidence and motivation dropped lower and lower. It did not take too long before the atmosphere within the team became affected too. The self-supporting team that Diane had inherited had become fragmented and de-motivated. Sadly, Diane was unable to understand why.

Unhappily, Shirley's story is one many people can identify with. Managers, in their desire to create a fully functioning team can sometimes overlook the easiest ways to achieve this. Diane could have avoided the situation she ended up with by talking to Shirley, finding out why she struggled with some of her duties and investigating ways to address this. In short, Diane could have tried an empathetic approach.

Empathy skills activity 4 – seeing another's perspective

This is an exercise to help you see another person's perspective. It is useful where you have an on-going 'difficult' relationship with someone. Often in this sort of situation we become locked into our own standpoint and our creative reasoning is lost.

Think about a specific person that you have difficulty with. Identify a specific type of situation that has happened a number of times in the past and is likely to happen again in the future.

Set up two chairs, both facing inwards. Sit in chair one and think about your perspective. This is the position from which you see the situation only through your own eyes. Imagine the other person is sitting in the chair opposite. Describe what is going on for you; say what you see. Use first-person personal pronouns, e.g. I, me, we, us. Use verbs and adjectives to describe what you see in their body language. For example, are they hostile, ingratiating, or insensitive? Are they listening, doodling or looking at you when you speak? This should be a very self-focused viewpoint. What sort of 'vibes' do you pick up from them?

Now stand up, take a moment to empty your head by focusing on something else in the room or briefly thinking about something unrelated, like what you had for breakfast. Then sit in chair two and take on the body language of the other person. This is where you are going to become the other person and see things from their perspective. You are looking at yourself through their eyes. Again, say out loud what you see. Describe your thoughts, feelings and beliefs about the situation, yourself (them) and the person in the other chair (remember – you are now the other person). Do you see someone who is upset, emotional, or calm? What about the body language? Is it tense or relaxed? Is the tone of voice level or sometimes highly pitched? You are describing yourself as the other person will see you – this is empathy.

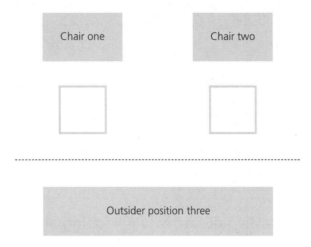

Next, stand up again and walk around for a moment. It's probably a good idea to shake your shoulders out a little and try to clear your mind, before you take up position three. This is where you will be a neutral observer standing outside yourself watching what is going on in a non-judgemental, but helpful way.

From the 'outsider' position review the situation again and notice any differences between the two perspectives. Establish what the person in first position (you) could do differently now they have a different understanding of the situation. Can you think of ideas for new and different behaviour that would improve this relationship?

Go back to sit in chair one position and ask yourself 'Can I do this new behaviour?' Make any necessary adjustments and then rehearse your next encounter with this person. How different will it be? How will the other person react? You could practise several possible scenarios and in doing so, become more confident and comfortable with your new approach.

(Adapted with kind permission of John Seymour Associates)

Empathy skills activity 5 – loss and bereavement

Everyone experiences loss at points throughout their lives, though of course there are degrees of gravity. All of us for example lose our youth; many of us lose a comfortable home when we move house. In more serious cases, we lose a close family member or friend through death, divorce or separation. In any serious loss the person suffering goes through the same cycle of emotions. Good empathy skills can be especially effective where you have contact with the recently bereaved. Very often we struggle to think of the 'right thing' to say. Some people are too afraid of causing further upset and so will simply be unable to broach the subject at all. This tactic seldom helps and an example of this is given below by Laura's story.

CASE STUDY – LAURA'S STORY

Laura's grandmother died suddenly and unexpectedly in hospital. The family were deeply shocked and quite distraught. Laura was very upset but still went to work the following day. She didn't want to be alone and thought that carrying on in a normal routine would help. What she found, however, was that she simply could not settle to her work; she could not stop herself from telling everyone what had happened. This carried on for several days with Laura becoming more and more frustrated as some colleagues avoided talking about her grandmother's death and, worse still – some avoided Laura altogether!

How would you have reacted to Laura? What do you think Laura might have wanted from friends and colleagues? More often than not, in this type of situation, people want to talk – let them. Don't be embarrassed. Try to imagine yourself in their position. Losing someone close to you is a devastating experience and there is no limit to how much support and compassion a person needs in order to come to terms with it.

Emotion, which is suffering, ceases to be suffering as soon as we have a clear picture of it.

(Spinoza)

Figure 9.1 below illustrates the five stages of loss:

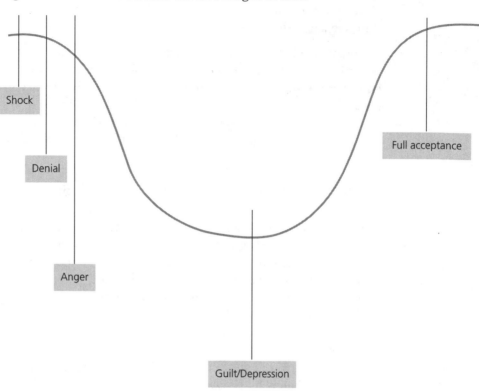

FIGURE 9.1

The five stages of loss

It's useful to be aware of what a person will be experiencing during each of these stages. Typically we struggle to find an appropriate form of words and behaviour when we are around people experiencing loss. Each stage is briefly described below, followed by some emotionally wise responses which should help support a person at each stage of the grief process. If you are around someone going through the bereavement cycle, instead of avoiding the issue you could consider these alternative responses.

STAGE 1   *Shock*

The initial reaction when there is a struggle to match the facts to an emotional reality. Where a death is involved, people might say silly things like 'But I only saw them yesterday', as if that guarantees continuing life. This is the stage at which people will say 'I can't believe it'.

Emotionally wise response

Acknowledge the feelings of the bereaved person. Show you care. Depending on the relationship, touching or holding the distressed person may be all that you can do. Try to encourage the person to express whatever it is they are feeling. You might say, for example, 'I can see that you are very shocked. What happened?' Let them talk. Be aware, however, that a very recently bereaved person may find it difficult to separate fact and emotion. Be sensitive to this – just be their sounding board.

STAGE 2   *Disbelief/denial*

The body's coping mechanism. Numbness and disbelief will occur, but the bereaved will continue to function and carry on with practicalities. They will half expect to find that the event hasn't happened after all. Or, that the partner who has left them for someone else will turn up saying they've made a huge mistake. The grieving person desperately does not want the event to be happening.

Emotionally wise response

Be aware that this stage is temporary although some people take a long time before the truth of the situation is fully appreciated. Encourage the person to be kind to themselves and others around them. If necessary, help with any lifestyle adjustments to allow time to cope with changes. Don't make any suggestions about what the bereaved should be feeling. Everyone responds in different ways – it is important to recognize and accept these differences.

STAGE 3

Anger

Anger is a very common part of the grieving process. And there is always someone to be angry with. The scattergun approach is common as anger spins off in all directions. Targets will be the guilty and the innocent. The partner for leaving; the other person they went off with; the doctor for not taking care of the loved ones; anger with the dead person for not looking after their health; driving too fast; the homework that's been forgotten; a partner/child/colleague who asks for something. Being irrational and unhappy are the overwhelming feelings.

Emotionally wise response

Acknowledge the person's right to be angry – don't tell them they're being silly. Anger is a response to something being wrong – consider what it is that's wrong. Encourage them to take any practical action if appropriate (speaking to a doctor for example). Or they could write a letter of forgiveness (see p. 80) or just write down whatever they are feeling. Sometimes it helps to use positive self-talk while writing. Visualization is another good technique here. After the feelings are written down, the paper can be torn up and thrown away, while the individual visualizes the negative feelings being thrown away too.

STAGE 4   *Guilt / depression*

There's always something to feel guilty about. Not making them go to the doctor; not paying them enough attention, not spending enough/spending too much time at work. Depression is common at this stage. Acknowledging the futility of seeking a scapegoat for the anger can mean it is turned in upon oneself.

Emotionally wise response

Encourage and help them to be around people who care – optimistic people. Again, suggest writing down feelings and maybe use visualization as above. Offer to help with practical things like shopping or cooking but be careful not to take over. If appropriate, speak readily about the special qualities of the deceased. Don't avoid the subject.

STAGE 5   *Acceptance*

Acceptance is only reached once the other stages have been worked through. This involves unravelling the real responsibility from the distorted one, but remember, it may be no one's responsibility. It is the ability to move on from the crippling grief and anger stages and pick up the threads of a new life. The length of time it takes to work from the initial shock to acceptance varies depending on the loss and the person. For a bereavement it could be as long as two years.

Emotionally wise response

Help them focus on new goals and how they can achieve them.

> *If you want* others *to be happy, practice compassion. If you* want to be *happy, practice compassion.*

(Dalai Lama)

Empathy skills activity 6 – empathy and body language

We will be looking at body language in more detail under Relationship Competence, Assertiveness activity 6 (p. 168), but in the meantime we also need to think about the interaction between body language and empathy. When you are listening or speaking to someone, you are unconsciously picking up on their movements and gestures. As we cannot consult a dictionary to translate these non-verbals into meaning, we have to rely on our instinct. This and the following activity should help you to extend your empathy skills through use of body language.

Walk alongside a friend, or your buddy, paying attention to the way they move. If they are agreeable, try to mirror their movements; hold yourself in the same way; swing your arms as they do. Tell them that you'd like to try to understand what they're feeling through their body language messages. As they walk, ask them to think about an experience they've had which invoked strong feelings in them. Now ask them to freeze, and freeze in the same position. Look at their facial expression; the angle of their shoulders; do they look relaxed or tense? Try to guess what sort of emotion they are feeling. Tell them what you think and check out your accuracy of perception. Try this a few times and maybe try it with different people. You should find that after several attempts, you'll become quicker at picking up the emotions behind non-verbal body language.

Empathy skills activity 7 – reflecting feelings

It goes without saying that when you listen to someone you should be listening to the content of what they are saying – the facts. This is only half the story though because you also need to listen to feelings. And sometimes feelings are not expressed directly and you need all your emotional wisdom to understand them.

Other people will truly appreciate your ability to pick up their feelings and it will deepen your relationship with them. You can show you understand someone's feelings by using rewording skills, in this case picking up on the feeling content of what was said. You can pick up the feeling content by:

- listening to what the person is saying
- listening between the lines
- watching the person's body language.

In this activity identify the words and phrases that the speaker uses that indicate feelings. Reflect back the feelings to them, starting your sentence with 'You feel' or 'You're feeling'. There is an example to show you how this works, read it through and then try the other situations below.

Betty to Barbara: 'I'm anxious about my mother, she has a lump in her breast and has to go for tests this morning.'
Betty's feelings were expressed by the word 'anxious'.
Barbara to Betty: 'You feel anxious about your mother's health.'

Kate to Stuart: 'My boss finds fault with everything I do, I worry I might get fired.'

Kate's feeling word(s):...

Stuart to Kate: ....

....

Jenny to Andrea: 'I've split up with Adam after just two weeks. I'm so afraid I'll never find someone permanent.'

Jenny's feeling word(s): ....

Andrea to Jenny:...

....

Dave to Scott: 'I'm so angry with my wife I'm afraid one of these days I might hit her.'

Dave's feeling word(s):..

Scott to Dave: ....

....

Empathy skills activity 8 – recognising feeling messages from others

At least three times each day listen more consciously to the emotions behind what other people are saying to you. Decide whether you will change the way you would have answered in the light of what you discover.

Now that you have had a chance to think about and practise your empathy skills, it's probably a good time to expand upon them. So let's move on to one of the skills which is complementary to empathy – effective listening.

Chapter 10

Relationship competence advantage 2 Effective listening

REAL LIFE STORY
John was at a work's party and several senior people were attending. One of them walked up to him and introduced himself. They began talking about a work situation. As he spoke, John noticed the manager's eyes constantly scanning the room. Eventually his boss spotted someone he thought more interesting. With barely an 'excuse me' he was off, leaving John in mid-sentence. John was livid.

Listening complements empathy as a core emotional intelligence relationship skill. Without effective listening we:

■ irritate other people
■ don't hear people giving us vital information
■ fail to understand the other person's point of view
■ negotiate poorly
■ damage relationships.

Even with good listeners there are many opportunities for the communication to go wrong. In the Personal Competence section we saw that all of us have our own unique way of looking at the world. This means that our world view may not coincide with other people's. Therefore we may be at odds because we actually disagree on something or we may not be clear with each other through simple misunderstanding. We unconsciously code our communication through the filters of our reality and the message is then decoded through the filters of the other person's reality. Figure 10.1 explains this graphically:

FIGURE 10.1

Communication coding

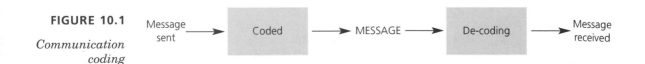

So you can see that there are many opportunities for communication to go wrong. Two emotionally intelligent tips to help you genuinely listen to the other person are:

■ make an effort to understand the other person before you put your viewpoint across

■ be honestly prepared to consider their viewpoint before you try to influence them to accept yours.

This section closely relates to the sections on Questioning (p. 132) and Rapport (p. 140) skills. It is difficult to be a good listener unless you establish rapport and use effective questioning.

Effective listening activity 1 – barriers to effective listening

This questionnaire is Part A of this activity and will provide you with an overview of your listening skills. To complete it, read the items on the left and, depending how often this behaviour is true of you, mark on the dotted line on the right. If you rarely exhibit this behaviour mark the line closer to the left where it is marked 'Rarely'. If this is common behaviour for you, mark the line nearer the right where it is marked 'Often'.

Barriers to effective communication

A. When listening to others do you:

1. Get distracted by inner thoughts that are nothing to do with what the other person is saying?	Rarely 1..2..3..4..5..6 Often
2. Stop listening because you are planning what to say next?	Rarely 1..2..3..4..5..6 Often
3. Start labelling the other person based on what they are saying?	Rarely 1..2..3..4..5..6 Often
4. Listen only through the filter of your existing knowledge of the person?	Rarely 1..2..3..4..5..6 Often
5. Interrupt?	Rarely 1..2..3..4..5..6 Often
6. Stop the other person from following their own train of thought?	Rarely 1..2..3..4..5..6 Often

7. Sit so that the other person has difficulty maintaining eye contact?	Rarely 1..2..3..4..5..6 Often
8. Give the person good non-verbal attention?	Rarely 1..2..3..4..5..6 Often
9. Fail to match the other person's body language?	Rarely 1..2..3..4..5..6 Often
10. Allow what is going on around you to distract your attention?	Rarely 1..2..3..4..5..6 Often
11. Apply labels by saying things like 'Well, he's a man, isn't he?'	Rarely 1..2..3..4..5..6 Often
12. Preach – just tell the other person what to do?	Rarely 1..2..3..4..5..6 Often
13. Diagnose too soon and provide what you think is the right answer?	Rarely 1..2..3..4..5..6 Often
14. Dismiss their concerns as silly or irrelevant?	Rarely 1..2..3..4..5..6 Often
15. Offer clichés such as 'It'll all come out in the wash?'	Rarely 1..2..3..4..5..6 Often
16. Trivialize the matter by telling the person it's really not worth getting upset about?	Rarely 1..2..3..4..5..6 Often
17. Offer false reassurance such as 'Don't worry, I'm sure it will never come to that!'?	Rarely 1..2..3..4..5..6 Often
18. Show impatience when the other person takes time to explain their situation?	Rarely 1..2..3..4..5..6 Often
19. Collude, when challenging is more appropriate, saying things like 'Yes, you're right, everyone knows that women are unpredictable?'	Rarely 1..2..3..4..5..6 Often
20. Not accept the other person's feelings, saying things like 'That's a stupid way to feel?'	Rarely 1..2..3..4..5..6 Often
21. Turn the conversation around so that it becomes about you, not the other person?	Rarely 1..2..3..4..5..6 Often

Ideally, your answers to each question will be close to the left of each line.

B. Working alone or with a friend, discuss the items above and note which unhelpful listening behaviours you use. Now discuss ways in which you can overcome this behaviour to become a skilled listener.

Unhelpful listening behaviour	Solution

Effective listening activity 2 – recognizing prejudice

Prejudice is a major block to effective listening. To be prejudiced towards someone we make assumptions about them as a whole person based simply on one or more observable characteristics. Whilst most people have minor prejudices they do not necessarily act on them. For example, someone may remind us of a teacher we hated at school so we find it difficult to be warm towards that person. Acting on serious prejudices such as racism or sexism is a sure sign of emotional illiteracy.

Here are some typical prejudices:

Labour voter / Guardian reader: left-wing, vegetarian, anti-blood sports, pro-abortion, into feelings, soft.

Conservative voter / Telegraph reader: right-wing, meat eater, pro-blood sports, anti-abortion, prefers facts, hard-line.

Social worker: wears leather sandals and jeans, young, Guardian reader, too soft.

Accountant: wears suits, likes facts rather than feelings, perfectionist.

Now write a thumbnail sketch of the following people and note which of the characteristics you identify you believe to be generally true. Then ask yourself 'What is the effect of my beliefs about these groups of people on my listening abilities when speaking to them?'

Social group	Characteristics	Effect on my listening skills
People with learning difficulties		
People with body piercing/tattoos		
People with a different skin colour to your own		
People with foreign accents		
People with broad local accents		
People with very posh accents		
People of the opposite sex		
People with a different sexual orientation from your own		
People with a different ability level from your own		
People whose age is very different from your own		

The eye sees only what the mind is prepared to comprehend.

(Henri Bergson)

If you're not sure what the effects of these assumptions might be, ask yourself 'What would my reaction be if someone of .... group knocked on my door late at night?' You will probably find that your reaction will vary with the group.

Prejudice stops us listening effectively because we make assumptions about the type of person we are listening to. These assumptions may be entirely wrong and can lead to miscommunication.

The 'Halo' and 'Nimbus' effects are well recognized phenoma of this type of thinking. When we first meet someone, we unconsciously make up our mind whether we like them or not very quickly indeed – some say within ninety seconds. From this initial impression we only notice things about what they say and do that reinforce our initial belief. The 'Halo' effect is when we like someone. From the start we look for the positive in them, and because we are looking we usually find it. The 'Nimbus' effect is when we dislike someone. From the start we look for evidence that they are not a person we would get on with. And in the looking we will usually find it.

If you think this doesn't happen to you, think again. Have you ever been in love? Remember those first heady days or weeks? Your loved one could do nothing wrong. You noticed all the wonderful things about them and were amused and delighted by their funny little ways. It was if they had a shimmering cloak around them dazzling you with its radiance. Gradually though, as you got to know them better, the cloak slipped and you noticed their 'faults'. You realised that they were (like the rest of humankind) an imperfect person and those funny little ways became major irritations. Eventually the relationship ended and now you wonder what you ever saw in them.

Effective listening activity 3 – overcoming prejudice

Recognizing prejudice is only the first step to effective listening. We must overcome it if we are to truly hear what the other person is saying. If you would benefit from overcoming these prejudicial feelings you might like to try one or more of the following activities.

Volunteering

If your difficulty is with people who are disadvantaged in some way, look for opportunities to work with them. Perhaps you know of a local group that works with children with physical disabilities for example. You'll learn more about disadvantaged people and have a good time into the bargain.

Learn more about the people who are different from you

If your problem is with people who are not disadvantaged but who are different from you in other ways, take time to learn about them. For example, you might like to learn about people from a different religion, race, nationality, or people from particular pressure groups. Work to understand their world view. You may never agree with it, but you may learn compassion towards their beliefs and this in itself will help your listening and communication.

Imagine yourself to be in that person's position

By being empathetic, you will naturally increase your listening abilities.

Build your self-confidence

Being very prejudiced against specific groups is frequently a sign of lack of confidence. Unconsciously, prejudiced people feel so small and insignificant that they look for a group that they can castigate. This enables them to feel better about themselves because they can believe they are superior to the other group. If you have any major prejudices you may like to refer back to the confidence-building section of this workbook or speak to a counsellor. Overcoming these negative feelings will certainly increase your self-esteem and give you emotional insight.

Effective listening activity 4 – listening to the opposite sex

Deborah Tannen, in her fascinating book *Working from 9–5*, points out that men and women have different ways of communicating. Neither is right not wrong, they are just different. However, in their difference each sex can believe the other to be poor communicators. Naturally, to make any comments about a whole group means to speak in generalities, but you will probably recognize the styles that follow.

Report talk

This is traditionally a male way of communicating. Men communicate by giving information in a direct and straightforward manner. It is goal-centred conversation: 'I need to give you this information and here it is.' In their efforts to communicate clearly men can sometimes appear domineering. This can be described as giving the message. Advantages of Report talk are that it may be much briefer than Rapport talk; it gets to the point, it is unambiguous.

Disadvantages of Report talk are that it ignores the response from the other person; it is not inclusive; it does not build relationships.

Rapport talk

This is more traditionally a female way of communicating. Women communicate less directly than men. Their talk is peppered with small talk, with incidental material, with efforts to include the other person in the conversation. For example, they often turn a statement into a question to encourage the other person to speak – so they'll put tag endings on to sentences, like 'Don't you think?' In their efforts to be inclusive, women can sometimes appear indecisive. This empathetic, inclusive way of speaking means that women communicate in metamessages. That is, they look at what's behind the words that are spoken. Advantages of Rapport talk are that it is inclusive; it builds rapport; it lightens the atmosphere. Disadvantages are that it takes longer; it can seem indecisive.

Here is an example of a conversation where Debbie is reading metamessages she believes are behind Tom's words:

> *Debbie*: 'How do I find the thesaurus on this computer?'
> *Tom*:   'I've told you before, its Shift F7.'
> *Debbie*: 'What are you trying to say – that I'm stupid?'

This conversation got off to a bad start because Debbie listened to a different message – one of imagined criticism. However, listening to metamessages is often very effective:

> *Ann*: 'Hello, Gail, how are you? I was so sorry to hear your husband died.'
> *Gail*: 'I'm fine, you know, getting on with my life.'
> *Ann*: (recognizing the strain in Gail's voice and seeing the efforts she is making to stop herself from crying) 'Come and sit down and tell me how it's going.'

Emotionally aware people are fully able to use both male and female ways of communicating. They are aware of which style will suit a particular occasion or person.

The challenge of this activity is to become aware of your own style of talking. When you are talking to someone of the opposite sex notice if their style is different from yours and what your response is. If you find yourself struggling to give attention to a different style, remind yourself of its benefits. In the section on Rapport skills (p. 140) we will explore these differences in communication style in more detail. You might like to read that section in conjunction with this.

It is one of the most beautiful compensations of this life that no man can sincerely try to help another without helping himself.

(Ralph Waldo Emerson)

Effective listening activity 5 – overcoming distractions

Internal and external distractions can both affect our ability to listen effectively. Internal distractions are those thoughts that get in the way and include thinking about:

- something unconnected to what the other person is saying
- what you are going to say next to the person
- your own experiences of whatever it is they are talking about
- your physical state (too hot, cold, itchy, etc.)
- your mental state (excited, bored, etc.).

External distractions include:

- people walking by
- the phone ringing
- external noises
- smells.

Good listening skills help you to keep your attention focused on what the other person is saying and the remainder of this section explores them in more detail. However, at present we'll concentrate on preparing for listening. This assumes that you know ahead of time that you are going to have a conversation with someone. Here is a checklist for you to use in preparation.

Preparation for listening checklist

Have you:	Yes	No
Disconnected the phone?	☐	☐
Placed the chairs so that you won't be distracted by people walking by?	☐	☐
Placed the chairs so that you can both talk comfortably? (chairs at right angles about 3–4 feet apart works well)	☐	☐
Asked people not to interrupt you or placed a 'Do not interrupt' sign on the door?	☐	☐

Internal distractions are best avoided by using the active listening techniques in the following activity.

Effective listening activity 6 – active listening skills

You might think that listening is a passive activity, after all someone else is doing all the talking. But if you have ever had a listener who took little part in the conversation you will know that you probably dried up fairly quickly.

Listening is indeed a very active activity. We use a range of skills to encourage the other person to speak and to help them to feel comfortable.

Active listening tip 1: look at the speaker

With a few cultural exceptions, when two people are in conversation they look at each other a great deal. Interestingly, the listener looks at the speaker much more than the other way round. The speaker, when thinking what to say next, darts their eyes in all directions. In fact, it is essential that the listener does look at the speaker. If this doesn't happen the speaker soon feels uncomfortable and the conversation grinds to a half.

Active listening tip 2: pay attention to the speaker's body language

The section on Body Language (p. 168) will tell you more about this fascinating subject and how to read the other person's body language.

Active listening tip 3: use listening body language yourself

When actively listening you should:

- have good eye contact with the person (unless they come from a culture where this is not the norm)
- nod from time to time to encourage the person to continue speaking
- make small sounds like 'mmm' to help the other person to continue with their train of thought
- hold your head slightly on one side
- have similar, but not exactly the same body language as the other person (you can read more about this later in section two on Rapport skills).

Over the next week consciously practise these three listening skills. Note how much your communication with others improves.

Effective listening activity 7 – separating viewpoints

When we listen to someone speaking it can be so, so easy to stop them following their own train of thought by making a statement or asking a question that comes from our own viewpoint. When asked directly for advice, this might be a valuable thing to do, but if the speaker still needs to continue telling their story, it is much more emotionally enlightened to stick with comments that come from their point of view rather than your own.

Here are some examples of conversations you might have with people. In each case there are two possible responses. Read through them and judge for yourself whether each response is from the other person's viewpoint (SP – speaker-centred) or from your viewpoint (SC – self-centred). Write in the space beside each statement which you think is which. The first example is worked for you to show you how this is done. Answers can be found on p. 306 at the back of this workbook.

EXAMPLE   *Speaker*: 'I'm really worried about Amanda. She seems to be very moody in the office at the moment.'

Listener:

SP: 'That's all you need!'

SC: ''You are worried that Amanda's behaviour is affecting things at work.'

1. *Speaker*: 'I hate being on a temporary contract. It feels very insecure.'

    ...... (a)   'Your temporary contract leaves you feeling unsure about your future.'

    ...... (b)   'I'm on one too, they're awful aren't they.'

2. *Speaker*: 'My appraisal is tomorrow and I'm really worried about it.'

    ...... (a)   'Don't worry about it.'

    ...... (b)   'You're worried that your appraisal won't go as well as you'd like.'

3. *Speaker*: 'Errol has gone off sex lately. I'm really worried he's seeing someone else.'

    ...... (a)   'All men go through periods when their sex drive is low.'

    ...... (b)   'You're worried that Errol is having an affair.'

4. *Speaker*: 'Teenage kids can be the very devil. My daughter didn't come home until 4 am last night. Goodness knows what she was up to.'

...... (a)   'You're worried what Tracy was doing last night.'

...... (b)   'My son's just the same, comes in at all hours.'

To further improve your skills in this area, you might like to try these two activities:

1. Listen to conversations around you or on television. Notice whether people give speaker-centred or self-centred responses to the person speaking.

2. Watch your own behaviour over a two-week period. Notice which behaviour you use most and ask yourself which response was best for each occasion.

Effective listening activity 8 – rewording skills

You may have noticed from the previous exercise that speaker-centred responses often merely reword what the person has said. The reason for doing this is that it allows the other person to continue with their own train of thought. You have experienced a situation where you started to tell someone a story but never got to the end of it because they either asked a question that took the conversation off in another direction or told you about a similar experience of their own. Often, in general conversation, there is no harm done by this behaviour. But if someone really needs to talk to you about a difficult issue it can be a great block to effective communication.

You may need to practise rewording skills because they can feel strange at first, almost parrot-like. However, with practice you can elegantly turn around someone's words so that they won't even know you've done so. They will be grateful for feeling listened to, though.

Here are some statements for you to reword. Try to think of two alternative ways of saying what the speaker has said. No answers are provided for this activity as there is no 'correct' answer – just a range of possibilities.

EXAMPLE   *Speaker*:   'Bob is such a pain in the neck. He's always interrupting me.'
Listener (a)   'You're frustrated with Bob because of his constant interruptions.'
Listener (b)   'You're feeling irritated with Bob's interruptions.'

Speaker statements:

1. 'I need to lose 20 lbs, I feel so unattractive.'

   (a) ....

   (b) ....

2. 'I hate it when Kate's home late, I really worry about her.'

   (a) ....

   (b) ....

3. 'I feel torn apart. I want to spend more time with my kids, but my job is so demanding.'

   (a) ....

   (b) ....

4. 'My boss is just so unreasonable. He doesn't see that I'm already overloaded with work.'

   (a) ....

   (b) ....

The following two additional activities will help you to improve this skill even further:

1. If you have a friend you can work with, practise rewording these and other sentences.

2. After a conversation with someone, reflect back over what was said. How well did you reword any relevant statements? Reflect on what you did well so that you can congratulate yourself and know how to do it again. Ask yourself also if there is anything you would do differently next time. Congratulate yourself on noticing areas for improvement.

Effective listening activity 9 – summarizing

Summarizing has three key benefits. Firstly, it shows the person that you have been listening. Secondly, it enables you to check understanding. Thirdly, it pulls together the threads of a conversation in a way that allows it to move forward. This can be very helpful if the other person is going round in a loop discussing a topic.

When we summarize we should:

- summarize what they have said in no more than one or two sentences
- withhold judgement
- not show our view on the subject
- convey the other person's views on the subject
- end with a question to encourage the other person to move forward.

Here are some ways to begin a summary:

- 'Let me just check if I've understood you. You're . . .'
- 'If I understand you correctly . . .'
- 'If I summarise that . . .'
- 'So let's see where we've got to . . .'
- 'If I've got this right . . .'
- 'Tell me if I'm wrong, but I think you're saying . . .'

Here is an example of a summary in action:

Ingrid to James: 'I love my work, it's so interesting and challenging. The trouble is I'm inclined to take on too much and then I get myself stressed. That means I either work late, which doesn't go down well at home, or take work home. Leaving the work undone just doesn't seem like an option – I feel too guilty.'

James to Ingrid: 'As I understand it, you're feeling stressed because you just have too much to do and it's affecting your home life. Is that right?'

Try these two for yourself:

George to Sarah: 'Maya is just so over-controlling, I don't know what to do. She organizes me within an inch of my life. I feel as if all my decisions are taken for me. I try to talk to her about it, but she just says she's being helpful.'

Your summary ....

....

....

Ken to Paul: 'I'm so angry with you that I'm thinking of putting in a formal complaint. You are over-critical and never listen to my point of view. I keep trying to tell you that we are under-resourced but you just don't get it. There aren't enough bodies to do all the work!'

Your summary ....

....

....

Effective listening activity 10 – checking progress

If you have been working through the activities in this section you have been developing a lot of skills. Now is the time to check your progress. Take note for the next day or two of how well you are listening and make notes in response to the following questions:

How well am I doing in these skills?

Active listening:

Rewording:

Summarizing:

Again, congratulate yourself on skills developed. Congratulate yourself also on noticing skills still to be developed. Noticing is the first step on the path to improvement.

Chapter 11

Relationship competence advantage 3 Questioning skills

Martha comes in late from work. Mark is exasperated because this happens regularly and spoils their plans for the evening. He has several possible ways of approaching her about it. Here are some possibilities:

- 'What time to do you call this, then?'
- 'Oh, remembered where you live, have you?'
- 'Why don't you tell that boss of yours that you finish at 5.30?'
- 'I was worried about you, are you okay?'
- 'I'm concerned that our evenings are spoilt by your lateness. Can we talk about it later this evening?'

It doesn't take a genius to work out that the first three questions in this scenario are likely to result in an argument. The fourth question doesn't allow Mark an opportunity to discuss what's worrying him so although it sounds kind, it is only half the answer. Only the last question is likely to have a positive effect on the situation.

Asking the right question is a crucial emotion intelligence skill, but not just for avoiding arguments. Have you ever been in a conversation where trying to get the other person to speak was like pulling teeth? When this happens we tend to blame the other person, and indeed it is true that all parties in a conversation have responsibility for making it work. However, sometimes we fail to encourage the speaker to enlarge on a topic by asking the wrong type of question. Being able to select the right type of question for our purpose is a major skill in relationship building. It enables us to collect information in the most effective way. We can also use this skill to make the other person feel comfortable. We can even use it to help an over-talkative person make their point more succinctly.

This funnel diagram visually demonstrates question types. At the beginning of the conversation we may want to encourage the speaker to give us as much information as possible, so we use open questions. To find out even more, we ask follow-on questions. We may use both of these question types several times. To

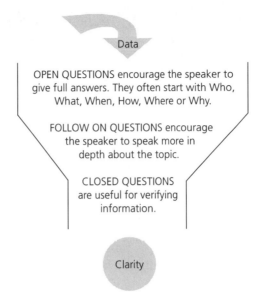

FIGURE 11.1

Question types

check our understanding and clarify the situation we may finish with a closed question.

Useful question types

Let's look at these question types in more detail.

CLOSED questions are useful for verifying information, and can often be answered with 'yes', 'no' or other short answers. In a situation where someone is rambling and you need a brief answer ask a closed question to provide focus.

OPEN questions are questions that encourage the other person to give a full answer. They are difficult to answer with a simple 'yes' or 'no' or one word answer. They often, but not always, start with 'who', 'when', 'what', 'where', 'how' and 'why'. A word of warning about 'why' questions: in some situations they can sound like an interrogation. 'Why' questions can, in any case, be replaced by other questions, for example 'Why haven't you done that yet?' sounds very accusing, but 'I see that report isn't finished yet. What's the problem?' sounds more constructive.

FOLLOW ON questions encourage the speaker to provide further information. They are often questions such as 'Tell me more', 'What happened then?'. Other types of questions you will find useful are:

PROBING   questions challenge the speaker, developing the discussion and getting the reasoning and proof behind the topic. Typical probing questions are 'How does that help solve this problem?', 'How do you know that to be the case?', 'What evidence is there?'.

EVALUATING ALTERNATIVE   questions are used for helping the speaker to make choices and to reach agreement. These are questions such as 'Which of these two options is better for you?', 'On the one hand . . . on the other . . .'.

PAUSE   is a very powerful questioning technique and is not a question at all. Pauses work so well because people feel uncomfortable with silence. If you want to encourage someone to continue speaking, look attentive and encouraging and keep quiet – probably the hardest skill for most of us to master.

CHALLENGING   questions challenge the person speaking to find a solution to their problem or to look at the problem in a different way. Examples of challenging questions would be:

'Is there another way you could look at that?'
'What else would be worth considering?'
'What would have to happen for you to reach your goal?'
'I wonder if you have considered your role in that?'

You can also use questions based on overcoming fuzzy statements below.

Clarifying questions for fuzzy statements

Sometimes people make statements which are unclear or fuzzy. Clarifying questions can help in this case by enabling the person to elucidate their meaning. Here are some different types of fuzzy statements and how to respond to them.

Statement	Question type
Generalized nouns or verbs People using generalized nouns or verbs often need help to be specific about what they are tryng to say.	Use *precision* questions to clarify. These often include the words 'exactly' or 'specifically'.
Example of a generalized noun statement: 'We're all fed up with this.'	Ask: 'What exactly are you all fed up with?' or 'Who, specifically, is fed up?'
Example of a generalized verb statement: 'The way she acts in team meetings sickens me.'	Ask: 'Which specific actions sicken you?' or 'What is sickening about her actions?'
Universal words such as everyone, no-one, all, none, never, always	When responding to these statements, challenge the universal word.
Example of statement using universals: 'No one thinks he'll get this project finished on time'	Ask: 'Is there anyone who thinks he will?'
Implied rules – words like should, must, ought, imply that there is some outside body or rule forcing people to behave in a certain way.	To deal with these statements ask questions to uncover the assumption behind the rule:
Example: 'I should do more gardening.'	Ask: 'Who says you should do more gardening?' or 'What would happen if you decided not to do more gardening?'
Comparisons – using non-specific words like better, worse, bigger, smaller, etc.	Where appropriate, encourage the speaker to be specific about the comparison.
Example: 'She's the worst manager in the company.'	Ask: 'Worse than who? In what way?'
Implied helplessness – using statements that imply the speaker has no personal power over the situation.	Use 'what' questions to help the person appreciate their personal power:
Example: 'I'm hopeless at maths?'	Ask: 'What would have to happen for you to be good at maths?

Question softeners

Sometimes, these clarifying questions can sound a little harsh. If you think this may be the case you can soften the question by prefixing it with something like:

- 'I was wondering . . .'
- 'Have you considered . . .'
- 'Someone once asked me . . .'
- 'Help me understand . . .'

Question types to be avoided

LEADING questions suggest to the listener what answer you expect. They are sometimes used innocently, but sometimes are deliberately manipulative, as it takes confidence to counter them. Examples of leading questions are:

> 'I expect you like the way the office is arranged now, don't you?'
> 'So you have a lot of experience with that software package?'

MULTIPLE questions are confusing because they ask more than one question in the same sentence. Here is an example:

> 'I heard you saw Tim last night. What's he up to these days and I heard his dog was ill, how's she doing and what's happened about his boss?'

WHY questions can be useful, but apply them with care. They can sound very accusing: 'Why haven't you done this?' , 'Why is this late?', 'Why didn't you tell me?'. So check your 'why' question before you speak. Be empathetic to the other person's perception of how it will sound and adjust your question to get the best result.

> *Treat people as if they were what they ought to be, and you help them to become what they're capable of.*
>
> (Goethe)

Questioning skills activity 1 – identifying question types

Test your knowledge of the different question types by identifying the type of question being asked in each of the following cases. The first two examples are worked to show you how to proceed. The answers can be found on p. 306 at the end of this workbook.

Code:

O = Open,   C = Closed,   F = Follow on,   L = Leading,   M = Multiple.

Some questions may be a combination, for example, of precision and open questions or question softeners preceding a closed question. In this case, put a P (for precision), or an S (for softener), in front of the code.

Question	Code
'I just wondered what you would think of re-arranging the room this way?'	S, O
'Are you 27?'	C
1. 'What strengths do you think you can bring to this job?'	
2. 'How are you feeling today?'	
3. 'Do you like living here?'	
4. 'What's the best thing that happened to you today?'	
5. 'What, specifically, makes you unhappy with my behaviour?'	
6. 'You worked in your last job, how long, three years?'	
7. 'Have you considered whether this relationship is the right one for you?'	
8. 'Where do you see yourself in five years' time?'	
9. 'Are you trying to contradict me?'	
10. 'Someone once told me that the two-second pause works when you're feeling angry, have you used it?'	
11. 'What's the best way for us to resolve this?'	
12. 'How, exactly, should we move forward on this one?'	
13. 'In what way are your kids driving you mad?'	
14. 'How, specifically, does that work?'	
13. 'Would you like a cream cake?'	

Questioning skills activity 2 – designing effective questions

Whilst we cannot plan ahead for every conversation we have, we often know in advance that we want to speak to someone about something. In this activity there are some typical situations where you may like to speak to someone. Read the situation and write a suitable question. There is no single 'correct' answer. However, by using your empathy skills combined with questioning skills, you will be able to predict the effectiveness of your question.

Situation 1

You are worried because one of your friends seems to be drinking a lot. You decide to speak to your friend about it. What question would you ask?

Your question: ....

....

Situation 2

Your colleague has made a major mistake that she has not yet noticed. You decide to raise the issue with her. What question would you ask?

Your question: ....

....

Situation 3

Your partner arrives home at 3 a.m. and you expected him home at 10.30. You decide to speak to him about it. What question would you ask?

Your question: ....

....

Now consider two future situations you are facing. Using your knowledge of different questioning types write yourself suitable questions for the situation.

Situation 1

Your question: ....

....

Situation 2

Your question: ....

....

Questioning skills activity 3 – practising question types

Real life presents us with many opportunities to practise emotional intelligence skills, and questioning techniques are no exception. When you are
talking to friends, check out your questions. Are you asking the right question
for each situation? You can improve your skills by:

- reflecting back over past conversations and checking your skill level
- planning for a future conversation
- watching interviewers on television tackle their guests
- working specifically with a friend to practise this skill.

Questioning skills activity 4 – conversations overhead

Listen to conversations around you and identify the type of questions that
people are using. Particularly notice those that are effective given the situation
and those that are not.

Chapter 12
Relationship competence advamntage 4 Rapport skills

Have you ever left a conversation feeling vaguely uncomfortable? You're not sure why things didn't go so well with the other person, but you know they didn't. This happens when you are not in rapport with someone. The art of establishing rapport, seemingly so effortless with some people, is actually a highly complex set of behaviours. Luckily, they are all learnable. Even people who generally have high rapport skills will experience occasions when they are not in rapport. This can happen when they are talking to someone they don't like or are talking about a difficult topic with someone they do like. It can also happen if they are distracted in some way.

So what are rapport skills? We have already looked at many of them: being empathetic, using good listening and questioning skills would be high on the list.

Rapport has been heavily researched and it has been found that when we are in rapport with someone we unconsciously become more like them in a variety of ways. These are shown in the diagram opposite.

Matching body language

Have you ever been chatting to a friend and you notice that you take a sip from your cup of coffee at the same time? That one minute you are both leaning forward with your chin in your hands and the next you're both sitting back? This is an example of *matching* – in this case body language. With most people this happens automatically when they are enjoying a conversation with someone else.

We accidentally *mismatch* when we don't like the other person or what someone else is saying. This is when the rapport stops and the conversation gets tricky. By ensuring that you continue to match the other person's body language in a difficult conversation you will keep the temperature down and be most likely to reach a satisfactory resolution to the topic under discussion. This works fantastically well.

We deliberately mismatch on occasions too. For example, someone comes up to chat to you at work when you're about to leave for home. You probably mismatch by gathering together your bits and pieces and putting on your coat. We can use mismatching deliberately too, for example if we want to stop someone chatting too long. Unless they have poor rapport skills themselves they will unconsciously pick up the mismatching message and bring the conversation to an end.

Tips for matching body language

- Don't exactly mirror the other person's body language, just make yours similar. Try, especially, to match the general posture – sitting forward or back.
- It can be difficult for women to match men's body language because men take up a lot more space and sit in positions that might be embarrassing if the woman is wearing a short skirt. The trick here is to simply match the upper body.

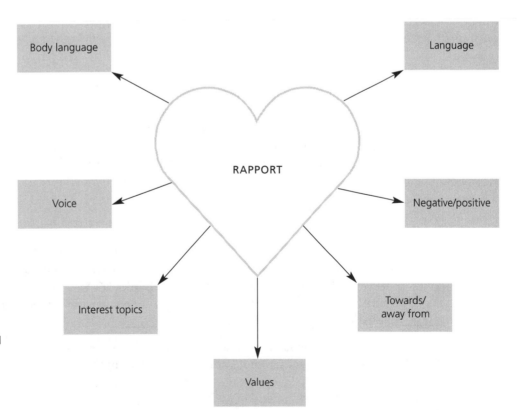

FIGURE 12.1

■ If the person you are speaking to gesticulates a lot, don't try to copy this – they'll have finished before you start. You can, though, just move a finger very slightly each time they wave their arm. It will get you in harmony.

■ If you are speaking to someone from a culture where the body language is very different from you own, don't try to make gestures that feel 'foreign' to you. Match general posture instead.

Matching voice tone or tempo

Different tones and tempos can lead not not only to lack of rapport but also sometimes to prejudice and distrust. People from slow-speaking areas can think that those from fast-speaking ones are always in a hurry, whilst people from fast-speaking areas may think slow speakers are stupid.

Tones can be high or low, loud or soft. Tempos can be fast or slow, with or without pauses. To establish rapport we don't have to match the other person exactly, just get a little nearer to their usual way of speaking. Don't make big, dramatic changes or they may be noticed, just shift a little towards the other person's tone and/or tempo. This is particularly useful over the phone, where the usual influence of body language is missing.

Language

You can make people feel more at ease by using the same type of language they use. For example, if a child calls its parents 'mummy and daddy', use the same words rather than 'mother and father' or 'mum and dad'. Notice whether people use long complex sentences or short simple sentences. Modify your speech to theirs. They'll feel more comfortable with you.

Interest topics

We all have perceptual filters through which we view the world. Our filters determine what we notice. Noticing what other people's interests are and talking about similar things is an excellent way to establish rapport. Filters include activities, other people, things, information, numbers, places, money, activities, etc.

Suppose you want to influence Pete, your boss, to give you some money out of the team's budget for some new equipment. Think about what influences Pete, what his bottom line is. Is it money saved? Time saved? How people feel coping without the equipment? The kudos of having the new equipment? Once you work out his angle, that's how you approach the topic. You'll have much more chance of success.

Positive/negative

Listen for whether the other person has a positive or negative view of the world. To establish rapport, join them in their view. If their view is negative, for a short time join them in negative mode: 'Yes, you're right, August is a miserable month!' If you approach them all cheery and bright, they'll just think you're out of touch and unrealistic. So by adopting their mood just briefly you can establish rapport. But: be careful not to get dragged down. From the base of rapport, work to bring them round to a positive viewpoint.

TRUE LIFE STORY
Fran's mother was known for her negative view of life. Nothing was ever right, everyone got things wrong, she'd had the worst operations, bouts of 'flu. You know the type of person. An insurance policy she held matured and she received her cheque. To her surprise a further £11,000 arrived three weeks later. It was a subsidiary policy she had forgotten about. What did she say? 'Hmm, fat lot of good that is at my time of life. What am I supposed to do with it? Would have been useful when you lot were small, but what's the point now.'

Towards/away from

Some people are motivated to change by moving towards pleasure. For example, they'll try a new product they saw advertised because it looked interesting. Others are only motivated to change by moving away from pain. In their case, they only shift once the *status quo* has become so uncomfortable that changing is an easier option. Once you recognize the other person's motivation, you use their viewpoint to persuade them. For example, to persuade your partner to help you with the household chores:

Towards: 'I'll be so pleased if you do this, that I'll cook us a nice lunch and we'll open a bottle of wine.'
Away from: 'If you don't help with the chores we'll sit here in a mess and you know how you hate that.'

Values

Identify what the other person's values are. What do they value most? What do they value least? Their value system may include topics such as being kind, value for money, being seen as strong, saving money, integrity, getting as much from the system as they can – the list is endless.

Rapport skills activity 1 – making small talk

Many people find small talk difficult, especially with unfamiliar people. They become awkward and embarrassed, and this causes a downward spiral of feelings. Sometimes these are accompanied by physical sensations such as sweating, a rash on the neck and face or stammering.

A good way to get into a conversation with another person is to ask them questions – most people like talking about themselves. You can use the PRONES approach. PRONES is a mnemonic for People, Recreation, Occupation, News, Education, and Surroundings. Here are some further tips:

PEOPLE You can talk about people you know in common, families, friends, people in the news.

RECREATION What is the other person's way of spending their spare time? What hobbies do they enjoy?

OCCUPATION Most people are willing to tell you what their job is. If you know something about that area of work, you have something to talk about. If you don't, you still have something to talk about because you can ask them to tell you more.

NEWS By being aware of current affairs, you can often find something to talk to others about.

EDUCATION Has the person attended any courses recently? Have you met on a course? What's in the news about education?

SURROUNDINGS Comment on your surroundings – the weather, the temperature, the building, pictures you can see.

When someone tells you a bit about themselves, tell them something about you in return. This reciprocity is the very stuff of friendly conversations. There is more information on this on p. 36 in the section 'Personal competence'.

Think back to the last time you were stuck for small talk. Imagine yourself right back there in that situation with that person or people. Using the PRONES prompts make notes about what you could have said to encourage small talk.

People

Recreation

Occupation

News

Education

Surroundings

Rapport skills activity 2 – discovering values

Understanding someone's values can be priceless if we want to influence their approach. People are motivated to achieve what they value and their choices are often made on this basis. However, they are sometimes unaware of the values that influence their decisions and judgements. By becoming aware, they can make more reasoned decisions.

In any situation dissatisfaction may be because of an important value not being met. For example, perhaps someone works hard because they value a high salary or an opportunity to help people. Perhaps they want mental stimulation or the company of others.

Over the next week or two try to find out the values of people you regularly meet. You can do this by asking the questions below:

- What is important to you . . . ?
- What has to be true for you to . . . ?
- What makes you . . . ?
- What do you value in . . . ?
- What motivates you . . . ?
- What else is important . . . ?
- What is even more important . . . ?

Rapport skills activity 3 – matching body language

There are two ways to practise matching body language. In the first work with a friend. Decide who will be A and who will be B. Have a conversation for five minutes about a topic of your choice. During that time A should subtly match B's body language. Now change around, and B copies A's body language. Now continue your discussion but this time A subtly mismatches B's body language. After five minutes swop around so that B is mismatching A's body language. When you have finished discuss the following questions:

- How did you feel when you were matching body language?
- What effects did mismatching have on your conversation?
- With whom do you match? Why?
- With whom do you mismatch? Why?
- In what situations would you benefit from matching more?

The second activity for practising matching skills is just to get out there and do it. You can feel a bit self-conscious at first so practise in easy situations where there will be no come-back if someone notices. Try matching at first just for very short bursts of time, perhaps a couple of minutes. If you regularly deal with someone you don't like, make an effort to match them during conversations. You will really notice the benefits.

Rapport skills activity 4 – using matching to calm down others

The matching rapport skills that we have identified can also be used to calm down angry people.

Matching body language

When you match the body language of someone who is angry, do not take on *all* of their non-verbal behaviour. Two people in angry pose are soon likely to get into a fight. Instead take on their general posture but without all the extras that demonstrate anger. These vary from person to person but some common signs you might see are: avoiding eye contact, 'eye-balling', jutting jaw, clenched fists, frowns, and sneers. Do not take on this body language.

So, take on the general posture of the angry person and when you think you may have begun to establish rapport, relax your body language and hope that they will follow your lead. This is called leading and pacing. If it doesn't work after about forty-five seconds, subtly take on their body language once more and then try relaxing again.

Matching voice

Often when we are trying to calm down an angry person we speak quietly, sometimes even saying 'Calm down' (a sure way to wind people up). Often this quiet speech works, but some people become more angry and think you are not taking them seriously. If you think this is the case don't shout back but raise your voice to show that you accept the importance and urgency of what they are saying. This is not the same as agreeing with them if you don't. Look at the statements below, which are the sorts of things you might say if you were dealing with someone angry. They can all be said either quietly or with urgency in the voice. They are options. If one tone of voice isn't working, try the other.

'I just want to be clear I understand what you're saying'	■ Summarizes; clarifies
'I can see you feel very strongly about that'	■ Empathizes, without necessarily agreeing with the content
'I'll sort that out now'	■ Promises action

Rapport skills activity 5 – checking assumptions

Often when we speak to someone we make assumptions about what they are saying or doing and fail to check out the truth of these assumptions. Author Chris Argyris calls this the Ladder of Inference. Here is an example of one such ladder. Judy is talking to her boss, Jane, about a problem:

Judy is worried that her boss frowned at her. On no other evidence than this frown she infers:

(a) that Jane is angry with her
(b) that she, Judy, must have done something wrong
(c) that Jane might fire her.

Judy failed to consider other options such as her boss having a headache, or being tired, or worried about something.

She might fire me
I must have done something wrong
Jane is angry with me
Jane frowned when I spoke to her

Ladder of Inference

Inferences come from a variety of places. We may make assumptions about someone's behaviour because of some old problem entirely our own. For example, Judy may have been fired ten years previously by another employer and lived in fear ever since that it would happen again.

We may also make assumptions based on incorrect interpretation of the other person's words or body language. We may also simply misunderstand what they say.

Chris Argyris talks about us having left-hand and right-hand thinking. Left-hand thinking is what we think but don't say to others. Right-hand is what we actually say – and this may bear little or no relation to what we think. Here is an example of left- and right-hand thinking.

Left-hand thinking (what I thought)	Right-hand thinking (what I said)
If he loved me, he'd know I'm tired and do the washing-up.	Joy: 'I've had a really hard day at work.'
Now he's telling me about *his* hard day. Why doesn't he listen?	Darren: 'Me too. The damn computer broke down three times and . . .'
I'm not interested in *his* day. I want him to listen to me and do the washing up.	Joy: 'Mmm. It's so tiring coming back to all the housework after being out all day.'
Now he'll get the hint.	Darren: 'Let's just leave it. It'll still be there in the morning.'
He's so insensitive.	Joy: 'And who'll do it then?'

You can see that this type of thinking and speaking can soon lead to misunderstandings and eventually to a row. Had Joy simply said to Darren 'I'm really tired, would you do the dishes?' she'd have had a much better chance of success.

Rapport skills activity 6 – observing a role model

Most of us know someone who is excellent at rapport skills. For this activity, we ask you to take conscious notice of your role model. In particular ask yourself what your role model does well that you could copy. You may like to try to observe him or her in the follow situations if possible:

- meeting someone new
- calming down a difficult person
- encouraging a quiet person to speak
- negotiating with someone
- speaking out in a meeting

or indeed in any other area of rapport where you would like to increase your skill level.

Rapport skills activity 7 – asking for forgiveness

Ever dealt with someone who will just not admit when they're wrong? Infuriating, isn't it? Now look at yourself. Do you always admit when you've done something wrong? The emotionally enlightened person is willing to admit to mistakes and work towards rectifying them. If you realize that you frequently have conflict with others, there is probably something in your behaviour that needs adjusting. Are you assuming that everyone should agree with you all the time? Do you think all mistakes are someone else's fault? Do you think that people should drop everything and do things when and how you want them? Are you sometimes sharp, downright rude, or bullying to others? If you can answer yes to any of these questions you might like to read again the Personal competence section of this workbook to find ways to adapt this behaviour. Your life will be much more pleasant as a result.

When we do mess up, often all that is needed is a simple 'sorry'. Sometimes, though, our emotional blockage or the sheer magnitude of what we've done wrong makes our apology more difficult. Here are some steps that will help you:

Steps for asking for forgiveness

1. Think about the situation and your part in it. What behaviour of yours are you unhappy about?

2. Make some notes for yourself to help yourself organize your thoughts.

3. Practise making your apology until you feel comfortable that you've got the words and tone right.

4. Apologize to the other person.

5. Don't make excuses or try to shift the blame. Take responsibility for your own actions.

6. Keep calm, listen to the response you get without getting defensive.

7. Offer to make amends if this is possible.

8. Forgive yourself. We all make mistakes. Our responsibility is to learn from them and try to avoid making them in future.

An honest apology counts for a lot. Think of it as a commitment to the relationship – an act of strength rather than an act of weakness.

Remember that the other person may not immediately accept your apology, they may be too angry. Allow time for them to calm down. You may need to make the apology again when they can hear you better.

And, if the situation is just too difficult, you can apologize in writing.

Chapter 13

Relationship competence advantage 5 Control and trust

In most relationships there tends to be one person who is more controlling than the other. Sometimes this is within acceptable bounds and causes no problems. Sometimes, though, the person is over-controlling and this has a very detrimental effect on the relationship, which quickly becomes dysfunctional. Over-controlling behaviour lacks emotional intelligence. Here are some examples of over-controlling behaviour:

■ wanting people to always do things when you want in the way you want
■ doing things for people even against their will 'because it's in their own best interests'
■ making others do things they don't want for the same reason
■ filling up every moment of someone else's day
■ constantly wanting to know another person's whereabouts.

Does this sound like you or someone you share your life with? If so, this section is for you!

Being over-controlling is often a sign of insecurity heavily disguised. Over-controlling people don't feel confident enough in themselves or the other person to allow flexibility of behaviour. They want to control everything that happens so that they can feel safe.

Emotionally perceptive people recognise that they are becoming over-controlling and learn to back off. They have the ability to trust others, or in cases where trust is abused, to deal with the situation assertively.

TRUE LIFE STORY
Mick was a committee member at his local sports and social club. He was secretary and liked everything to be just so, believing that no-one else could do anything as well as he could. A very tense man, unable to trust anyone, he believed that everyone was out to get him. This meant that he misinterpreted everything that was said to him. An offer of help was seen as a criticism that he wasn't doing it right. Even a mild challenge sent him into a fury, banging his fists on the table and threatening to resign.

> Eventually the group got tired of his behaviour and voted him off the committee. The very over-controlling behaviour that he thought would keep him safe had in fact worked against him.

Control and trust activity 1 – stop being controlling

Overcoming controlling behaviour takes time and persistence but it certainly pays off. You will feel more relaxed, less stressed and you'll find that others like you better. Here are some questions to ask yourself. Complete the sections below in relation to one situation where you believe you were over-controlling. We would highly recommend that you copy this worksheet and keep a record over a few weeks so that you can see if any patterns emerge.

1. Congratulate yourself for noticing that you have been over-controlling on this occasion. The noticing is a very emotionally intelligent thing to do. What was it that made you realize that you had been over-controlling? How can you notice more quickly in future?

2. What were you thinking and feeling at the time? What fears were in your mind (they may be well hidden)? What did this over-controlling behaviour do to and for you?

3. What did you say or do that was over-controlling?

4. What was the effect on the other person or people?

5. Consider alternative ways of acting and the responses they would have had.

Alternative 1	Response
Alternative 2	Response
Alternative 3	Response

6. Look back over this worksheet or your collection of worksheets and try to detect patterns of behaviour. For example are you over-controlling:

- ■ with your children because you're afraid they'll make the same mistakes you did?
- ■ with your partner because you're worried you might be deserted?
- ■ with your staff member because you fear their poor performance will reflect on you?

7. Look at your attitudes that are behind your behaviour. They will reflect your beliefs about the person or situation. Ask yourself 'What would be more helpful to believe?'. Examples might be: 'I'll show my children a good example, give them lots of love and attention, and trust them to find their own way'; 'Other people have good ideas too';, 'Having a good relationship is more important than controlling others'.

More helpful beliefs:

8. How could I act to live these new beliefs? (For example, you might offer less direction, listen more, or let others do things their own way.)

9. Write down the new behaviours on a card and place them where you see them regularly. This will keep reminding you to behave in the way you want. It is also very helpful to visualize yourself behaving in the way you want to.

10. Congratulate and reward yourself every time you behave in a less controlling way.

Control and trust activity 2 – coping with a controlling partner

If you have turned straight to this activity, you would probably find it helpful to read Activity 1, Stop being controlling, where the reason for controlling behaviour is explained. This will help you to gain perspective on your partner's behaviour.

If your partner is not willing to change their behaviour you must decide what you can and can't live with. Here is a worksheet to help you to deal with emotional wisdom with your controlling partner.

1. Write down a list of the controlling behaviours that your partner has. Divide them into those you can and those you can't live with.

Can live with these behaviours	These behaviours must stop

2. Make notes about why these behaviours annoy you. Ask yourself:

    ■ Is this behaviour really over-controlling or is my partner simply trying to get me to take my share of responsibilities?

    ■ Does this behaviour remind me of something from my childhood?

    ■ Do I feel in control in other areas of my life?

3. Identify which behaviour is truly over-controlling and which is related to your wish to do your own thing or some experiences from earlier in your life. This is to help you separate those behaviours which truly relate to your partner. (You may notice after doing this that your feelings of irritation with your partner decrease)

4. If you decide to speak to your partner in an attempt to get a change of behaviour, you can use the format for giving criticism in the Assertiveness skills section of this workbook (pp. 176). Plan what you will say in the space below:

TIPS
■ Remember that being over-controlling is often to do with lack of confidence or trust. Work to build your partner's self-confidence. Also, be trustworthy at all times. Be where you say you will, do what you say you will do, and remain faithful.

■ If your partner is overly intrusive, wanting to know where you are and who you've been with at all times, give straight honest answers but refuse to prolong the conversation. Explain calmly that you have replied honestly and that your partner's behaviour has slipped into being over-controlling.

■ If your partner does change, show that you appreciate them. Reward them with a hug and thanks. Doing this will reinforce the new behaviour and make it more likely to happen again.

The area of control is one where you might like to remember the three choices outlined in the Relationship Competence Section:

Choice 1. Change yourself – how you feel about the situation.

Choice 2. Change the situation – if this possible.

Choice 3. Get out.

Control and trust activity 3 – start trusting others

If you have found people untrustworthy in the past it can be difficult to risk trusting others for the first time. Your past experience probably means that you home in on noticing untrustworthy acts, unaware of the people who have earned your trust. Give yourself a pat on the back for being courageous enough to try this new way of acting. These guidelines may help you:

1. Notice people you interact with on a regular basis. Objectively observe whether they are people of integrity. Do they respect other people's feelings? Do they do what they say they will do? Do they keep confidences? When you have identified someone who has this integrity, you can begin the next step.

2. Decide on one small thing you are going to trust this person with. This could be:

   - a small secret
   - talking over a problem
   - a favour
   - to lend you something
   - feedback on something you've done
   - anything else that comes to mind.

   Make sure it's something that won't have serious consequences should the person fail to do as you wish (even reliable people have off-days).

3. Try out this new trusting behaviour with the person.

4. Assess the result. If all goes well, try trusting the same person or someone else with something else. Gradually build up the number of occasions when you trust others.

5. If things don't go to plan, don't assume this means that no one is trustworthy. Even the most trusting of people have occasional let-downs, it's all part of life's rich pattern. Try again. You will gradually find that your opinions are changed as people respond to your trust by being trustworthy.

6. Remember to be trustworthy in return.

Chapter 14

Relationship competence advantage 6 Assertiveness

Assertiveness is the ability to act in a way that is consistent with our beliefs and that respects ourselves and others equally.

Assertiveness has been in and out of favour for a number of years. It has probably been most closely associated with women's development and, as a result, some people have attached certain connotations to it. For the purposes of emotional intelligence, however, assertiveness is about meeting the needs of all parties involved in a situation and is gender-neutral. It is about balancing your rights with your responsibilities.

There are many excellent books written on this topic, which cover for example assertiveness in specific vocations, assertiveness in the workplace, or assertiveness as a generic skill. If you have not already read or attended courses on assertiveness, then this is something that you may now want to consider. Similarly, you may feel that you already have a good understanding of how to be assertive. Excellent – you have a head start in this section! Remember though, as we said in the introduction, if you want to gain best value from this book, you will only do that by working through all the exercises.

Assertiveness activity 1 – assertiveness rating

Assertiveness is very closely linked to conflict management and we will move directly into dealing with conflict next. But let's start by taking a quick look at your own assertiveness rating. Read the statements 1 to 10 in the table below and tick the box which most closely describes how you would respond.

Skill	Mostly	Sometimes	Hardly ever
1. I can accept a compliment			
2. I am confident about asking for a salary increase when I feel I've earned it			
3. I worry about situations involving confrontation			

158 The EI Advantage

4. People take me for granted
5. I feel comfortable around people in authority
6. If I feel strongly about an issue I express this
7. I pay others compliments
8. I let others know that I value them
9. If I am unhappy with a service I've received I set about addressing this
10. I am happy to invest time and energy in meeting new friends

Now circle the corresponding scores from the following list, total each column and add the three together to give you a grand total.

Question	Mostly	Sometimes	Hardly ever
1.	5	3	1
2.	3	2	1
3.	1	2	3
4.	1	2	3
5.	3	2	1
6.	6	4	1
7.	5	3	1
8.	3	2	1
9.	6	4	2
10.	3	2	1
Totals			

Grand total: ......

Scoring: up to 15 passive
over 26 assertive

How did you get on? Do you see a clear picture emerging of yourself as an assertive or a passive person? Perhaps you scored over 26, but realize that you are assertive in some situations but not in others. This is a simple exercise just to encourage you to think about the different levels of assertiveness you use across a range of situations. Be mindful that other behaviours sit along the continuum between assertive and passive styles. For example, aggressive and indirectly aggressive responses may be used on different occasions. We will discuss these in more detail from p. 161. It is very common for people to be assertive in one area of their lives but passive at other times. Likewise people often say they are assertive with some people but not with others. For example, many people report that they find it difficult to be assertive with older people or those in authority.

Being assertive IS:	Being assertive is NOT:
Respecting yourself and others equally	Bullying others
Feeling confident about yourself	Getting your own way at all costs
Averting potentially aggressive situations	Ducking out of difficult situations
Listening to opposing viewpoints	Being sarcastic
Having maximum flexibility in your approach to people and situations	Always responding to situations in the same way
Being willing to say when you don't know something	Failing to stand up for yourself
Helping others to be assertive	Compromising your principles to avoid conflict
Being aware of your behaviour and its effects on others	Sulking

Assertive rights

Assertive rights are about believing that you and others have certain rights simply as human beings, and they stem from the right to be treated with respect. For example, we all have the right to:

- be treated with respect
- support from family, colleagues and managers
- finish work at a reasonable time.

You can benefit from thinking of assertive rights this way. You know that you have rights in other areas of your life. For example, you have consumer rights. If you think you have had a poor deal in a shop you can check your rights and feel more confident in returning the goods. You have legal rights. If someone libels you, you can see a solicitor and take them to court. You may not like any of these actions but you will feel more confident because you know you have rights in the matter. In the same way, believing in your assertive rights will help you to confidently tackle situations that you face in your everyday life.

What other rights do you think you have? Write them below.

1. ....

2. ....

3. ....

4. ....

5. ....

6. ....

All rights carry responsibilities, otherwise they could be seen as a charter for selfishness. If we look at our three earlier examples, you can see that each has a corresponding responsibility.

Right	Responsibility
1. Be treated with respect	1. Treat others with respect, even if we don't agree with what they say or do
2. Support from family, colleagues and managers	2. Give support to family, colleagues and managers
3. Finish work at a reasonable time	3. Arrive at work on time and work effectively

What responsibilities go with the rights you have identified?

1. ....

2. ....

3. ....

4. ....

5. ....

6. ....

Always begin with the lowest level of assertiveness. Just as you don't need to use a hammer to crack an egg, it is not necessary to launch into a heavy assertive stance for a relatively minor situation. Choose a level of assertiveness to fit the occasion. If this is ineffective, then move to more complex levels, but only if necessary. This approach can also be applied to writing an assertive letter, which we will cover on p. 180. It's inappropriate, and often counter-productive to use heavy assertion techniques too early.

Four styles of behaviour

The basis of assertion is respect for yourself and others: a belief that 'I'm OK and you're OK'. This equal respect is much easier said than done. For example powerful 'parent messages', explored in more detail on p. 48, tell the growing child about their position in life, their value and what to think about others.

So, if you have poor self-esteem you will find it difficult to treat others equally because you'll have underlying feelings that they're more important than you. Likewise, any prejudices you have will dictate how respectful you are towards others.

You could find yourself in a situation where you need to be assertive with someone who, for all sorts of reasons, you do not respect. This can be difficult, but it is important that during this interaction, you regard this other person as an equal. For assertion to be effective, each person involved needs to know that their feelings will be treated with respect.

The following diagram sets out four styles of behaviour and the levels of self-esteem underpinning them:

Assertive	Aggressive
'I'm OK, you're OK'	'I'm OK, you're not OK'
Passive	Indirectly Aggressive
'I'm not OK, you're OK'	'I'm OK, you're not OK, but I won't tell you I think that'

The aim of:

- assertive behaviour is to achieve as close as possible a 'win–win' situation
- aggressive behaviour is to win, probably at the expense of another person; 'for me to win, you have to lose'
- indirectly (passive) aggressive behaviour is to win without others realizing that you are out to do so
- passive behaviour is to avoid confrontation and please others.

Assertive behaviour is:

- respecting yourself and others equally
- standing up for what you believe in without damaging others
- feeling confident about what you say, even if sometimes you have to say you don't know something
- working to achieve a win–win situation with others
- being clear in your communication
- having flexibility in your approach towards others.

Aggressive behaviour is:

- aiming to get your own way at all costs
- showing lack of respect for others
- communicating with others by shouting, swearing or other aggressive speech.

Passive behaviour is:

- avoiding conflict at all times
- not asking for what you want
- not saying 'no' when you want to
- building up resentments
- not speaking out for what you believe in.

Indirectly aggressive behaviour is:

- disrespecting the other person in an indirect way
- sarcasm, put-downs
- sulking
- silence rather than sorting out a problem

- looking for people to blame
- not accepting responsibility.

Another way of looking at this is by plotting level of need on an axis:

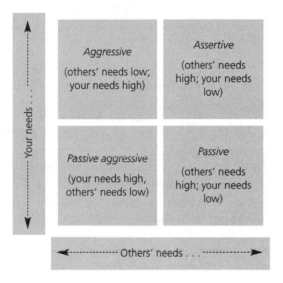

Think about some situations common to you. Look at the following examples. Where would you sit on the axes above?

- A colleague asks for a lift home which will take you out of your way and you are already late.
- You have planned and are looking forward to a quiet evening with your partner. Friends whom you've not seen for some time call to say they are in the area and want to visit.
- You have been saving for a new jacket. Your partner needs to buy equipment for work and asks if you can help out with the expense.
- At work you have washed up/made the tea twice in a row when a manager asks if you'd mind doing it again.

You could well find that your response differs depending on the context. It is useful for you pay attention to what this reveals, for example, you may be passive at work and passive aggressive at home. If this is the case, then why might this be so?

Assertiveness activity 2 – asking for what we want

One major reason why people don't get what they want is simply because they don't ask for it. This is typical passive or indirectly aggressive behaviour.

People often sabotage their chances of getting their needs met because some aspect of their belief system gets in the way. Surprisingly these belief systems often involve an expectation that the other person should be a mind reader:

- 'If he was any sort of manager he'd know I need help to do . . .'
- 'If she was a decent colleague she'd know that I need someone to talk to right now.'
- 'Nobody in this house ever clears up behind them.'
- 'She is deliberately withholding that information from me.'
- 'No one tells me anything.'
- 'No one noticed how well I handled that situation.'

Conversely, we can be irritated if others expect us to mind read: 'Well, how could I know that's what she wanted, I'm not a mind reader, am I?' And so we stay locked into the cycle of complaining how hard done by we are when the reality often is about not taking responsibility for ourselves and our failure to communicate clearly.

Assertiveness activity 3 – assertiveness scale

To check how confident you are about getting your needs met, complete the simple questionnaire below:

Need to be met	Comfort level (1 = very uncomfortable 10 = very confident)	What stops me feeling confident
Ask a colleague to take on some work for you		
Asking your line manager for some time off		
Ask your partner to clean the bathroom/lounge/kitchen		
Ask a colleague not to smoke in your car		
Ask for a refund for sub-standard goods/services		

The reality is that those who ask are more likely to get what they want. This is simply because others will be aware of their needs. It is your right to ask for what you want. If this seems too bold, remember that it is the other person's right to say 'no'.

Giving clear request messages

For many of us, making assertive requests is a real struggle. If this is a problem for you, there is a technique to making requests clearly you could try:

Phase 1
What do you want?
↓
Phase 2
Who do you need to ask?
↓
Phase 3
How will you request impact upon the other person?
↓
Phase 4
When will you ask?
↓
Phase 5
How will you ask?

PHASE 1   *Decide what you want*

Seems obvious, but this is often surprisingly difficult. It can be simpler to work out what we don't want. If this is easier for you then use this as your starting point and work through a process of elimination to gain an idea of what does appeal.

PHASE 2   *Decide who to ask*

Again, it seems obvious not to ask the wrong person, but this needs to be carefully thought through. It could be that the person who could grant your request is unwilling to do so. If so, you have to be prepared to find an alternative route to achieve what you want.

PHASE 3   *Consider the effects of the request on the other person*

Will the other person be able to meet your request? Is it reasonable to ask them or might it add to their work load ? Will they be flattered to be asked to help? What's in it for them to say 'yes' to you?

PHASE 4   *Decide when to ask*

Choose your moment! Don't rush in with your request in an attempt to 'get it over with'. Quite often this most basic principle is overlooked when people make requests.

PHASE 5   *Decide how to ask*

Keep it uncomplicated – 'I need to' or ' I'd like to' is much easier to understand and respond to than a vague 'I was wondering if maybe . . .'

Assertiveness activity 4 – your unmet needs

Make a list of your needs which are not currently being met:

1. ....

2. ....

3. ....

4. ....

5. ....

Taking each item in turn plan how to request that your need be met using the guidelines discussed above. Copy this list five times (or more if you need to):

Step 1 – What exactly do you want?	Step 2 – Who is the best person to ask?
Step 3 – What are the effects of the request on the other person?	Step 4 – When is the best time to ask?
Step 5 – What is the best way to ask?	Additional notes

Assertiveness activity 5 – broken-record technique

'Broken record' is an excellent technique to use when the other person either won't hear you or tries to deflect what you are saying. It is a very simple and effective technique when people won't take 'no' for an answer, don't listen to your point in meetings, or in any other situation where you need to make your point strongly. It involves repeating your message several times – hence its name. This is how it works:

1   *Decide what you want to achieve*

Example: your manager tends not to notice the number of occasions you work late and does not suggest that you take time off in lieu. You want to change this pattern.

2   *State your case including your 'broken-record' statement*

Example: ' I have worked late twice this week. I'd like to leave at 3.30 pm on Friday to make up for this.'

3   *Listen to what the other person has to say and decide if you will change your mind*

Example response: ' Oh, I'm afraid that's going to be difficult. I need you to lock up on Friday as I have an out-of-office meeting that afternoon.'

4   *If you have not changed your mind, respond briefly to their comment and then repeat your broken-record statement*

Example: 'Then can we look at finding someone else to lock up? I have worked late twice this week. I'd like to leave at 3.30 pm on Friday.'

5   *Repeat the above two steps up to five times*

Be prepared for the other person raising an issue which is not immediately relevant.

Example response: 'I am under a lot of pressure at the minute. I need your support'.

Respond to this with, 'That's important, we'll discuss that in a minute but now I . . .'

Discussing the discussion as opposed to what the discussion is about is very helpful if you are getting stuck. This would involve phrases such as 'I'm concerned that we seem to be having difficulty coming to an agreement'. 'It seems as if we have conflicting views here, is there some compromise we can reach?' This in itself could become the new broken record.

By using the broken-record technique you can prevent the other person deflecting or manipulating you with diversionary tactics and keep the focus of your discussion where you want it.

Assertiveness activity 6 – understanding body language

'It's not what you say, it's the way that you say it', so goes the old song and there's a lot of truth in that. If we contradict what we say with our body language or our tone, we will not be convincing or assertive. In fact, the message we give other people is far more through our body language than anything we say (see Figure 14.1 opposite).

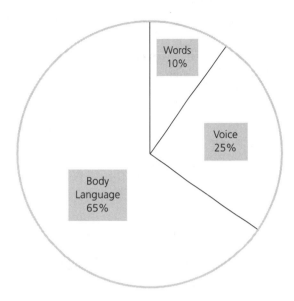

FIGURE 14.1

The message we give others

You can see that a staggering 65% of the message we give others is non-verbal. Imagine a teacher of assertiveness standing in front of a class wringing her hands, looking at the floor and saying 'I can teach you to be assertive'. Would you believe her? Of course not. You'd be seeing a massive discrepancy between what she said and what she demonstrated.

Most people are experts at body language, even though they may be quite unaware of their skill. Most of us can pick up whether someone is happy or sad, tense or relaxed. We can usually tell when two people are in love or having a row without having to hear what they're talking about. It's useful though to have this knowledge in our conscious awareness so that we can pull it out of our emotional intelligence toolkit to use when necessary.

Before we look at different meanings of this type of non-verbal communication it's worth saying that body language is different across cultures. Indeed, hardly any body language is common throughout the world. With that in mind we must be particularly careful if we interpret the body language of someone from a different culture to our own. For example, in Turkey they shake their head to say 'yes' and nod their head to say 'no' – very confusing when bartering for goods in the covered bazaar in Istanbul!

These differences can have a big impact on what we think of people from a different culture so be careful before passing judgement. The body language talked about here is mainstream British or American body language (although even here there are differences between the two, but our exposure to each other's culture via the media means that they are reasonably familiar).

When considering body language remember that you should never make a decision based on one piece of body language alone. For example, most people think that crossed arms are a sign of defensiveness. And it's true. Up to a point. But it's also a sign that the person is cold or that they're relaxed. It's the combination of this single gesture with others that gives the complete picture. The person who is cold will probably be sitting forward hugging themselves with shoulders pulled in and back bent. The person who is relaxed will be sitting back, arms stretched forward. The person who is defensive may be sitting rather upright and rigid, although even there there are other non-verbal ways of communicating defensiveness.

Non-verbal clues and the passive person

Facial expression: looks anxious, ingratiating, smiles and nods, neutral

Eye contact: minimal, frequent combined with anxious look, downcast eyes, roving eyes, avoiding contact

Gestures: fidgets, nods frequently, hand over mouth when talking, other nervous gestures

Posture: slumped, pulled in on self, neutral, shrinking

Tone of voice: hesitant, weak

Non-verbal clues and the assertive person

Facial expression: attentive, interested

Eye contact: open, frequent, friendly

Gestures: open gestures, calm

Posture: sitting upright or forward, open and approachable, relaxed, friendly

Tone of voice: measured, appropriate volume

Non-verbal clues and the aggressive person

Facial expression: frowns, rolls eyes, squints, pinched mouth

Eye contact: 'eye-balls', looks away in disgust

Gestures: abrupt, points finger, leans forward suddenly, taps fingers, slams doors, pounds fist

Posture: upright, leaning forward, rigid fists, clenched

Tone of voice: shouting, sneering, over-controlled, shrill

Non-verbal clues and the indirectly aggressive person

Facial expression: insincere smile, avoids eye contact, bored look, lack of expression

Eye contact: direct, roving eyes

Gestures: raises hands, mocking

Posture: upright, leaning forward, head on side, chin forward

Tone of voice: questioning, sarcastic, whining, drawling

Posture often provides the strongest clue to someone's feelings, reflecting their state of mind. Stand an assertive person next to a passive one and you will immediately tell the difference. The assertive person will have upright yet relaxed stance, while the passive person will be trying to make themselves smaller with scrunched shoulders and lowered head.

Sitting postures also reflect emotional state. Sitting relaxed, just slightly slumped and with upright head and alert eyes indicates confident interest. Just a small change to sitting with your bottom a long way forward on the seat, legs extended and head forward now suggests superiority. Sitting on the edge of the seat with arms folded inward, legs crossed and head down is likely to indicate nervousness.

It's easy to look assertive. Sit with your weight evenly distributed on your bottom. Now imagine a string pulling you up from the top of your head. This should bring your eyes level, your shoulders down and your back comfortably straight. It looks fantastic. Standing assertively is the same except this time the weight is evenly on your feet instead of your bottom. Just changing your body language really changes how you feel because your body and mind are so linked. Just think about it: expressions such as 'stand on your own two feet', 'taking a firm stand', '. . . 's standing in the community' reflect this assertive posture. Expressions like 'I'm not sure where I stand on this' and 'shifty character' reflect an unbalanced body weight and subsequent poor image.

Non-verbal leakage

When we feel uncomfortable about something but are not expressing our feelings openly, they often 'leak' in some way. For example, we may say we're calm but may actually be tapping our fingers impatiently. We may say we're happy but have drooped shoulders and downturned mouth. In fact, non-verbal leakage is any body language that is inconsistent with what the person thinks they are projecting.

You can use your knowledge of non-verbal leakage effectively. Next time you see someone demonstrating leakage, ask yourself what the conversation is about and why they may feel uncomfortable. This is your opportunity to learn more. You may even simply say something like 'You don't look happy with that'. Hopefully they will tell you what is wrong. Sometimes though, it's just that they're worried about missing their bus or want to go to the loo.

Next time you are with other people and are not expected to have too much involvement watch their body language. This could be in a restaurant or other social gathering. What do you think each person is thinking or feeling? How do they feel about each other? How do they feel about what is being said? How do you feel about them? As much as possible try to judge these points without actually listening to what is being said.

Assertive activity 7 – your body language

Over the next week become consciously aware of your body language. What message do you give people non-verbally? Try changing your body language when you are feeling negative. What effect does that have?

> *If you won't be better tomorrow than you are today, what do you need tomorrow for?*
>
> (Unknown)

Assertiveness activity 8 – responding to criticism confidently

We all receive criticism, sometimes justified, sometimes not. The way in which the criticism is delivered will often dictate how we respond. For example, when criticism is given aggressively, we tend to become defensive. For example:

You've made a total mess of this report! What's the matter with you?	Well if I only had one thing to do at a time instead of twenty, I might be in with a chance
These figures are all wrong! Where on earth did you get the information?	If I'm given information I naturally assume it is correct. I don't have time to go around checking it all!

In whatever form criticism is given to you, an emotionally intelligent response is to use it constructively; make sure you consider why it was given and how you can gain something from it. Tune into your emotions, keep your breathing regular and don't become defensive. Recognize that you *will* learn something from it and try to show willingness to change. This makes it easier to discuss possible solutions. The flow chart below gives an outline of how you might do this:

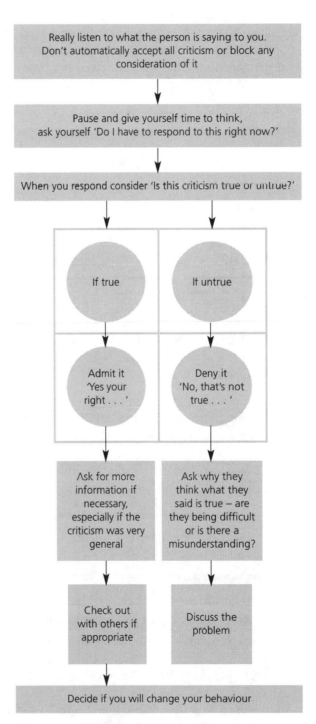

FIGURE 14.2

Assertiveness activity 9 – assertive statements for use in handling criticism

Think of a time recently when someone has levelled a criticism at you. This could have been at work or at home. Summarize the situation in the box below and then think about how you felt at the time. Write your feelings in the space allocated.

Situation	Feelings

Now think about the outcome – did you adapt your behaviour as a result of the criticism? Did you feel the comments were justified? Did you feel resentful or hurt by some of the remarks? If you felt unhappy, what might have made you feel better about it?

Listed below are some emotionally enlightened responses that can be used in response to criticism. Read them through and think about whether you could have used any during the example you've written above:

- 'I'd like to explain why I did that/think that way'
- 'I feel frustrated about the difficulty we are having discussing this'
- 'Could you give me some specific examples?'
- 'I feel you may be agreeing with me even though that is not what you believe'
- 'Do you have any suggestions for resolving this situation?'
- 'I'd really like us to be able to find a compromise'
- 'I'd like to check I understand you correctly'
- 'We seem to have dissimilar ideas/views on this'

Now try replaying your example again, with your buddy or someone you feel comfortable with. Make a note below of the way that you would accept the criticism now and then think about how this makes you feel. Discuss this with the person you are practising with.

Revised response	Feelings

We can all benefit from genuine criticism, provided it is given in a way which helps us strive for improvement. At all times keep calm, do not crumple or attack the other person. Use criticism as a learning experience!

Make sure that the words you speak today are sweet, because tomorrow you may have to eat them.

(Chinese proverb)

Just desserts

Fran Johnstone

Assertiveness activity 10 – assertive statements for use in giving criticism

Since we've spent some time looking at how to deal with *taking* criticism and using it creatively, we need to move on and look briefly at how to *give* it. We've looked at how easy it is to be defensive when we receive disapproval. We've all probably experienced unwelcome criticism. Whatever form it is presented in, criticism is hard to accept, though it is possible to give it in an emotionally insightful way. Your aim should be to word the criticism in the way the person is most likely to hear. Basically, this comes down to focusing on the action – not the person. Try using the four-step approach:

STEP 1   *Describe what you are unhappy about*

- ■ 'Can we talk about time-keeping?' instead of 'You're late again'
- ■ 'This piece of research needs more evidence' instead of 'You haven't finished this yet'.

STEP 2   *Invite the other person to speak*

Expanding upon this, you could then invite the other person to give their input, for example:

- ■ 'Are you aware that you've been late several times recently? Can you tell me what is causing this?'
- ■ 'Are you having difficulty accessing information. How could we help you with this?'

STEP 3   *Consequences: positive and (if necessary) negative*

Allowing that most people are more motivated by a carrot than a stick, try to identify something good that will be true for the other person if they change their behaviour:

- ■ 'If you are able to complete the report by Friday lunch time, we could probably leave work early.'

If this is not an option, then you need to be blunt about the consequences:

- ■ 'If you continue to be late, you will be given a written warning.'

STEP 4   *Try to reach agreement*

After two-way discussion, summarize the agreed action, making sure that the other person is clear about what is expected of them:

■ 'So, we've agreed that from now on you will . . .'
■ 'OK, we're clear now that you are going to . . .'

Remember that your goal is to aid the person change a behaviour. To achieve this you do not need to use sarcasm, bribery, flattery or aggression.

Think of a criticism you might have to give someone in the near future. Write yourself a 'script' using the four-step format. If possible ask a trusted colleague to role play the situation with you.

■ STEP 1 – Summarize the problem
■ STEP 2 – Explain how you feel
■ STEP 3 – Describe what you'd like to happen instead
■ STEP 4 – Consequences – positive and (if necessary) negative.

Your script

STEP 1 – Summarize the problem

STEP 2 – Explain how you feel

STEP 3 – Describe what you'd like to happen instead

STEP 4 – Consequences

Summary guidelines for giving criticism:

1   *Use 'I' statements*

A statement that starts with 'You' often ends up as a blaming, disrespectful statement. Start with 'I' statements as the foundation of what you are saying, move from basic assertions to more complex statement as, and if, the situation warrants.

2   *Be concise*

Only one or two sentences are necessary before giving the other person a chance to respond. When we have rehearsed a situation we can forget that negotiation is a two way exchange. One person speaks, waits for a response and then responds to what the other person says.

3   *Pick up non-verbal communication*

Be sensitive to the tone of voice and body language in others. Use these clues to help you gauge levels of support, hostility or fear.

4   *Focus on the here and now*

Do not allow old feelings and incidents from history colour the current interaction.

5   *Be prepared*

Remember the Boy/Girl Scout motto! Go into assertive negotiations with your thoughts marshalled. Have your facts straight and have whatever materials you need to be convincing – receipts, the contract, whatever the situation requires.

6   *Use assertive listening*

While it may seem awkward to say back to the other person what you heard him/her say, it keeps the communication clear. Most importantly, assertive listening keeps us from falling into the trap of *assuming* that the other person is on the same track we are.

7   *Use summary questions*

For example: 'Can I just be clear that you are saying ....'. See pp. 116–31 for more on effective listening skills and assumptions.

Assertiveness activity 11 – using choice

Our lives are filled with a series of interactions and compromises. The level of compromise we are prepared to make differs greatly between individuals. The reasons behind this can be very complex. For effective assertive behaviour you need to have some understanding of how far you are prepared to compromise with others and why. You need to consider the balance between your own need and that of the other person.

Make a list of all the things you have to do in a day. This can be as detailed as you want and you might want to use a separate piece of paper to begin with. Start with the time that you get up in the morning:

- get up
- shower, dress
- prepare breakfast/packed lunch
- feed cat/dog/goldfish
-
-
-
-
-
-

Now read out aloud, to your buddy if you have one, all the things which you have listed, prefacing them all with: 'I have to . . .'

- I have to get up, shower and get dressed
- I have to prepare breakfast/packed lunch
- I have to feed cat/dog/goldfish . . .

When you've finished and are working with a buddy, let them do the same thing. Now, take your list and repeat the whole exercise again, but this time, preface each statement with 'I choose to . . .'.

- I choose to get up, shower and get dressed
- I choose to prepare breakfast/packed lunch
- I choose to feed cat/dog/goldfish . . .

Think about the statement that you are making as you say it. Realizing that you do have a choice about almost everything you do can be extremely liberating. For example, you might think that you 'have to' rather than 'choose to' cook dinner, because no-one else will. But, you *could* choose not to. Perhaps this would create all sorts of other issues and therefore you 'choose' to cook dinner because you don't welcome the alternatives. So, it's clear that some of these are not easy choices, but *you* are making the decision.

Assertiveness activity 12 – assertive letter

An assertive letter has enough detail to explain the problem, but not so much that the problem gets lost in all of the sentences. Sometimes an assertive letter can employ humour but be careful not to confuse sarcasm with humour. Generally keep the letter as simple as possible.

When you write an assertive letter, consider who needs to see it. For example, if you are writing to your manager then maybe you need to give a copy of the letter to the next line of management. An every-day example most of us can identify with is where your bank has taken unauthorized debit from your account. Here are some example assertive letters which you could use in this sort of instance, beginning with the mildest approach.

Letter 1

The Manager　　　　　　　　　　　　　　　　　　　　　　　Date ......
Anybank
Anystreet
Anytown

Dear ......

Re Account Number ......

My recent bank statement, received on ...... shows a direct debit which I do not recognize. I enclose for your information, a copy statement with the debit highlighted.

Please would you investigate this and advise me of your findings as soon as possible.

I look forward to hearing from you soon,

Yours sincerely

....

Letter 2

The Manager   Date ......
Anybank
Anystreet
Anytown

Dear ......

Re Account Number ......

I refer to my letter of ...... drawing your attention to an unauthorised direct debit from my account. As I have not yet received a response I am enclosing a copy of my original letter and look forward to hearing from you within the next week.

Yours sincerely

....

Letter 3

The Manager   Date ......
Anybank
Anystreet
Anytown

Dear......

Re Account Number ......

With reference to my letters of ...... and ...... which remain unacknowledged , I now write to express concern that this issue remains unresolved. This is now a matter of urgency and as such, I request that you telephone me with an explanation before ...... As I am dissatisfied with the lack of response to my previous communications, I am copying this letter to the bank's regional customer service manager.

I look forward to your response,

Yours sincerely

....

cc Regional Customer Service Manager

Refer back to the examples above and write your own assertive letter in response to the following situations:

- a member of sales staff in a shop is rude to you when you return a faulty item
- your child has been inappropriately disciplined by a class teacher
- you have been given a verbal warning from your manager for alleged misuse of company email.

We've covered a lot of background to assertiveness and this is probably a good point to pick up on some basic principles.

Assertiveness activity 13 – saying no

Frequently when we are asked to do something we find it difficult to say no. The reasons for this typically come from our belief systems for example:

- they won't like me
- if I refuse, I won't be able to make requests of others
- their need is greater than mine
- they'll be hurt if I say no
- they'll be angry with me if I refuse
- it will look as though I can't cope.

So, because of these beliefs, you could find yourself saying 'yes', when you really want to say 'no'. This can lead to you being in the position of taking on too much and then in turn, quite possibly feeling resentful towards the person who made the request. Ironically, you are angry with yourself for not saying 'no' but direct this anger outwards. Have you ever found yourself in this type of situation – soldiering on with your burdens while leaving a distinct whiff of burning martyr in your wake?

Let's consider how you might be more emotionally skilful in this respect. The key here is individual rights. Others have the right to make requests; you have the right to refuse. If your right to refuse is limited by either your job description, or perhaps family dependency, then you have the right to state what problems the request will trigger. Some tips for saying no assertively are:

Keep it simple and brief

You don't need to ramble on about your reasons for declining. Just say 'I don't want to do that . . .' or 'I'd prefer not to . . .'

Give reasons, not excuses

This includes apologizing, as in 'I'm so sorry but . . .' as well as 'Oh dear, I won't be able to do that because . . .'

Don't use decoys

Be clear that you are refusing the request. Don't dress your refusal up as if it's coming from someone else, for example, 'Oh, my manager would not be happy for me to do that'.

Be sensitive to your body language

There is a world of difference between saying 'I don't want to do that . . .' in a sulky or aggressive manner rather than in an assertive manner. Make sure you use appropriate non-verbal behaviour and that it is consistent. For example, it is no good using an even tone of voice, but avoiding eye contact or fidgeting with your sleeve at the same time.

Use broken-record technique

Where and if none of the above hints appear to be working, broken-record technique as explained above, is a useful fall-back!

Try out some emotionally competent responses to the following situations.

Situation	Response
1. You've had a difficult day at work during your boss's absence and are looking forward to a quiet relaxing evening. As you are packing up to go, your boss telephones to say that she is on her way to the office and needs an update on the day before you leave. You know that this will take at least an hour. What do you say to her?	

2. You take your elderly parent on holiday every other summer, alternating with your brother. This year it is his turn but he asks if you could take the responsibility again as he has financial problems. You've not yet made any bookings but had made plans with your partner/family for a holiday which would not suit an elderly person. What do you do?

Chapter 15

Relationship competence advantage 7 Conflict management

The key to good conflict management is accepting that you cannot guarantee to change the other person. You can however, control your own responses, which in turn can influence the relationship, hopefully in a positive way. In emotional intelligence terms, dealing with conflict means involving your creative side. Don't allow the 'emotional hijack' situation to take over. If you find yourself thinking

- s/he's not listening to me!
- no way!
- they can't!

then you will very probably have the associated physical reactions. Your heartbeat increases to about ten beats a minute above your normal level and adrenaline is surging through your bloodstream. This is 'flooding'. You are in danger of letting your emotions dictate your behaviour – a good time to pause for a few minutes! Of course it is not always possible to agree to take 'time out' in a difficult situation but as you will need to be as calming as possible, do try using this tactic first.

So, coming back to using creativity, we can see that when we most need it, our emotional state means that our creativity has just flown out of the window! Fear and distress activate the limbic system at the base of our brains. This shuts off the cerebral cortex, where our creativity and problem-solving ability originates. So, what can we do? Well, to begin with, we can look at what conflict is and then work through some activities to practise more creative responses.

Take a moment to think of some words that you associate with the term 'conflict'. Perhaps you thought of some of those listed in the following:

- arguments
- upset
- unpleasantness
- hostility
- disagreement
- war
- quarrel
- struggle
- dispute.

These are the terms which people most often relate to conflict, but there are also positive aspects of conflict. For example:

- change
- negotiation
- renovation
- resolution
- difference
- intervention
- transformation
- makeover
- conciliation.

Perceiving conflict as 'difference' is perhaps a more positive way to approach it. Looking at conflict in this way removes a good deal of the negative emotion and opens up potential for creative responses. Conflict management is not about what other people do, it's about our reactions to it. Watch anyone who is skilled at handling people who are upset and you will undoubtedly see how they 'de-personalize' the interaction. For example instead of 'You've done that wrong', they say 'There's an error here.'

Another useful tactic is to know when and where to take make a stand and when to compromise. It's unnecessary and unhelpful to have to be the victor in all disagreements. 'It's better to lose the battle but win the war' is a useful cliché to bear in mind! That is not to say that you should concede in a way which makes you feel uncomfortable – remember the assertiveness skills and exercises from earlier in this book.

A MODERN DAY FABLE
Toni needed a fresh lemon for a meal she was in the middle of preparing. Realizing that she didn't have one, she decided to pop quickly to the supermarket. Approaching the fruit section, Toni met her friend Anne. They chatted for a moment and found that they were both looking for a lemon. Unfortunately, there was only one lemon on the supermarket shelf. They asked a member of staff to bring out some more, but were told 'sorry, waiting for delivery – maybe tomorrow'. Both Toni and Anne felt they needed the lemon and neither had time to drive to another store. As they were friends and anxious to avoid unpleasantness, they decided to buy it and asked a supermarket assistant cut it in half. Then Anne drove home to grate the peel from her half of the lemon, whilst Toni went home and squeezed out the juice from hers.

This short modern day fable is just a way of illustrating how easy it is to lock into your own perspective in a potentially difficult situation. By concentrating on how important it was to have the lemon, Anne and Toni were unable to assess the bigger picture and work out that there was a win–win outcome; Anne only needed the peel and Toni only needed the juice!

Guiding principles for emotionally intelligent conflict resolution

In any type of conflict situation – large or small scale, the emotionally intelligent aim is to achieve resolution. This could mean you are acting as a mediator between others. This type of situation may demand a significant investment of time as you will need to give each party an opportunity to have their say – to 'vent' without causing further damage to the relationship. Here are a few pointers for achieving this.

- Chose neutral ground for the discussion to take place.
- Let each party have a pre-agreed amount of time to give their side. (If feelings are running particularly high it might be better to do this with each party separately. Come back together to resume after the 'venting').
- Find the common ground. This may initially seem like an impossible task but there will always be a common denominator. It could be something totally remote but as the mediator, you need to find it.
- Check that both sides feel heard. Keep feeding back, confirming that each person is comfortable with the way the process is developing.
- Call time-out if you get into a stalemate situation. When you start going round in circles, it's time to summarize how far negotiations have got to and to suggest a break. Agree time to reconvene.

Conflict management activity 1 – negotiation skills

Spend half an hour with another person(s) trying out the responses to each of the situations below. Take a few minutes to set the scene, including any props, before acting out each of the reactions given. Give yourselves no more than five minutes on each type of reaction. You might want to jot a note of how you felt and what you felt about the other person at the end of each situation.

Situation 1

You have reserved a training room for a high level meeting which you are chairing and feeling very nervous about. You're setting out the agendas when a manager from another department walks in, insisting that she reserved the room for an external function. She accuses you of taking over her reservation and threatens to call in your senior manager. What do you do?

(a) You get drawn into an argument – 'Hang on a minute. What makes you think that your booking is more important than mine?'

(b) You take an adversarial stance – 'You should have got here a bit earlier if you wanted this room'.

(c) You become fixed in your own situation and perceive her as the enemy – 'I don't believe this. I made this reservation months ago. You must have been aware of it. This is a huge mess-up.'

Situation 2

You are the first male (or female) to join a formerly all female (or all male) team and they are testing you. Some of them are pushing the boundaries with risqué jokes; others are giving you technically challenging tasks to see if you are up to the job. What do you do?

(a) You let the tactics get to you and become irritated – 'This is really childish behaviour. You all need to grow up.'

(b) You become emotional, your voice pitch rises – 'I am just as well qualified to do this job as any one else here. You are making me nervous.'

(c) You weakly try to defend yourself, become their 'victim' – 'Come on you lot, give me a break. Please just leave me alone to get on with my work.'

Situation 3

You are about to reverse into the last space at your work car park when a colleague pulls straight into it!

(a) Your anger flares. You use the car horn to demonstrate your frustration.

(b) You drive off fuming, resolving to tackle the individual as soon as you get into work.

(c) You drive across them, initiating a direct and immediate confrontation.

Having completed this exercise, talk through with the other(s) involved what you think an emotionally intelligent response to each situation might be. Going back to the Anne and Toni fable above might help to set the context.

Conflict management activity 2 – conflict skills practice

Role play (as above) some or all of the following conflict situations using empathy to try and handle the conflict. Discuss the outcome.

1. A friend borrows something of value but does not return it.

2. A colleague keeps using your desk as his/her filing tray.

3. A close relative repeatedly causes aggravation within the family.

4. You have delegated some work which is not completed to an acceptable standard.

5. You arrive home to find your son/daughter has invited half a dozen friends round for supper and loud music!

Conflict management activity 3 – accepting responsibility

You will hopefully remember the issue of taking responsibility in Section One. Just as it is a key element in the group of EI personal competencies, accepting responsibility is an important factor in relationships. This next part will build on the progress that you will have made already from the exercises on personal responsibility in Section One, this time looking specifically at how these skills can help in conflict management.

Many people sabotage themselves and their relationship with others by failing to accept responsibility for their own actions. The aim of this emotionally illiterate behaviour is to blame others. This is much more comfortable than realizing that the buck stops with you.

The down side of blaming others is that you lose control and feel like a victim. Accepting responsibility puts you back into a powerful position, realizing that you have the ability to work to change situations.

Look at the differences in the ways of expressing meaning below. Reflect on ways in which you fail to accept responsibility and add them in the blank boxes, along with a more constructive way of thinking.

Instead of:	Try:
'Good grief, can't he understand that yet?'	'How else could I explain it so that it becomes clear to him?'
'You make me so mad!'	'I feel angry when you . . .'
'I can't change, it's just the way I am.'	'I tend to be that way, but I am working be more flexible.'
'You haven't received the letter yet? Our secretary is useless.'	'I'm sorry there's been a hitch. Let me get that letter faxed to you immediately.'
'This sort of thing always happens to me. It's fate.'	'I can see a pattern emerging here. I need to think what to do to break the pattern.'
'I'm too unfit to do that type of thing'	'I can work at improving my fitness so that I can join you.'

Conflict management activity 4 – own your feelings

When you are in conversation with others or even when you are having a conversation with yourself, use more 'feeling' words. Where it is true, say 'I feel . . .', 'I'm concerned that . . .' or whatever is true for you at that time. Using the word 'I' stops you from blaming your feelings on others and encourages you to accept responsibility for your own feelings and actions. Do this at least once a day for a week. Use the table below to record one experience every day.

Day	Situation	Feelings
Sunday		
Monday		
Tuesday		
Wednesday		
Thursday		
Friday		
Saturday		

Conflict management activity 5 – summary exercise

Let's come back to dealing with conflict and recap on some practical strategies.

1. Use empathy. Try to see the situation from the other person's perspective.

2. Get your point of view across using neutral language.

Try:	*Instead of:*
I can see that you are upset about this.	You make such a big deal out of everything.
I'd like to hear your views on how this has happened.	This is chaotic – how did you get into such a mess?

3. Demonstrate that you are willing to talk things through rather than being drawn into aggression.

4. Stress the benefits of co-operation.

Try:	*Instead of:*
If we could arrange to have regular team meetings it would improve communication across our departments.	There's just no point in trying to set up meetings with your team, you are only interested in your own targets.
I'd like to discuss how we could work around this problem.	I'm fed up with always having to give in here.

5. Use summary statements to confirm you have understood correctly.

6. State your position.

Try:	*Instead of:*
Let me be sure I've understood this correctly. You are disappointed because I didn't make the meeting.	Nobody let me know that this meeting was going ahead. How am I supposed to know if I'm not kept informed?
I didn't make the meeting because it was in my diary as unconfirmed.	You didn't let me know it was a confirmed meeting.

7. Talk through problem areas.

8. Resolve!

Try:	Instead of:
Can I just check that we have understood each others' position? Let's discuss our options.	I'm fed up with trying to have an adult discussion with you. You simply don't listen to my point of view.
I think there's some middle ground here where we could both feel comfortable with the outcome.	This is absolutely hopeless!

As you become more practised and comfortable in using emotional intelligent responses to conflict situations, the chances are that these will become your normal reactions.

Go out armed with all the skills you have gained in this section and use them with confidence!

Leadership competence
How to be an inspiring leader

Leadership competence in emotional intelligence is important because it enables us to:

- recognize and use the key leadership competencies to lead others
- have greater flexibility and creativity
- influence others skilfully
- achieve our goals
- demonstrate commitment
- have initiative and optimism.

This section contains information and activities on:

- leading others ethically, either formally because of job role or informally through family and network relationships
- flexibility
- responsibility
- rewards
- setting and achieving high standards
- clarity of communication
- gaining and keeping commitment from others.

This section is about using your emotional intelligence skills in relation to leading others. Using these skills not only makes you a more valued leader, it's good for your organization and your career.

Let's look first at what some researchers have found out about management competence. For decades they have tried unsuccessfully to link 'traditional' intelligence with business success. It was only when the link was made with *emotional* intelligence that researchers really found out what made a leader successful. Starting in the 1970s the late David McClelland, a Harvard University psychologist, tested a range of business leaders for their emotional intelligence and found a significant link between their level of EI and their effectiveness at work. Daniel Goleman continued this research and found that the costs of emotional illiteracy were indeed real and quantifiable. His books on emotional intelligence provide a good deal of evidence that low EI at work causes upset, stress and friction. Leaders with low EI are often impatient, insensitive or careless in their relations with others causing wasted time, bad feelings, poor motivation and apathy. Team members who have low EI work less effectively and harmoniously.

One piece of research looked at leaders in a large company. Among those leaders with high emotional intelligence, 87% were in the top third for annual salary bonuses based on their performance. Further, their divisions usually out-performed others' yearly targets by an impressive 15% to 20%.

Six leadership styles

This section looks at the six leadership styles Goleman identifies as necessary for effective leadership and provides activities to help you to further develop these skills or learn more helpful skills. You will see that all six styles have their place in the leader's toolkit; your challenge is to know how and by how much to apply each in any given situation. There is a questionnaire at the end of this section that will help you to identify your usual leadership style. From this you can refer to the relevant leadership competency to develop your leadership emotional intelligence. Having said that, because all styles are necessary, you will find it very beneficial to work your way through the whole of this section of the workbook.

In each section you will be guided towards the skills required for that leadership advantage. You will also be shown which skills may be lacking if this is your overly predominant style.

Some skills are used across more than one management style and where this is the case you will be guided towards that section to complement the one you are reading. Likewise some skills have already been addressed in this workbook. Again, you will be guided to the relevant page.

Seven characteristics of emotionally intelligent leaders

1   They are emotionally intelligent, they

- are aware of their emotions, and can control them to best effect
- are empathetic
- are flexible in their communication with others
- aim for win-win solutions to negotiations.

2   They are committed to continuing professional development, they

- regularly take courses, read, etc.
- reflect on experiences in life and learn from them
- continually develop new skills
- learn about areas related to their own discipline.

3   They are empowering, they

- see themselves as being a support for their staff as well as vice versa
- empower others at every opportunity
- keep the customer in mind at all times.

4   They trust others, they

- work closely with others to achieve the best results in any situation
- see the strengths in other people, and work towards remedying weaknesses
- treat people equally and fairly
- know the limits of their abilities and consult specialists as necessary

5   They are optimistic, they:

- see the best in people and situations in a realistic way
- have a 'can-do' attitude
- concentrate on solutions rather than problems
- use their breadth of knowledge synergistically – bring together the best of what they know.

6   Have a life outside work, they

- have a social life
- read non-work related books and magazines
- are aware of and involve themselves in current issues while actively pursuing their own interests.

7   They look after their physical and emotional well-being, they

- exercise to ensure good health
- keep their weight within healthy limits
- have regular health checks
- are aware of their emotional needs and get help in the most appropriate way for each situation.

Questionnaire – Your leadership style

There are four questions in this questionnaire. For each one circle the response that most closely rings true for you. For example, in question 1 'My style of leadership means that I . . .', if the statement that is most true for you is 'have a clear vision and enjoy leading people towards it', then circle b. When you have worked through all four questions total your score according to which letter you have circled most.

1. *My style of leadership means that I . . . :*
   a. expect my staff to do what I say immediately without question
   b. have a clear vision and enjoy leading people towards it
   c. love working closely with people to build effective working relationships
   d. like to work as part of the team rather than taking the lead
   e. have clear standards and expect my team to reach them quickly every time
   f. like working one-to-one to coach people towards effective performance.

2. *I am most likely to say:*
   a. 'This is what I want you to do'
   b. 'Join me in achieving the dream'
   c. 'People are my most important asset'
   d. 'Right team, what shall we do?'
   e. 'Achieve this standard, now'
   f. 'Let's work together so that you can develop this skill'.

3. *My emotional intelligence drives are:*
   a. Self-control, initiative, need to reach the goal
   b. Self-confidence, need to achieve a win-win situation, to achieve change harmoniously
   c. Building close relationships, communicating effectively, understanding others
   d. Being part of the team, collaborative working
   e. Need to succeed with speed, use of own initiative
   f. Desire to develop others, self awareness, relationship-building.

4. *My style seems to work particularly well when:*
   a. there is a crisis, when dealing with a poor performer
   b. change is needed, when clear vision and objectives are required
   c. teams or individuals are facing stressful situations
   d. the team needs to own a project, to get the best out of skilled and valued staff
   e. good results are needed quickly
   f. employee's skills need developing.

Total a ......   Total b ......   Total c ......

Total d ......   Total e ......   Total f ......

If you answered mostly a, your style is Coercive, mostly b, your style is Authoritative, mostly c, your style is Affiliative, mostly d, your style is Democratic, mostly e, your style is Pacesetting and mostly f, your style is Coaching.

It is likely that you have more than one predominant style and this is a benefit because to be an effective leader you need to have all styles available to you. However two of the styles, Pacesetting and Coercive, should be used sparingly otherwise they have a negative effect on staff.

By working through this section of the workbook your can further develop the positive styles and learn how to overcome the negative effects of the Pacesetting and Coercive styles.

Chapter 16

Leadership competence advantage 1
Authoritative leadership style

Authoritative leaders get results by inspiring their staff. They have clear vision and can convey this vision in a way that encourages others to achieve. Through their clarity of vision they develop a team that pulls together towards a common goal. They have confidence and enthusiasm, are empathetic and make excellent agents for change.

Skills needed for authoritative leadership are flexibility, creativity, the ability to inspire others, being an effective change agent, and having a clear vision.

If this is your predominant style be careful your enthusiasm does not lead you towards being overbearing and ignoring others' needs. Also, beware of a possible tendency to be pompous.

Many of the emotionally intelligent skills covered earlier in this book are very relevant to this leadership style. In particular you will need to have empathy (see p. 100) for those people who find change difficult. You will need to be confident (see p. 46) in sharing your vision and allowing your staff to contribute ideas and have flexibility in how goals are reached. You will need to be able to set clear goals, discussed in this section and on p. 53 in Section One on Personal competence.

Authoritative leadership activity 1 – defining the vision

Having a vision is important at any level of management. Without vision organizations and teams would get stale and fall behind their competitors. If a vision of the future doesn't come naturally this is the activity for you. To find your vision you will need to do some research to find out what is current and upcoming in your area of work. Here are some areas which should prove fruitful:

What is happening within the organization that will impact on your team?

What are the latest trends among your competitors? You may need to look both within your own country and abroad for answers to this one.

What ideas do your team have for how improvements could be made?

What do your customers want? Remember internal as well as external customers.

What ideas do you have?

What legal or professional specific legislation or regulations are likely in the future?

When you have gathered together all this information, you can begin to draw your vision. Remember to involve your team at all possible stages so that they are as committed to the goal as you are.

Authoritative leadership activity 2 – inspiring others

When we have a dream, a vision, we need to inspire others towards it so that we can achieve a common goal. Great speech makers know well how to use language to inspire others. Is there anyone who is unmoved by the Martin Luther King 'I have a dream' speech? Luckily, this is a skill we can all learn.

Your first step of course is to decide exactly the point you want to get across. Other considerations are:

- Who are my audience?
- What do they already know?

- What do they need to know?
- What do they want to know?
- Why do they need to know what I am telling them?
- What part of what I'm saying will they connect with happily?
- What parts of what I'm saying will they be resistant to?
- What pictures can I encourage them to paint in their minds that will inspire them towards the dream?
- What sounds do I want them to imagine to move them towards the dream?
- What feelings do I want to arouse to make the dream compelling for them?

With this information you can begin to plan your inspirational talk. Obviously you want to use your talk to provide information about your dream but the words you use can help or hinder the listener in developing a mental picture of their own vision. Choosing the right words is vital. Your goal is to get your team to envisage the goal for themselves, to picture their part in its success. For this reason, as well as giving specific information you will sometimes also be 'artfully vague' so that people can develop their own picture in their mind.

Here is the beginning of an inspiring speech a senior manager or training consultant might make about inspiring others to change. On the left is what the speaker would say, while on the right is why these words were chosen. You will see that there is reference to 'towards' and 'away from' speech. Understanding people's motivation towards or away from change is important and is explored on p. 219. In case you haven't read that section yet a resume of this is that some people are motivated to change by moving towards pleasure whilst others will only change to get away from discomfort.

Inspiring speech – trainer or senior manager to leaders who must manage change

Speech	Why used
I have a mission!	Self-disclosure
As you know, we are all subject to the challenge of change . . .	Unifying statement, not too specific
. . . some of us hesitate under these challenges whilst some of us blossom	Acknowledges difficulties but saying 'some of us blossom' last should make that stick in the mind
My dream is to overcome these challenges by showing you a variety of ways to inspire others to change	Convincing leadership words

. . . to help us and our staff become empowered people, going forward to make changes for the better	Stating your goal, appealing to common values, still not specific
This is what learning change management skills is all about . . .	Empowering assumption that you can do it
. . . it's like the tool chest of the gods!	Metaphor
My mission is to see people like us pulling together in leadership, showing others the future so that they can experience a sense of flow as they move forward into the future . . .	Repeating mission, involving a sense of movement and vision
. . . a mission to develop a way forward in times of change	'Towards' speech
. . . away from old unhelpful working systems	'Away from' speech
Today, I invite you to become role models by:	Explaining your model strategy

- embracing a new attitude
- modelling respect for others
- challenging where appropriate
- inspiring a focus of solution rather than blame
- walking your talk, and leading the way

Just imagine being that role model now! . . .	Installing a picture in the listeners' minds
. . . and notice how good it feels to be making such a positive move . . .	Good feelings
. . . and never doubt, that you can empower your staff to make these changes comfortably	Empowering belief
So, I invite you to think on these things – and take a few moments right now to imagine yourself back at work embracing this mission for positive change . . . and notice what that is like!	Taking the image into the future

Adapted from material by Anna Dalton, John Seymour Associates Ltd, 0117 955 7827

This speech would then go on to give specifics of how to manage change. You may also have noticed that a metaphor is used in this speech. Metaphors can be a very powerful way of influencing people. A metaphor is a word or story that represents something else. So, for example, we might call someone who is fierce a 'lion'. Metaphors can inspire or demotivate.

> **TRUE LIFE STORY**
> Brian, an ex-military man, was called in to do some team-building work with staff from the caring professions. He entire presentation was peppered with military terms 'When your captain makes a decision . . .', 'You are the flotilla . . .' , 'When you advance into battle . . .', 'You need to attack when . . .' He turned them off in the first half hour and for the rest of the day they were resistant to learning from him.

Your challenge for this activity is to write an inspiring talk for your staff and to include one appropriate metaphor.

Wrong choice of metaphor

Fran Johnstone

Authoritative leadership activity 3 – increasing creativity and flexibility

Creativity and flexibility are key characteristics of the emotionally intelligent leader. These skills come easier to some than others. Luckily there are many ways to increase creativity and flexibility, and the good news is that they are fun to experiment with. A few of them are described here.

Edward de Bono's six thinking hats

Edward de Bono is a prolific writer on thinking creatively and this is just one of his many ideas for developing this skill. The purpose here is to encourage you to get out of your habitual way of thinking and to look at situations from a variety of viewpoints. This allows you to take all points of view into account, recognise flaws in your argument before you present it and anticipate objections. As you read the descriptions of the different 'hats' (way of thinking) ask yourself which one you use most often. Which hats do your staff wear?

You don't literally have to don different hats, of course, they are a metaphor for different thinking choices.

White hat – cool and neutral

When you are wearing your White hat you are objective, collecting data and information in an unbiased way. Relevant questions will be:

■ What information do we have?
■ What information is still needed?
■ Where can we find the information?

No opinions are passed in White-hat mode.

Red hat – fiery and hot

Wearing your Red hat you'll be involved with feelings, intuition, hunches, and emotions. Typical Red-hat questions are:

■ 'I feel . . .'
■ 'My gut reaction is that . . .'
■ 'My intuition leads me to expect that . . .'

Intuition is important because it is the sum total of our experience and knowledge processed unconsciously. Be wary of trusting it entirely though, because it may be based on prejudice or incorrect learning.

Black hat – cautious and critical

Black-hat thinking is critical and cautious. It stops us acting impulsively or illegally. Black hats always see the difficulties in situations rather than the solutions. In this mode you'll say:

- 'That's against the current legislation.'
- 'We tried that three years ago, it didn't work then and it won't work now.'
- 'We can't possibly meet that deadline.'

Black-hat thinking is a useful foil to the Yellow-hat optimist or the Red hat impulsive side of our nature. But don't use it too often or you'll demotivate people and stifle innovation.

Yellow hat – sunny and cheerful

Yellow hat mode is optimistic and pragmatic. In this mode you will be focussed positively on solutions rather than problems. Yellow hat is none the less logical and practical. In this mode you'll be saying things like:

- 'That's a brilliant idea, though it will take two more days than you allowed.'
- 'The company would get a real increase in market share from that move.'
- 'There may be difficulties but let's try it for a week and then do a review.'

We all need some Yellow-hat thinking to aid creativity and flexibility.

Green hat – luxuriant and creative

Green hat is really inventive and creative, considering a range of alternative ways of approaching situations. Green hats enjoy looking at possibilities. They say things like:

- 'Hey, I can think of a couple of ways that might work.'
- 'What other ideas does anyone have?'
- 'How else can we look at the problem?'

Green hat enjoys making creative suggestions and encouraging others to do the same.

Blue hat – helicopter mind/overview

Blue hats like to get an overview of situations and think through the processes involved in a logical way. In fact, they like to think about thinking and love processes even more than the end product. They establish the boundaries of the topic under discussion and like to control others and encourage them to do the same. They are calm, logical and objective. Blue hats use chairing skills of summarizing, reaching conclusions and making decisions. They sometimes point out the thinking processes of individuals or groups. Blue hats say things like:

- 'Let's have some Black-hat thinking on this topic.'
- 'Could you summarize the points you've been making?'
- 'Let's stop for a minute and look at this from a White-hat perspective.'

Blue hats are useful for chairing meetings, assessing priorities and recognizing constraints.

Increasing creativity in your team

If your team are in a well worn rut, with little creativity or flexibility, you might like to introduce them to the idea of six thinking hats. Ask them to don an unfamiliar hat at the next staff meeting. You could give them an extra stretch by asking them to change hats half way through the meeting. Hat terminology could become part of your everyday speech. You could say to individual people, for example, 'Let's have a bit of Yellow-hat thinking on this subject.'

It's worth it just to get the inevitable moaner and whinger into a different mode!

Authoritative leadership activity 4 – develop your own creativity, flexibility and risk-taking skills

If you would like to increase these vital skills you need to keep giving yourself small challenges, and even occasional big ones. Here are some to try, none are too huge in themselves but they will make you more creative as they increase your ability to think outside the box.

1. Take a different journey to work at least once a week.
2. Read a different newspaper at least once a week. Try one that has a different slant on life from your usual one.
3. Read a magazine you haven't read before.
4. At least once a week watch a TV programme you haven't seen before.
5. Sit in a different chair.
6. Instead of booking a package holiday, book a flight and accommodation separately. Better still, just get on a flight and find accommodation once you arrive.

7. Learn a new skill.

8. Do a crossword puzzle or similar occasionally.

9. Try a new food at least once a fortnight.

10. Smile and speak pleasantly to someone you usually avoid.

11. Take a few minutes to sit quietly and do nothing, allow your unconscious to get to work.

12. Listen to a different radio station.

13. Tell your brain that you would like an answer to the problem by a certain time (you'll be pleasantly surprised by how often your brain responds).

14. Learn new techniques for improving creativity. There are several books and websites dedicated to creativity.

15. Use mind maps – Tony Buzan's book on the subject is excellent.

16. Find a role model and copy their skills.

Authoritative leadership activity 5 – managing change

Change is a constant! It's the one thing you can depend on in your working life. As a manager you are likely to have to lead people through times of change on a regular basis and many of the skills already learned throughout this workbook will help you towards this goal. Other relevant skills still to come in this section include motivating others, being principle-centred, gaining consensus and valuing diversity.

But let's look at a five-stage approach to change.

STAGE 1   *Develop a vision*

We have already looked, in Activity 1 – Defining the vision, at ways to develop a vision. This vision is your starting point for change. Of course, you will not be developing this vision alone, you will be involving your staff and any other relevant people.

STAGE 2   *Gaining political support*

Change almost always has a political aspect. The politics could be large – for example at government level. They could equally be small – the politics of your workgroup for example. At whatever level they will need to be negotiated if you are to succeed as a change agent.

Questions to ask yourself are in relation to gaining political support are:

- 'Who is affected by the change?'
- 'Who is for the change and who is against?'
- 'Who do I need to influence for resources?'
- 'Who do I need to influence to sway the people?'
- 'Who are the stakeholders in this process?'

Your task then is to influence these people. The Rapport skills part of the Relationship competence gives excellent guidance when you need to influence others. It is especially important to remember that prior to any influencing activity you should put yourself in the other person's shoes (empathize). By doing this you will be able to see what their angle on the situation will be. This gives you the power to present your case in a way which will most appeal to them.

STAGE 3

Creating the climate for change

Many people find change difficult to cope with. Frequently people going through change will experience many of the same emotions discussed in the Bereavement part of the Relationship competence section. This means that you may find yourself faced with one or more people who are apathetic, angry or depressed. Create a good climate for change by involving people as much as possible before the change begins. Use your influencing skills to bring them on board. Make them feel that they and their opinions are valued.

STAGE 4

Lead the transition

Change is about taking people from one state to another and is a time when your leadership skills need to be exceptional. Include everyone involved (including internal and external customers where possible) in making the decisions that will lead to successful transition. Keep people informed as fully as humanly possible. These actions in themselves will reduce resistance to change by the old diehards. Be especially sensitive to those people who struggle with change; they may be afraid although the fear may show itself as aggression. Check if they need additional training to be successful in the new situation. Explore ways to make them feel valued and even more involved. If people are dragging their feet, give them clear deadlines and check at regular intervals that they are working towards them. Show everyone how what they regard as a threat is also an opportunity.

STAGE 5   *Ensuring momentum*

Naturally, you don't want things to slip back to the old ways so you must provide the momentum to reinforce the changes. Make sure that people have the resources to do the job. Ensure that they have the skills and confidence to perform well. Reinforce new skills through informal activities like encouragement and praise as well as formally through appraisals.

Your challenge for this activity is to consider a change you would like to make in your workplace and plan for it using the five-stage approach above. Other EI skills that relate to change are empathy, motivation, leadership, creativity, coaching and decision-making.

Authoritative leadership activity 6 – establishing standards

The authoritative leader not only inspires others with clear vision and goals, but also sets the standards that people must reach. When you set a standard you make clear to your staff what is expected in relation to the task. You clarify the boundaries and exact specification to be reached. The results should be measurable in terms of quality, quantity, resources and time.

Sometimes standards are ours to decide and at others they are imposed on us. For example, we may decide on the standard for turning around work or for answering the phone. We have little choice on standards to be reached in matters such as legislation and organizational policy.

To help you think through these issues you may like to complete this section of this activity:

What standards are used within your team that are external to your organization, e.g. legal, contractual, industry standards?

What standards are used within your team that are set by the organization, e.g. organizational standards?

What standards are used that are set within your department or team? Remember to consider less obvious standards such as dress code, punctuality, customer service, and tidiness.

Next, consider how you let people know these standards. Many are passed on explicitly through quality or procedures manuals, others through team meetings or briefings. Others though are vague and unspecified. You may not even be aware that there is a standard until someone transgresses it. Maybe you've never defined a dress code until someone comes to work in short shorts or with multiple body piercing. Maybe you've never defined tidiness until a new member of staff shows what untidy really means.

Agreeing standards in the workplace

Where standards are institutional, your role is explaining what they are, and why they exist, in a way that is relevant to the individual. To pass this information on effectively, you need to know your staff and understand the reason for the standard yourself.

Where standards are your responsibility, you have several choices you can:

- take a democratic approach and discuss the standard with your team, asking them to work out appropriate standards
- work with individuals in your team on particular issues to establish standards.
- make decisions yourself about what standard is appropriate for each task, and inform the team accordingly.

You can combine these methods depending on your need. Think through the areas in your workplace where standards are not clear and decide which would be the best approach for defining the standards.

Where people fail to reach standards you will need to use a range of emotionally wise interventions such as empathy (p. 100 of Relationship competence), listening skills (p. 116 of Relationship competence), questioning skills (p. 132 of Relationship competence), goal setting (p. 52 of Personal competence), and feedback skills (p. 235 of Leadership competence).

Chapter 17

Leadership competence advantage 2
Affiliative leadership style

Where the authoritative leader inspires people to action, the affiliative leader makes it clear that people come first. This leadership style is very people-based and the leader aims to keep people happy and have a harmonious working environment. This builds close bonds between staff and leads to dedication and loyalty. This style leads to clear and close communication where people are willing to take risks and think creatively and flexibly. The Affiliative leader is like a wise parent who provides the boundaries within which people work while allowing them as much leeway as possible to decide how to achieve the task to the required standard. This leader offers much positive feedback and will often be involved in social activities with employees.

This leadership style is particularly important if you are trying to build an effective team. However, like all the other leadership styles, this one should not be used exclusively. There are times, for example, when a member of staff is performing poorly despite positive feedback and coaching, that praise will not work. At this time another management style may be more appropriate.

This style works particularly well when combined with the authoritative style. Using these styles together you will be offering clear direction and vision combined with a positive motivational approach.

Some of the skills needed for this style are addressed elsewhere in this workbook. Empathy and communication are clearly two key skills in the affiliative approach and you can find material on these in Relationship competence p. 100. You also need to trust your staff and there is an activity on control and trust in Relationship competence p. 152.

> *By now, most executives have accepted that emotional intelligence is as critical as IQ to an individual's effectiveness.*
> (*Harvard Business Review*, March 2001)

Affiliative leadership activity 1 – positive feedback

Positive feedback is sadly lacking amongst leaders and staff often feel the only time they get any feedback from their boss is when things go wrong. No wonder they get demotivated. Positive feedback is one of the most effective ways of reinforcing good behaviour. Lack of positive feedback can lead to resentment and sabotage.

Some leaders say 'I'd like to praise my staff but I don't know how to say it and they might think I'm insincere'. Certainly, when you try out this new approach they might be somewhat taken aback and suspicious. However, as long as your praise is sincere and not 'plastic' they'll soon get to value this aspect of your leadership style.

Praise doesn't have to be big and flowery. Here are some ideas on different ways to show appreciation:

- A simple 'Thanks for doing that' or 'Thanks for getting that in on time'.
- Talking specifically about what the person has done rather than a general 'That's good'. So, for example instead of saying 'That report was good' you'd say 'I really liked your report, your headings and charts were particularly helpful in getting your message across'. This helps the person to know what to do well next time.
- Take in a bag of doughnuts or ice creams and call an impromptu coffee break occasionally.
- With staff who have poor or variable performance reinforce good work by noticing even small things they do well (you should still give clear feedback about areas for improvement). Teachers call this 'catching the little so-and-so's being good'.

This activity involves you in taking note for the next week of how often you praise your staff. If this is not something you do naturally, gradually increase the amount of praising you do to develop your skill and delight your staff. This tactic works well at home, by the way!

Affiliative leadership activity 2 – strokes and motivation

Psychologist Eric Berne invented a theory called Transactional Analysis (TA) as a way of explaining human nature. A very valuable idea from this theory is that of 'strokes'. In TA terms a stroke is a unit of recognition and recognition is a basic human need. There are three types of strokes: positive strokes where we give caring recognition; negative ones where we blame or criticize; and zero strokes where people are ignored.

Sadly many leaders give predominantly negative or zero strokes. As a trainer I frequently hear people tell me how annoyed they feel when their boss ignores them in the corridor or criticizes as a sole way of giving feedback. These strokes demotivate people quickly and lead to reduced effectiveness and high staff turnover.

Let's look first at your stroke balance – the balance between positive, negative and zero strokes. Make notes in the spaces below:

I get positive strokes from:	The form these take are:
I get negative strokes from:	The form these take are:
I am ignored by:	The form these take are:

On reflection my stroke balance is ....

If you realize that your stroke balance is not positive make plans to get more positive strokes. Giving them is one way – people will learn to reciprocate. Asking for them is another. This can feel risky but asking in an emotionally mature way such as 'You seemed pleased that I got that project in on time. Are you happy with it?'

Now consider each of your staff. What do you think their stroke balance would be in relation to your communication with them? Do you need to make any adjustments?

Your difficult member of staff

By the way, it is worth noting that there is one personality type in TA called the 'rebellious child'. This person has been largely ignored as a child except when naughty. They have therefore learned to get attention by being naughty. As an adult this translates into being a worker who constantly fails to come up with the goods even though you know they are capable of doing so. It's as if they had a sign on their back saying 'kick me'. They can often be quite nice people but nonetheless in relation to their work they can make you feel furious and impotent to motivate them.

Worse still, this person may have only received praise as a child when the parent wanted something: 'You're a good lad, go to the shops for me'. The person with this upbringing will not only fail to recognize praise (no practice as a child) but will also be suspicious of it, wondering what you want from them.

Do try giving this person positive strokes, all hope may be not be lost. Also give coaching and training so that they have a chance to develop skills. Alongside that however, give very clear instructions. Get the person to repeat them to you and follow them up in writing. If you find yourself heading down the discipline route, make notes of everything that happens so that you have evidence. You'll need it because this person is an expert at blaming others for their own failings.

> **TRUE LIFE STORY**
> Tom was the manager of a busy social work team. This was his first manage-ment role and he was leading a child-care team even though his previous experience was in working with elderly people. Tom didn't go out of his way to learn about child-care issues, relying on picking them up as he went along. This meant that he could not offer good supervision to his staff and often said the wrong thing in multi-disciplinary meetings. Worse, he avoided making tough decisions by hiding in the men's toilet for hours on end if necessary (it was an all-female team). He also consistently arrived late for meetings without cause, giving a very unprofessional impression. He was a very pleasant and intelligent man, well able to learn. His rebellious child nature though ensured what eventually happened – he got fired.

Affliative leadership activity 3 – strokes and knowledge of staff

Strokes are not just about praise because a stroke is a 'unit of recognition'. This means every time we acknowledge that someone exists we give them a stroke. A stroke can be a simple 'Hello', a smile, asking about family, any number of things.

To give your staff appropriate strokes, you have to know quite a lot about them. This activity will test your knowledge. Choose one of your staff and ask yourself the following questions:

1. How knowledgeable am I about this person's career to date?
2. What is my view of their capability to do their current job and to take on extra responsibility?
3. How emotionally intelligent do I believe this person to be?
4. What is this person like as a team player?
5. How high is this person's integrity level?
6. What age is the person?
7. Is the person in a steady relationship?
8. Does this person have children? If so what are their names and how old are they?
9. What are the person's hobbies and interests?
10. Does the person have any particular worries inside or outside work?

Naturally, some people are open about themselves and their lives while others are more private, and you should respect this. However, if you struggle to answer most of these questions you are probably insufficiently knowledgeable about your staff and they will know this. Get chatting!

Affliative leadership activity 4 – praise and acknowledgement

We should praise our staff, it is a vital part of motivating others. However, we can go beyond simple praise and use a more advanced skill, the skill of acknowledgement. But before we explore this, let's look at one aspect of how people are motivated.

Some people are what is called 'self-referenced', that is they judge for themselves how well they have performed a task. Other people are 'other-referenced', they find it difficult to judge the value of what they have done without reference to others. This can be why some of your staff are constantly asking for your approval on work while others rarely do.

Whilst we do need to praise other-referenced people we also want to teach them to be more self-referenced. It empowers them by making them more aware of their abilities and it saves you time.

Acknowledgement is very different from praise inasmuch as it develops this skills of self judgement. When you give acknowledgement you identify one or more aspects of the person's personality and/or skills that are worthy of note. Naturally you will only give genuine acknowledgement otherwise it will be rejected.

Whereas praise is usually about behaviour, acknowledgement is aimed at who the person is, their identity. In the following examples you can see the subtle difference between praise and acknowledgement.

Praise	Acknowledgement
■ You did a great job, good for you	■ It was a stretch to deal with that situation
■ I'm impressed with how you handled that	■ Your determination and skill certainly paid off
■ That was very creative, I'm impressed	■ It took real guts to tackle that
■ You are certainly developing your skills	■ You often show your wisdom with the advice you give
■ I'm so delighted with you	■ You are excellent at fine detail

You can also ask powerful questions to encourage other referenced people to judge their own performance:

■ What personal attribute enabled you to succeed then?

■ What strength have you just demonstrated?

■ What type of person must you be to have achieved that?

Affliative leadership activity 5 – motivation: pleasure and pain

One way of looking at motivation is to think that we are motivated to action or inaction by moving towards pleasure or away from pain. Thinking about your own motivations, did you:

■ leave your last job to get away from it or to go towards a new challenge?

■ change your car because it was playing up or because you wanted a newer, better one?

■ write up your notes of that difficult meeting because you wanted to cover your back or because you find writing down what was said helpful?

Most people use a mixture of the pleasure and pain drives, but some people are primarily motivated by one or the other.

When you want to motivate someone try to establish whether they are a towards (pleasure) or an away-from (pain) person. You can often do this just by listening to the way they talk. They might say things like 'I'd better do this or I'll get it from the boss' (away-from) or 'I'd really like to have a go at that, it looks exciting' (towards).

Once you know whether someone is towards or away-from, you present your case to them in that mode – it will be much more compelling to them. Here are some examples:

Towards	Away from
'I wondered if you'd considered taking on this task, it might lead to bigger things.'	'Not taking on this task could affect your promotion prospects.'
'If you get that in on time, you'll be more likely to get your bonus.'	'If you don't get that in on time you might lose your bonus.'
'If you prepare well for your performance review, you'll be more likely to get that upgrade.'	'If you don't prepare for your performance review you could be stuck where you are for another year.'

If you can't tell if someone is a towards or away from person try both – one will probably hit the mark.

But what about yourself? Being a towards person is a more positive approach, giving you more options and more ability to deal with change. It's certainly true that we all want to get away from people and situations – we'd be unrealistic if we thought this were never true. But if this is your habitual way of thinking, it's more negative than starting from a towards position. And it could mean that you repeat the same behaviour time and time again. This of course means that you end up with making the same mistakes over and over again.

By keeping your positivity log as outlined in Personal competence, you can begin to change your outlook from away-from to towards.

Your challenge for this activity is to assess whether you are a towards or an away-from person and judge whether any changes in approach would help you. When you have done this, do the same for your most difficult member of staff.

The important thing to recognise is that it takes a team, and the team ought to get credit for the wins and the losses. Successes have many fathers, failures have none.

(Philip Caldwell)

Chapter 18

Leadership competence advantage 3
Coercive leadership style

The coercive leadership style is directive and autocratic and people using this style tell people what to do rather than involve them in decision-making. Coercive managers often have excellent drive and initiative and enormous self-control. They can be decisive decision-makers and are able to take tough decisions without hesitation. However they reign by bullying and fear, demotivate others and have high staff turnover.

It is certainly true that there are times when you need to coerce people. Crises are probably the best example. When the building is burning down you can't call a staff meeting to ask people how to handle the situation. When legislation or policy changes are introduced people have to comply (although even in this case there is often an opportunity for staff to have a say in how the changes are implemented).

Overuse of this leadership style leads to high levels of dissatisfaction amongst staff. Because of the fear of retribution staff will avoid taking creative risks, won't tell you things are going wrong until they have gone thoroughly wrong, cover up mistakes and sabotage you whenever they can.

> *Conquest is easy. Control is not.*
>
> (Captain Kirk, Starship Enterprise)

Coercive leadership activity 1 – bullying

Bullying is a major problem in the workplace and increasingly it leads to litigation. This activity will help you to identify whether you are a bully or not and provide suggestions for alternative ways of dealing with situations.

Read each statement and if it is more true than untrue for you put a mark in the 'yes' column. If it is more untrue than true put a mark in the 'no' column.

Statement	Yes	No
1. I regularly put my own self-interest before the interests of others		
2. I sometimes deny saying things I have said		
3. I often say one thing and do another		
4. I think that others are too sensitive		
5. I often wonder why I'm surrounded by fools		
6. I often put people down		
7. I regularly notice that people make lots of mistakes		
8. I notice one person's mistakes more than other people's mistakes		
9. I often tell people of my successes so that they are clear how worthwhile I am		
10. If I can't fault someone over one issue, I'll find another		
11. I fail to praise people		
12. I am happiest doing repetitive, predictable work		
13. I like to make sure that I receive credit for my work		
14. I am often sarcastic		
15. I can be charming for short periods of time		
16. I tend to have mood swings		
17. I like jobs done *my* way		
18. I like to let people know who is in charge		
19. I can act like a controlling parent at times		
20. I tend to concentrate on what's *not* done by others rather than what *is* done		
21. I am able to misinterpret what people say to suit my needs		
22. My sense of humour is different from other people's		
TOTAL		

If you have more than 5 'yes' answers you should look carefully at your behaviour as there's a good chance you are bullying others. You may have realized that it is not you who is the bully but one of your staff. Either way action is vital. A bully is:

- selfish and acts out of self-interest and self-protection constantly
- very willing to criticize and humiliate others, often in public. The bully pretends this is because s/he wants to improve the other person's performance, but in reality it is about control over others
- someone who constantly monitors others through their own lack of ability to trust
- autocratic – telling others what they 'should' and 'ought' to do
- sometimes a poor performer, although often able to deal with repetitive work effectively
- a poor influence on others, de-motivating, sometimes even causing others to have breakdowns
- extrovert, enjoying an audience while bullying, or
- introvert, either bullying in private or sitting in the background and encouraging others to do the bullying for them
- inflexible to new ideas
- moody and unpredictable
- low in emotional intelligence, especially empathy
- unwilling to accept responsibility for his/her own actions
- always looking for someone to blame
- someone who when tackled will either deny the accusation ('Can't you take a joke?'), attack back, or pretend he/she is the victim ('You're always picking on me!')

If you recognize that you are a bully, or have some bullying tendencies, give yourself a pat on the back for being courageous enough to get this far. By working through this workbook you will be able to go some way towards reversing these tendencies. You will find the sections on control and trust, empathy and listening skills in Relationship competence especially helpful.

No one gets to be a bully without a reason and bullies are often unhappy people deep down. If this sounds like you, you might also like to consider getting counselling.

If you realise that you have a bully in your workplace refer to your organization's anti-harassment policy. A very useful web site on this topic is www.successunlimited.co.uk.

TRUE LIFE STORY
Jane was a happy, enthusiastic 18-year-old when she started her new job. Three years later she was nervous, insecure and her personal relationships were suffering. She was the victim of a bully. As happens to many bullied people, the bully had convinced her she was worthless and it took her three years to apply for and get another job. When she handed in her notice she told her boss about the bullying. Her boss replied 'Well, I'm not going to replace you. I thought you'd be able to cope with her (the bully), but if you can't no-one will.' The bully is still in post. Worse, so is the boss.

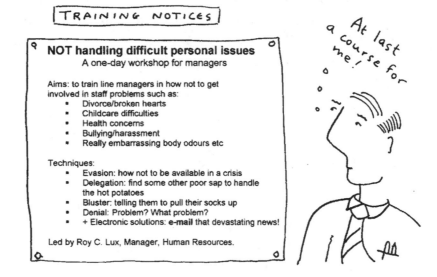

Training notices

Fran Johnstone

Coercive leadership activity 2 – developing a no-blame culture

Not everyone who is into blame is a bully. Some leaders can be reasonable in other areas but lack skills in getting problems sorted constructively.

This activity will help you to decide whether your culture is to blame or to not blame. Read each of the statements and then mark one of the three boxes on the right depending on whether the statement is frequently, sometimes or rarely true for you.

In your workgroup:	Frequently	Sometimes	Rarely
When something goes wrong you/the group look for someone to blame			
People tend to hide their mistakes until things go seriously wrong			
There is little creativity in finding solutions to problems			
People lack motivation and a can-do attitude			
People grumble			
There is high staff turnover			
You as the boss are the last to hear when things are going wrong			
There is a competitive rather than a co-operative atmosphere			
Information is closely guarded			
Communication is poor			

Those areas where you've marked 'frequently' or 'sometimes' are areas for improvement. Let's look at them one by one.

Looking for someone to blame

It's certainly true that people must accept responsibility for their work but looking to 'blame' someone is counter productive. It builds resentment in people who probably already feel bad about making a mistake. It also damages your relationship with them. By finding other ways to resolve problems you improve motivation and your relationships with your staff.

People hide mistakes

A blame culture leads to people covering up mistakes for fear of retribution. This means that things have already gone thoroughly wrong before you find out about them. Naturally, this makes them harder to put right.

Creativity is reduced

Creativity means trying new approaches and is inherently risky. Blame culture reduces people's willingness to take creative risks and reduces their confidence. This means that your staff will get stuck in a rut, reluctant to try new, improved ways of working.

Developing a no-blame culture

Blame looks to the past 'What happened?' 'Whose fault was it?'. A no-blame culture looks forward 'How can we fix this?' 'What can we do to make sure it won't happen again?'. It is a problem-solving approach.

There will always be mistakes, but people and organizations should not continue to make the same mistakes over and over again. While people must take responsibility for problems, their main responsibility is to ensure that they correct the problem and avoid it happening again. They have to learn from the mistake.

Here are some tips for speaking to someone about a problem that allow you to discuss it within a no-blame framework.

- When you speak to people about a problem separate the person from the issue.
- Speak to the person in private.
- Don't get into name calling. Act respectfully at all times.
- Ask the person for ideas on how the situation can be resolved. Explore their ideas, adding any of your own until you find one that is mutually acceptable.
- Help them to identify what they have learned from the situation so that they can avoid it happening in future.
- Take note yourself of any responsibility you may have in the situation. This could be inadequate training, poor resources, faulty systems or insufficient monitoring and feedback.
- Give praise. Using the full range of leadership styles and developing an open approach and excellent team work will go a long way towards developing a no-blame culture.

If, once you have put this framework into place, a member of your staff continues to make the same mistakes, you have a training issue on your hands. If that fails you may get to disciplinary action, but even here use the same respectful way of speaking to the person.

My sense of humour

Fran Johnstone

Coercive leadership activity 3 – encouraging feedback in the workplace

Do people in your team give each other feedback? Do they avoid telling each other things they are unhappy about? Do they tell each other by using 'jokes' or sarcasm? Do they give each other positive feedback?

Having a healthy climate for feedback with staff skilled enough to give effective feedback leads to a productive working environment and happy staff.

You can encourage feedback by being seen to give positive feedback yourself. Remember, negative feedback should be in private, but some positive feedback can be in public. Make sure you praise your staff to others whenever possible.

Test your ability to encourage constructive feedback by looking at the statements below. Give yourself a rating between 1 and 10. 1 is 'I rarely do this' through to 10 – 'I frequently do this'.

Statement	Score
I praise people in public	1..2..3..4..5..6..7..8..9..10
I praise people in private	1..2..3..4..5..6..7..8..9..10
I ask for ideas for improvement or innovations in our work	1..2..3..4..5..6..7..8..9..10
I encourage everyone to make contributions to team meetings	1..2..3..4..5..6..7..8..9..10
I ask my staff for feedback on my performance	1..2..3..4..5..6..7..8..9..10
I encourage my staff to read widely to keep fresh ideas flowing	1..2..3..4..5..6..7..8..9..10
I use team building activities with my staff	1..2..3..4..5..6..7..8..9..10
I encourage my staff to socialise	1..2..3..4..5..6..7..8..9..10
I avoid sarcasm	1..2..3..4..5..6..7..8..9..10

The higher the score, the happier your staff will be and the more likely to give each other constructive feedback. If your score is low on any item, the statement itself gives an indication of changes to make to develop this positive climate.

Coercive leadership activity 4 – words that wind people up!

Do you find that you sometimes wind people up even when you don't mean to? It's easy to wind people up – just try some of the words and phrases on the left. Alternatively, for a nicer life, increased popularity and a happier staff group, try the ones on the right.

Wind up words	Calming alternative
'You should . . .'	'I wonder if you've considered . . .'
'You shouldn't . . .'	'I find that . . .'
'You must . . .'	'It is helpful if you . . .'
'You idiot'	'How can we avoid that happening again?'

'You ought to . . .'	'One way of doing that would be . . .'
'You always . . .'	'On three occasions in the last week . . .'
'You never . . .'	'I've noticed that you rarely . . .'
'You wrote this number down wrong'	'This number is incorrect. Do you have the correct one please?'
'Can't you get anything right?'	'I've noticed this work is incorrect, what do you think needs doing to get it right?'
'What do you call this then?'	'Could you explain this to me please?'
'What time do you call this to come in?'	'I'm worried about your timekeeping. Can we discuss it please.'

Over the next few days check your speech patterns. Do you use 'universal' words such as 'always', 'never', 'no one', 'everyone'? Do you tell people what they 'should', 'must' or 'ought' to do? Is your tone accusatory?

As well as selecting the right turn of phrase in the first place, you can ease a difficult message by use softeners such as 'I was just wonder if you had . . .', 'It occurs to me that . . .', 'Someone once told me that . . .', 'I was reading that . . .'. The key is to sound empathetic rather than aggressive. And if you have to give advice don't do it in a 'Look what I know, I'm cleverer than you' way. Share your knowledge rather than hit someone with it.

Coercive leadership activity 5 – learning from feedback

Coercive leaders rarely ask for feedback. They tend to believe they (and only they) do things right. Because of this, they don't value other people's opinions. Yet we all need feedback. In Johari's window (p. 36 of Personal competence) we saw that by asking for feedback you can unlock your potential for improvement and this is a skill potential that the coercive leader especially needs to develop.

Asking for feedback can be threatening if you haven't done it before. Suppose they say something we find difficult to hear? Suppose we feel very angry with what they say? Using the emotional intelligence skills already covered in this workbook (especially Effective listening in Relationship competence and Overcoming anger in Personal competence) in addition to this section, you will have the skills to cope with feedback and benefit from it.

Spend a few minutes thinking about the answers to these questions:

- How often have you asked for feedback?
- If you have asked, who did you ask?
- Are there people you would definitely not ask to give you feedback? Why?
- In what circumstances would you ask for feedback?

Reflecting on your answers, did any pattern emerge? Have you avoided asking for feedback altogether? Have you asked for feedback only from people who are not direct when they have difficult things to say? Do you only ask for feedback when there are serious consequences if you don't improve (such as a threat to your job)? If you can see a positive pattern of asking for and using feedback constructively, congratulate yourself. If your pattern is destructive plan now for a more productive approach.

To help you to benefit from feedback you might like to work through this process.

Think about three significant occasions when you have received critical feedback.

- What were your reactions?
- How was the feedback given to you? Was it direct, indirect or assumed (by you)?
- Was the feedback given in an emotional or objective way?
- Did you find yourself becoming hooked by the emotional content?
- What were your inner thoughts when you were receiving the criticism? Did you think the criticism was fair? Did you think you were being victimized? Did you feel guilty? Did you want to place the blame on others?
- What were your physical reactions?
- What feelings did you have? Anger? Guilt? Shame? Embarrassment? Passivity? Remorse? Contrition? Hostility? Rage? Relief?
- How did you respond?

Now reflect on what you did that you are pleased about. Congratulate yourself. If, in retrospect, there was anything you would change what would it be? Could you adjust your inner dialogue? Could you use a calming technique? (See Changing a negative mood in Personal competence, p. 78). Could you have asked for time to think about the criticism before responding?

Asking for feedback

Fran Johnstone

How to ask for feedback

■ Ask the right person. Ask someone who knows you in the area in which you want feedback. Also ask someone who is able assertively to give you feedback in a way that won't damage you. Make sure too that they have enough time to talk to you about this. If not, arrange to see them when they are less busy.

■ Explain why you want the feedback. Be positive by saying something like 'I'd like to be better at my . . . skills'. Make it clear that you want to learn from what they have to say.

■ If the person struggles giving you feedback, pose direct questions. 'I've noticed that my staff go to Amir for help but not to me. What do you think stops them?' 'I realise that customers often get upset with me on the phone. Can you comment about my tone of voice please?' 'My staff are very demoralized. Is there anything I can do to help them?'

■ If possible, get feedback from several people. Different people throw different perspectives on a situation.

■ Practise your calming techniques if you feel anxious about hearing the feedback. Respond in a polite way, and ask further questions if necessary.

■ Thank the person for giving you the feedback.

■ Congratulate yourself on taking this step.

You may like to spend a few minutes now deciding what feedback would be helpful to you in developing your range of leadership styles. The questions below will prompt you.

I would like feedback on	1.	....
	2.	....
	3.	....
I will ask	1.	....
	2.	....
	3.	....
I will ask them on (date, time, etc.) . . .	1.	....
	2.	....
	3.	....
My approach on each of the three situations will be	1.	....
	2.	....
	3.	....

Sometimes we are unprepared for negative feedback that is unexpectedly given to us. At times like this it can help to have a strategy for coping – after all, this is not a situation many of us like.

You will find guidelines for dealing with negative feedback in Personal competence on p. 173. If you have not already worked through that section you might like to do so now.

Coercive leadership activity 6 – being an inclusive leader

Inclusiveness is about valuing the differences that people bring to the workplace – their diversity. A team that is made up of people who are too alike does not work well. We need people with different backgrounds, personalities and abilities to enable a team to work effectively and creatively. Such diversity means being comfortable with people of different ages, sexuality, gender, ability level, interests and race, from our own.

One of the better known cases for the success of inclusiveness is the British home improvement chain B&Q. In 1989 they made a decision to employ older people in one of their stores. They were delighted with the results. When compared to their other stores:

- profits were 18% higher
- staff turnover was six times lower
- there was 39% less absenteeism
- there was 59% less shrinkage
- there was improved customer perception of service and increased staff skill base.

B&Q have also worked hard to improve their stores to cater for the needs of people with disabilities and people of all ethnic groups. To read their inspiring story you might like to look at their website www.diy.com.

Do you value diversity? Read the following statements and give yourself a score from 1 to 10 by circling the applicable number in the box on the right of each statement.

Statement	Score
1. I reflect on my thinking and behaviour to check for discriminatory thinking	Always..1..2..3..4..5..6..7..8..9..10 Rarely
2. I appreciate the differences people bring to my team	Always..1..2..3..4..5..6..7..8..9..10 Rarely
3. I challenge discriminatory behaviour or remarks	Always..1..2..3..4..5..6..7..8..9..10 Rarely
4. I prefer to reflect on someone when I meet them rather than trust my first impressions	Always..1..2..3..4..5..6..7..8..9..10 Rarely
5. I am interested in cultural differences	Always..1..2..3..4..5..6..7..8..9..10 Rarely
6. When I appoint a member of staff from a different cultural background I make time to find out about that culture	Always..1..2..3..4..5..6..7..8..9..10 Rarely
7. I ensure that people with disabilities can use our workplace	Always..1..2..3..4..5..6..7..8..9..10 Rarely
8. When appointing staff I try to find ways in which disabled candidates can do the job with the right resources	Always..1..2..3..4..5..6..7..8..9..10 Rarely
9. I understand body language differences in different cultures	Always..1..2..3..4..5..6..7..8..9..10 Rarely

10. If a transgender member of staff joined my team I would feel confident about handling all relevant legal, organizational and interpersonal issues

Always..1..2..3..4..5..6..7..8..9..10 Rarely

The lower your score the more inclusive you are as a manager. In questions where your score is higher ask yourself:

- What do I need to learn about this issue? How can I learn it?
- What attitudes, if any, do I need to reconsider?
- What might I be missing by not valuing diversity?
- What can I learn from the B&Q story?

Chapter 19
Leadership competence advantage 4
Pacesetting leadership style

Pacesetters, as the name suggests, set the pace for work in their team. Pacesetters have drive and initiative and are conscientious. They expect high standards both in terms of speed and quality. This style can work well when staff are highly competent and self-motivated. Sadly, though, pacesetters can de-motivate others who do not have these characteristics. They can have unrealistically high expectations of what others can achieve and be too controlling. They often give poor or no feedback to their staff. And sometimes in their haste for a quick result they forget to give people the big picture about the work they're involved in.

In this way, there is much in common with the coercive leadership style. Both styles are a necessary part of the leader's toolkit, but both need to be used in moderation.

The skills a pacesetter needs to learn to be an accomplished leader are listening, questioning, empathy, motivation and trust. Other skills are part of this section.

Don't take life too serious. You'll never escape it alive anyway.
(Elbert Hubbard)

Pacesetting leadership activity 1 – feedback for improved quality

In their haste to achieve high quality in minimum time, pacesetters can sometimes give criticism in a destructive rather than an empowering way. Giving criticism in this way not only de-motivates others, it kills creativity because people are so scared of making mistakes that they won't take risks at all. If you realize that people react badly to your criticism you will find the format below helpful. You will also benefit from reading through the material on developing a no-blame culture on p. 224.

All leaders have to say difficult things to their staff occasionally and giving criticism is a turn of phrase that has little joy. If you think instead about giving someone constructive feedback to help them develop their performance your frame of mind will be more empowering.

Six steps to giving constructive feedback

This approach helps you to think through what you want to say before you say it. Unless someone is in imminent physical danger feedback should never be given in anger or haste. Spend your time planning what to say in a way that the other person can hear and act on.

STEP 1   *Get in the right frame of mind*

Tips:

- Wait until you are calm before tackling someone about a difficult issue. If you go in with all guns blazing you'll have a showdown you could do without.
- Use a relaxation technique before you start. There are some suggestions for this in the activity that follows.
- Always give difficult feedback in private – no one wants to be shown up in front of their colleagues.
- Don't make guesses at the person's motives for their behaviour. It's very frustrating when people say things like 'I expect you're doing this because . . .'
- Plan the conversation ahead of time, choosing your words carefully (some suggestions for wording can also be found in 'Words that wound' later in this section).
- Remember that most people find negative feedback difficult and they may respond by getting aggressive, or crumpling.

STEP 2   *Describe the specific behaviour you are unhappy about*

Tips:

- Be specific, don't use 'universal' words such as 'always', 'never', 'everyone', 'no one' unless they are entirely true.
- Remember that you are describing the behaviour, not the person. Again see the section 'Words that wound'.

STEP 3   *Explain how you feel about what is happening and the effect it is having on the work and/or other people*

Tips:

- You may need to modify your language. If you are absolutely furious, you may progress better by saying that you are 'angry'. It is possible to say this in a calm way!
- At this stage check that the person agrees with your analysis of the situation. Invite their comments.
- State the positive consequences of improved behaviour for the person themselves. This will be motivating for them.

STEP 4   *Ask for suggestions as to how things could be improved*

Tips:

- People are more likely to go along with solutions they have reached themselves rather than those that they feel are forced upon them.
- Have a solution in mind in case they don't have one or don't suggest an acceptable solution. Don't try to ask for too many changes at once.
- Keep an open mind – their idea may be better than yours.
- Consider what you might be able to offer by way of negotiation.

STEP 5   *If necessary, state negative consequences*

Tips:

- Try never to get to this stage. A good leader will always try to work closely with staff to develop practical or behavioural skills.
- Never make idle threats or threaten anything you won't carry through.

STEP 6   *Follow through*

Tips:

If appropriate arrange a time to review how progress is going. Be specific at the initial discussion as to the timing and format of the review. Here is a sample of how a conversation like this might go:

John: 'Have you got a moment Sarah? I'd like to speak to you about that customer who just came in.'

Sarah: 'Sure.'

John: 'I couldn't help but notice that you were not very quick serving her even though you weren't busy. I also noticed that you didn't look at her throughout the whole conversation. Were you aware of this?'

Sarah: 'Well, I suppose I was a bit slow but she didn't really come up to the counter straight away, did she?'

John: 'You're right, but if you'd been keeping an eye out you'd have noticed her buying signals. I have noticed you doing this on two or three occasions before, sometimes when you are busy talking to Tracy. Do you have any ideas how this could be resolved?'

Sarah: 'God, I feel as if you've been watching me all the time! (Heavy sigh) I suppose I could keep my personal chats to Tracy to the break times.'

John: 'That's an excellent idea, thanks for suggesting it. There was one other thing if you remember. I have noticed that you rarely have eye contact with customers and it's an important part of customer service. Customers see it as rude if someone doesn't look at them. I've noticed that you have good eye contact with Tracy and other people so you can do it. How could you remember to look at people when you serve them?'

Sarah: 'I suppose it's just a case of reminding myself.'

John: 'That's great. I think that if you do this your sales will go up and your commission will be higher. Why don't we discuss this again tomorrow afternoon and see how it's been going. If I can help in any way do let me know.'

Think now about some feedback that you would like to give someone. Plan how you will say it using the format below.

Step 1 – Get in the right frame of mind

Step 2 – Describe the specific behaviour you are unhappy about

Step 3 – Explain how you feel about what is happening and the effect it is having on the work and/or other people

Step 4 – Ask for suggestions as to how things could be improved

Step 5 – If necessary, state negative consequences

Step 6 – Follow through

Pacesetting leadership activity 2 – relaxation techniques

Pacesetters push themselves as hard as they push others and this can lead to high levels of stress. This is not only poor for your own physical and mental health, it can be devastating if you take your stress out on your staff. Learning some relaxation techniques can make all the difference to your stress level throughout the working day. You might like to try the Two second pause on p. 87. Here are some others you may benefit from:

Calming picture

As you sit reading this allow yourself to picture a beautiful piece of scenery with some gently rippling water. Enjoy making the picture as clear, bright and colourful as you can. If you can, hear the sound of the gently rippling water and any other restful sounds associated with the picture. If this is difficult for you, say slowly to yourself 'Calm'. As you do this allow any tension in your body to slip away.

You can train yourself to use this visualization any time you are feeling stressed. Do this by becoming aware of the first sign in your body that you are becoming stressed and learn to associate this with switching into the calming visualization. Practise this several times until it becomes automatic.

Stress releasing shower

When you are alone stand still for a few seconds with your hands raised at your sides. Imagine a gently cooling shower rippling over your body washing away all your tension.

Muscle relaxation

Sitting down, allow your muscles to relax by tensing and relaxing them. Start with your scalp and work your way down to your toes. You may like to imagine the tension dripping off your toes and fingers when you relax these muscles.

No act of kindness, however small, is ever wasted.

(Aesop)

Pacesetting leadership activity 3 – words that wound, sounds that soothe

Sometimes we upset people with a careless use of words. We can give difficult messages much more effectively by choosing our words carefully. Remember that the more aggressive our approach, the less the other person will feel able to really hear us and take on board our message.

Here are some examples of words that wound and suggested alternatives. Write down any wounding words you may use and think of a more positive way to give the same message:

Words that wound	*Sounds that soothe*
'You're hopeless. You always get things wrong.'	'I've noticed the same mistake happening again and again. Let's work out how we can avoid it in future.'
'How could you have messed this up so thoroughly?'	'Let's see if we can sort this out quickly.'
'If you think you can just walk in here and take our resources, you're mistaken.'	'Can we discuss what you need, to see if we can find a way to satisfy everyone's needs.'
'That's a lie and you know it.'	'I'm uncomfortable with that . . .'
'If you ask me how to do that once more I'm going to explode!'	'How can you help yourself to remember this for the future?'

Chapter 20
Leadership competence advantage 5 Democratic leadership style

Democratic leaders act more like members of the team than its leader. This very hands-on approach can win approval from the team, who realize that the boss really knows the work and is willing to knuckle down to it with the best of them. The democratic leader, through close links with the team, knows what's going on at any one time. This leader usually has good listening skills and involves people in decision-making. Decisions are made through consensus and people feel involved at all times.

Unfortunately if this is your only leadership style you are probably actually de-motivating people. This is because you will be seen as unwilling to make decisions alone, hold endless meetings and do not provide a clear vision for everyone to work towards. Furthermore your style may mean that poor performance is allowed to continue. (In this case you will find the next chapter on Coaching leadership style especially helpful.) You may also be poor at making decisions at times of crisis.

This style works well when the leader is unsure about what decision to make. It also works well with a self-starting team whose goals are given to them from elsewhere.

In fact, the occasions when a whole team can, and should, make the final decision on a topic are more rare than you might think. Generally, a good leader will consult with the team but retain the power to make the final decision. The consultation should, of course, be genuine. People quickly see through leaders who pretend to consult and then do what they had planned all along. Very soon people stop putting forward suggestions.

If the democratic leadership style is one you lean on most, you need to develop other styles, especially the authoritative style. By combining decisiveness, clear vision and your existing teamwork skills you will have much to offer your staff and your organization. Additional skills that will help you are described in Establishing standards on p. 212 and the coaching skills on pp. 252 and 254.

Democratic leadership activity 1 – effective decision-making

Democratic leaders often find decision-making difficult, preferring to leave decisions to the team. On one level this is an excellent tactic because people are much more likely to work towards goals they have helped to form.

However, it is not always possible to reach a consensus and as we have already seen, this sometimes leads to lack of direction and subsequent poor quality and de-motivation.

Effective decision-making is a vital part of the leader's role. The responsibility for final decisions usually rests with you. Don't let your team, your organization and yourself down. Here is a simple yet effective decision-making format:

STEP 1   *Define the problem*

To do this you need to take all factors into account:

- the needs of the organization, the customer and the team
- resource implications, including your human resources
- timescales
- other pressures on the team at the time
- criteria for success.

STEP 2   *List all possible solutions and undertake a SWOT analysis of each*

SWOT is a mnemonic for Strengths, Weaknesses, Opportunities and Threats and is usually laid out this way:

Strengths (things that are on your side in the decision-making process)	*Weaknesses* (things that are against you – time, resources, etc.)
Opportunities (to use your strengths and overcome weaknesses)	*Threats* (to achieving your goal)

There are ideas for increasing creativity on p. 206. Other ideas you may like to try include brainstorming with the team. To do this pose the problem to the team and write suggestions on a flipchart. Suggestions should not be commented on until everyone has run out of ideas. Ideas can be as sensible or wacky as people like to make them – often excellent ideas grow on the back of seemingly absurd ones.

You could also use a process flow chart where you make a diagram showing the steps in the task sequence. The diagram tracks the flow of resources and time through the system.

STEP 3 *Look at your solutions in the light of your success criteria*

Eliminate any solutions that don't meet the required criteria.

STEP 4 *Compare solutions against the criteria*

The solution with the best match is the winner – provided your criteria have been properly defined.

STEP 5 *Implement your chosen solution*

Remember, you won't always make the right decision, no one does. However, using a logical and justifiable approach is better than no decision at all or one based purely on gut feeling.

Democratic leadership activity 2 – clear boundaries

CASE STUDY – SUE'S BLURRED BOUNDARIES

Sue and Tamsin worked together for three years. They spent ages chatting about how awful things were at work and what they'd like to change. They socialized together and shared many secrets. Although generally good workers, they both took occasional sickies and sometimes let things slide.

Then Sue got promoted above Tamsin. They continued to be close friends but things got very tricky when the company hit hard times and Sue had to be more accountable for the work her team did. She wanted to make sure that everyone worked effectively and that there were no more 'sickies'. When Sue got the promotion she and Tamsin didn't discuss their changed relationship, and now she didn't even know where to begin to get Tamsin to go the extra mile. The friend/boss boundaries were unclear.

Democratic leaders frequently have poor boundaries. It's as if, within the workplace, they hardly know where they end and the team begins. Their role as leader is ill-defined and they are pretty much just one of the team. With such poor boundaries it is difficult for the leader to have authority with staff. This can be especially difficult when there are issues of performance management to be addressed. It follows therefore that if your boundaries are unclear you need to take steps to clarify them.

One way you can have clearer boundaries is to be an effective decision-maker, perhaps using the guidelines above. Another is to very slightly distance yourself from your team. No more getting drunk with them after work on a Friday, no more disclosure of very private information. So, what's appropriate in terms of disclosing information about yourself? Here's a formula that should help you sort this one out.

- With each person ask yourself, 'What is my orientation to this person? Am I higher or lower in rank? Am I in a supporting or receiving role?'
- If you are lower in seniority than the other person you are not their peer but you can turn to them for advice and support. They should not look to you for this support.
- If you are higher in seniority, you are not *their* peer and you do not turn to them for this support, you offer it instead.
- If you are level in seniority with the other person you *are* their peer and you can offer each other mutual support. If you are doing peer things with someone who is not your peer, then your boundaries have been crossed.

These clear boundaries mean that you do not gossip with one worker about another. You do not moan about your boss or the organization to your staff. You do not run down your team to others.

Your challenge for this activity is to clean up your boundaries. Spend some time thinking about the people with whom you interact regularly. Then ask yourself the following questions:

- 'If this member of my staff is also a close friend, which relationship is most important to me?' (You may need to chat to the member of staff about keeping work and non-work talk separate.)
- 'If this boss is also a close friend, what effect will that have if I have problems with my performance?' (You may need to clarify this with your boss.)
- 'What information about myself is appropriate to share with my team?'
- 'What information would be better kept private?'

There is another sort of boundary that should be clear – who does what work. If you have been working as part of the team and neglecting to lead it, it's possible that you are doing too much of the team's work. Take some time soon to re-assess the situation. Leading a team takes time, and that means the time can't be spent doing all the team's work yourself. They'll thank you for it.

By cleaning up your boundaries you'll find you have better relationships at work and begin to assert your leadership in a positive way.

Democratic leadership activity 3 – asserting your leadership

If you now realize that your style has been too democratic you can begin to assert your leadership in an appropriate way by talking to your team about future plans for where the team and the organization are headed. If you've been working alongside the team you have probably many times discussed how things could be done better (probably blaming senior management errors and omissions). How is your chance to make things happen.

Spend some time thinking about the improvements you'd like to make in the team, how quality could be improved, how people could be happier and more motivated. Write your ideas down.

Next, spend some time speaking to each member of your team separately, saying that you'd like to improve things for them and the organization and that you'd appreciate hearing their ideas. You should give them some warning of this meeting so that they can get their thoughts together. Write down their thoughts, thank them for their time and at the end of the interview tell them that you plan to do the best for them and ask for their support. If they don't give it, problems have been raised and that's better than them festering under-ground. You can then work towards resolving them. If you get the support, all well and good.

When you have spoken to each member of the team, put together their ideas and your own and work out a plan for quality development over the next six or twelve months. Always bear in mind your organization's strategic plans. Call a team meeting and share your ideas with people, emphasizing how much you have valued their input. Ask for further suggestions and make any necessary changes to your recommendations in the light of them. At the end of the meeting ask the team, 'Can I count on your support to help me see this through?' Again, it is better to have any dissenters speak now than to find out later that someone is unhappy and out to sabotage you.

This whole process sets you aside as the boss in a way that is very positive for you, your team and your organization. It is a win–win–win situation.

If asserting your authority is an issue for you, you might like to carry out this process. You can combine it with carrying out performance reviews (appraisals). These again set you aside as the leader. They also allow you a constructive time when you and the team member can discuss their performance. If you are hesitant about conducting a performance review, do undertake some training before you begin. It takes a long time to win round a team after botched reviews, better to do it right first time. Your emotional intelligence gained through developing the skills in this workbook will stand you in excellent stead now.

Democratic leadership activity 4 – delegation

Let's just be clear about terminology before we discuss this topic. Delegation is when you give people *your* work to do. This contrasts with allocation where you give people *their* work to do. Democratic leaders are often quite good at allocation but rarely good at delegation. It's a difficulty shared with several other leadership styles.

So why do leaders hesitate to delegate? I've heard them all: 'They might do it wrong', 'They'll say it's not in their job description', 'They might do it better than me', 'They're too busy', 'It'll take more time to explain the job than do it myself'. All these and other reasons are sometimes true but sometimes just excuses, justification for fear of letting go. It's true that delegation does involve risk, you have to risk that your coaching of the other person is sufficient for them to perform the task well. This involves trust. If trusting is a difficult issue for you, you might like to work through the activity Control and trust on pp. 152–7.

It is also true that delegation takes time. It's rather like basic parenting skills – you have to spend time to save time. If you didn't take time training your child to tie its shoe laces, and grit your teeth when they take ages doing it when you want to get them off to school, they'd go off to college still unable to put their shoes on properly. It's time well invested and it gives you freedom to concentrate on more strategic issues.

In fact, participants on courses who go back to the workplace and delegate work invariably report that the whole experience went very well. People were flattered to be asked, they enjoyed the challenge and the opportunity to develop their skills. And in fact, even busy people usually find time to do things they really want to do.

So, let's see how comfortable you are at delegating.

STAGE A   Look at the statements below. If you fail to delegate because of any of these reasons, tick the 'yes' box. If this reason is not true for you, tick the 'no' box.

Reason for not delegating	Yes	No
1. I like doing everything myself		
2. The staff member may not do the task as well as I can		
3. It takes too long to explain the task		
4. If they get as good as me my job may be under threat		
5. They may do the task in a different way and I like it done my way		
6. They don't have the right skills		
7. I'm not sure when I should delegate		
8. I don't enjoy coaching people		
9. I find it difficult to trust people		
10. My people are just too busy to take on anything else		

STAGE B Alone or with a friend, look at any of the reasons where you have answered 'yes' and ask yourself why this may be so. Then discuss what steps you can take to help you feel more comfortable. For example, if you ticked number 8, you could get some coaching training so that you feel more confident in this aspect of your management role. It is useful to make some written notes.

There are some useful questions you can ask yourself if you are unsure whether or not to delegate. These are:

- Is there someone who may be more skilled than you at performing the task?
- Is there someone who may do the job more slowly or in a different way, but who can still reach an acceptable standard of performance?
- Is there someone who is paid less than you, so that even if they take longer the cost of performing the task will be lowered?
- Is there someone whose professional development would be helped if they undertook the task?

Answering 'yes' to any of these questions means that you have a delegation opportunity.

What is delegation about?

Delegation means giving a member of your staff some of your work to do. To do this you need to agree on several points:

- the nature and scope of the work
- the measurable standards expected
- the timescale for task achievement
- assessment methods
- resources required
- the authority required for successful task achievement.

Guidelines for effective delegation

- Identify an appropriate task to be delegated.
- Select a person who has the correct skills or can be trained to the correct level. Ensure that they have enough time to perform the task.
- Speak first to the person and anyone who needs to know about the delegation.
- Use good coaching skills – see Coaching leadership on p. 254 if you are unsure about these skills.
- Delegate whole tasks whenever possible. If this is not possible explain how the part of the task fits in with the whole.
- Agree measurable criteria for success before the work begins.
- Delegate, don't dump! Some people are tempted to delegate unpleasant work and this won't make you popular. Remember, though, that different people have different ideas about what is 'pleasant' work.
- Before the work starts, build in your support system – check points throughout the work process.
- Delegate then TRUST your member of staff. Be available to help but don't appear to be constantly looking over their shoulder.

Man who says it cannot be done should not stand in the way of man who is doing it.

(Old Chinese proverb)

Democratic learning activity 5 – dealing with difficult people

Democrat leaders so like to be part of the team that they can sometimes fail to deal with difficult members of staff. Often they justify this by saying that they don't like to upset people, or it's more trouble than it's worth. If this is true for you, you must remember that while you are avoiding upsetting your difficult person, you are certainly upsetting everyone else.

Don't say anything to the person who habitually comes in late? You've just told him that tardiness is OK. Don't tackle the bully? You've just told her that bullying is acceptable. Don't coach the poor performer? You've made it clear that poor quality work is good enough. Every time you ignore poor behaviour you are reinforcing it.

Of course, there are many different types of difficult person and it's a subject that deserves a book on its own. In the book list at the end of this workbook there is some suggested additional reading. One type of difficult behaviour – bullying has been addressed under Coercive leadership (p. 221) and coaching to improve performance will be addressed in Coaching leadership to follow. Here we'll look at some of the more common types of difficult people.

Other skills covered in this book that will help you to cope with difficult people are empathy, assertiveness, giving constructive criticism and the section on Words that wound in the Pacesetting leadership section (p. 240). But let's look at some typical difficult types.

Indirectly aggressive people

Such people love to put you in your place, but won't be direct and open about their feelings. Instead they deal in sarcasm, put-downs, sulking, coldness and manipulation. They love to take a pot shot at you when they're on their way out of the door or give you the cold shoulder to let you know their displeasure.

These people bolster their own ego by trying to make you look small. If you don't give them the satisfaction, they'll probably take their aggression elsewhere. As Robert Bramson says in his excellent book *Dealing with Difficult People*, 'You won't cure these people, but you'll get them away from your desk, and hey, that's not so bad.'

So, how do you deal with people who are sarcastic and try to put you down? Well, a good trick is to treat their comment as if it weren't sarcasm but a straightforward comment. Here are a couple of real life comments someone I know made to students she taught, followed by appropriate responses:

Sarcastic comment:	(on noticing the student's scrunch-dried hair) 'I'm not sure about your hair. Is it supposed to look like that or are you always in a hurry?'
Response:	'Don't you like my hairstyle then?'
Sarcastic comment:	(when returning an essay) 'You're not nearly as intelligent as you look, are you?'
Response:	'I take it that you weren't happy with my essay.'

This type of 'straight' response is likely to throw many sarcastic people who don't expect the other person to respond at all. If, however, you're dealing with someone who needs stronger action, add to the end of your reply, 'But I think I heard a dig there, did I?' and then wait for the reply.

If the reply is 'Can't you take a joke?' Your response is 'Well, I didn't think it was a very funny comment, and I think that was a dig too. Was it?' And wait for a reply.

When the sarcastic person learns that they won't get away with it, they will almost certainly turn their attention away from you. And as Robert Bramson says 'hey, that's not so bad, is it?'

The aggressive person

Aggressive people attack first and ask questions later. They try to get their own way by force and appear to value aggressiveness and confidence in others.

To deal with this person, learn good assertion skills. Keep your body language assertive. Do this by sitting or standing with your weight evenly centred and imagine a string pulling you up from the top of your head. This should get your head upright and your back comfortably straight. Your eyes should be looking forward, not down, allowing you to maintain eye contact with the aggressive person and look confident at the same time.

Here is a step-by-step guide to dealing with the angry person.

What to do	Hints	What to say (example)
Step 1 Stop, listen to the angry person, use active listening skills, let them run out of steam before attempting to seriously join the conversation.	Keep calm, have good inner dialogue, concentrate on listening to the person and observing body language.	(To yourself) 'I can handle this' – but if worried about physical violence, leave immediately.

Step 2
Respond assertively, check if you have understood correctly (angry people are often unclear).

This allows the other person to feel heard or correct you.

'Can I just be clear I've got this right? What you're upset about is . . .'

Step 3
Make an empathetic comment, the person will realise you understand how they feel.

Do not compromise your integrity – you can say you notice the feeling without agreeing that what the person says is correct.

'I can see that's really annoying you.'

Step 4
Point out any contradictory comments the person has made.

Only do this if you feel it safe to do so. If you think they'll become more angry go with whichever interpretation to you feel correct and check your understanding.

'On the one hand you're saying . . . and on the other . . . I'm not clear which one is of most concern to you.'

Step 5
If aggression continues repeat above steps.

Continue to assess your level of safety, do not leave yourself open to physical attack.

'It seems that you're saying . . .'

Step 6
If aggression continues let the other person know you are unhappy about the situation.

Keep calm, make sure your body language is congruent. Don't threaten consequences you won't carry through. If dealing with a customer, check policy on terminating interviews or putting down the phone.

'I'd really like to help you sort this out but I can't whilst you're shouting at me. Let's sit down and discuss this quietly. Otherwise I'll have to end this conversation now.'

Step 7
End the discussion or start discussing the discussion.

Discussing the discussion is often a useful way to take things forward. You do not discuss what the discussion is about, but the process itself.

'I have tried several times to sort this out with you. Is there some way we can resolve this matter?'

Moaners and whingers

These can really test your patience. They find fault with everything except themselves. They whine incessantly and always believe that someone else should do something about the situation.

Although it's tempting to lose patience with moaners remember that they really do feel impotent and hard done by. They offer an excellent opportunity for you to use empowerment. Work with the moaner to develop their skills and encourage them to see where their own responsibility lies. When they moan about something always put the responsibility firmly back with them. For example, if they moan about someone else, say 'Have you spoken to them about that?' (You may have to coach them on how to tackle situations.)

To test your skills when dealing with moaners, work out a response to each of the following sentences. No 'correct' answers are provided as there is a wide range of responses possible. Remember, though, that you are aiming to make the person responsible for dealing with their complaints themselves. The first example is worked through for you as guidance.

Complaint	Your response
'No one ever tells me anything.'	'What can you do to ensure that you are kept informed?'
'It's not my fault I was late. Things just get in the way.'	
'Jo always gets her figures to me too late.'	
'I have to do everything around here.'	
'I'm fed up with people taking it out on me.'	

Democratic leadership activity 6 – how to get people to listen to you

Asserting yourself as the leader when you have worked as part of the team requires a range of new techniques. One of them could be getting people to listen to you – as the leader. Here are some tips that will help you achieve this confidently:

- Plan for what you want to say. Make sure that your content is coherent and presented in a logical manner. Prepare also any audio or visual aids you require.

- Make eye contact with the listener. If you're speaking to the whole team, direct your attention to each individual, one at a time. As you make eye contact speak directly to that person for the required time. If your team is big, you can also glance at small groups of people, usually two or three.

- Vary your tone and speak clearly – people will stay interested. If this is something you find difficult consider investing in one or two sessions with a voice coach. It can make all the difference.

- Involve your audience by referring to things they know well.

- Ask questions, this way your audience will continue to feel involved. Lectures are rarely effective.

- Be brief, get to the point and stick to it.

- Having said that, illustrate your points with appropriate figures and metaphors: 'We scored big that time', 'Let's avoid an own goal', etc. See Authoritative leadership 2 on p. 202 for more details of this.

- Choose your place. Locations with a lot of distractions will detract from your message.

- Summarize at regular intervals and at the end, and check understanding and agreement.

Your task for this activity is to look in your diary for the next week or two and identify opportunities for you to put this new approach into action. You might like to practise with your learning friend beforehand.

Chapter 21

Leadership competence advantage 6 Coaching leadership style

The Coaching leadership style is a very empowering one, enabling staff to be developed to their full potential. This obviously benefits not just the staff member themselves but also the organization.

Most managers coach their staff at one time or another yet many miss valuable coaching opportunities in the emotional intelligence areas. Allowing that emotional intelligence has been so closely linked with success this is surprising. And yet, in another way it is not surprising because the low EI can be more sensitive to tackle.

In this section we will look at coaching both hard and EI abilities so that you can get the best from your people.

Coaching leadership activity 1 – coaching practical skills

In The Emotional Intelligence Advantage, you were introduced to the idea of the learning cycle (p. 15). Understanding this concept is vitally important for a coach and you may like to remind yourself of it before you move on.

In it we saw that to learn from experience people must complete the learning cycle. We also saw that people will have one, or sometimes more, preferred learning styles. This means that they will feel most comfortable with one or more stages of the learning cycle. If you try to teach someone using the wrong learning style for them, you will find yourself in trouble. The person will fail to learn easily because there will be a mismatch.

Whilst there is a questionnaire you can complete to determine someone's learning style, this may not be practical in everyday life. I find that one way to determine a person's learning style is to ask them a simple question: 'How did you learn to use your video recorder?'

Some people will say that they fiddled with the controls until they got it to work. These people like having lots of experiences and are known as 'activists'. Activists often get bored half way through learning something new, so they'll only learn the basics on the video recorder until they need to know more.

Other people like to try one or two things with the controls and then sit and think carefully before trying anything else. They like stage two of the learning cycle, reflecting on the experience, and are known as 'reflectors'.

People who like to read the manual before they touch the controls are people who are happiest in stage three. They are called 'theorists'.

And people who like the planning stage are called 'pragmatists'. They like to see the practical application of the video recorder, or anything else for that matter.

So if you are going to teach someone a practical skill ask them the video recorder question and then plan your teaching style accordingly. Can you imagine what would happen if an activist tried to use an activist style with a reflector? The reflector would feel too hurried and become anxious because they wouldn't have enough time to reflect on what they were learning.

Imagine a theorist trying to use their own style to teach an activist or a pragmatist. The learners would become very impatient and want to get on with it. Here then are pointers to your approach with each of these styles.

Style	Teaching approach
Activists	Activists enjoy enthusiastically immersing themselves in new experiences and are open-minded. Give them plenty to do (but check their quality). Allow them to make quick decisions, give them deadlines to work to, give them opportunities to generate new ideas. If they can do this with others and in the limelight so much the better. Remember too, that they like to have fun.
Reflectors	Reflectors like to ponder unhurriedly on experiences. They are cautious, slow people, often with a low profile. While they sometimes avoid taking action at all, when they do it is usually well-considered. To teach them most effectively give them plenty of time to digest information. Give them deadlines that aren't too tight and don't expect them to learn too quickly. However, once they have learned something, they will probably have learned it well.
Theorists	Theorists like to see where their work fits into the scheme of things. They like systems, models, concepts and theories so if there is any theory that will help explain your topic use it. Draw diagrams, provide hard data. Give them time to make sense of what they're learning in relation to what they already know. Stretch them intellectually. Teach in a structured way, presenting well-reasoned arguments. Give them an opportunity to improve the way things are currently done.

| Pragmatists | Pragmatists like to see how things work in practice so ensure that this is part of your initial explanation: 'We're going to learn . . . which will be useful for . . .'. They like to learn from an expert and enjoy looking at charts and other visual aids. Keep your talk concrete and not too theoretical. |

Understanding your 'pupil's' learning style is therefore a prerequisite for planning your coaching session. The guidelines below will direct you through the whole process.

Coaching for skill improvement

Stage 1. Preparation

- Establish the learner's learning style so that you can plan the most effective way to teach them.
- With the learner, set SMART objectives for the coaching session (see p. 53).
- Agree teaching method, timing, deadlines, resources, review method.
- Prepare beforehand any documents needed for the session, including diagrams, pictures, statistics, equipment, etc.

Stage 2. The coaching session

- Put the learner at ease by using a relaxed and friendly approach.
- Use the learner's learning style to ensure maximum retention.
- Relate the new skills to the learner's existing knowledge.
- Remember to consider Health and Safety issues.
- Agree responsibility and support you and any others will give.
- Watch body language for signs that you are going too fast or boring the person by going too slow.
- Use the four step approach:

  1. Demonstrate the whole task through quickly, so that the learner can see it from start to finish.

  2. Repeat the task. This time, work slowly, explaining at every stage what you are doing. Encourage the learner to ask questions and discuss what they are learning. Ask learning questions yourself, such as 'What do you think I should do now' or 'What problems might happen here?'

3. Get the learner to undertake the task. Encourage them to do it slowly, explaining to you what they are doing at each stage. This will aid retention of information.

4. If sufficient learning has taken place the learner should now be able to perform the task straight through. This of course will depend on the complexity of the task. It could be that stages 2 and 3 have to repeated several times.

Stage 3. Evaluation, feedback and monitoring

At all times give positive feedback. Even if the person is doing something wrong do not criticize. Instead ask empowering questions such as 'What will happen if you do it that way?' or 'How else could that be done?' Ask questions that check knowledge of why the person has done what they have done. It could be that they just struck lucky this time.

After the teaching session ensure that you offer on-going support. This is especially important if the person does not perform the task often – they could have forgotten what they learnt.

Your task for this activity is to get together with your learning friend and practise a coaching session. You can teach each other anything – a card game, how to fold a paper napkin, how to use part of a software package – anything that you know well and they are willing to learn.

Coaching leadership activity 2 – coaching EI skills

Every day leaders are presented with opportunities to coach their staff in their EI skills. Remember poor emotional intelligence can lead to poor performance, unmet deadlines, interpersonal conflict, poor customer service, sulking, bullying – the list is endless.

Coaching in emotional intelligence requires all your tact and diplomacy skills. Other EI skills you will need are empathy, good listening and questioning, clear communication, and the ability to read body language. These guidelines complement those for giving constructive feedback on pp. 236–7.

Guidelines for coaching Emotional Intelligence topics

STAGE 1   *Identify the problem*

Step	What you say
Be sure of your facts before you start.	(This is before you speak to the person.)
Introduce the subject in a friendly, non-threatening way, make it sound as if you are just discussing a shared problem (which indeed you are).	'I've noticed that sometimes you don't speak to your colleagues for several hours and look very withdrawn.'
Establish a desire for a solution.	'I wonder if you are upset about something and we could explore how to resolve this?'

STAGE 2   *Work together towards a solution*

Step	What you say
Seek the person's ideas on how to resolve the situation. Listen actively to the suggestions. Avoid forcing a solution unless it is a policy or Health and Safety issue.	'So you're sometimes upset that they don't do their share of the work. How else you could deal with this?'
Offer suggestions if necessary.	'Would you like to be more assertive so that you feel confident to tell them how you feel?'
Build on their ideas.	'I think attending an assertion training workshop is a great idea. We can follow it up with role play between us as well if you'd like.'

STAGE 3   *The follow up*

Step	What you say
Set review dates.	'Why don't you look for a suitable course and get back to me by the end of the week.'
Confirm what support you'll give.	'I'll get approval for the cost of the course and together we'll plan how to get the best out of it for you.'

This type of approach follows the basic rules for EI coaching:

- Talk about the behaviour not the person.
- Don't get personal – no name-calling.
- Give feedback in private.
- Don't use this as an opportunity to hit someone with your anger – use it as an opportunity for their EI development

Your challenge for this activity is to work with your learning friend and practise coaching each other on one or more of the following situations.

How would you coach a member of staff who:

- often turns up late
- bullies others
- is being bullied
- makes sexist comments in the workplace
- has temper tantrums
- is very passive and can't say no, resulting in their being overworked
- is sarcastic to others.

What kind of a leader are you now?

If you have been working through the activities in this section your leadership capabilities will have improved considerably. You might like to check this out by asking someone you trust what changes they have seen in you. You could reflect back to the way you managed before you began your programme of leadership development.

You could also assess your improvement by asking yourself the following questions. Since I began developing my EI leadership abilities:

- Has the level of staff turnover changed?
- Are individuals more motivated?
- Is the team working together more effectively?
- Am I less stressed?
- Can I make decisions more confidently?
- Can I deal with difficult situations more easily?
- Am I controlling my negative emotions more often?
- Have we made more profit?
- Have we reduced wasted time?

Congratulate yourself on your success. Leadership is often a difficult task, but with emotional intelligence an enjoyable one!

Future competence
Understanding and managing continuous personal development

Future competence in emotional intelligence is important because it enables us to:

- determine our personal goals
- know what motivates us
- identify an acceptable work/life balance
- network successfully
- encourage others in our lives to be emotionally intelligent.

This section contains information and exercises on:

- lifestyle appraisal
- motivation
- visualization
- networking
- career development
- celebrating success.

If you have been working through this book you will already have realized that your future is in your hands – that you have the personal power to work towards making your life what you want it to be. In Emotional Intelligence terms this is often referred to as 'Energy Management Competency'. It involves linking the skills of self-motivation, commitment, and locus of control (the level of control you have over your personal destiny). These are all 'emotion'-based abilities.

As the last section in the book, Future competence, it is essentially about using your emotional intelligence skills to start achieving your maximum potential now. No divergence there from the recognized EI competencies. Where this section deviates, however, is by giving what we feel is a practical 'value added' EI advantage – how you can use accumulated skills and creativity to carry you through your future, long-term development. This will involve looking at the things that motivate you, what you want more or less of in your life and then offering some practical strategies on how to accomplish your goals.

But first, before you begin to work through this final section, you may want to take a little while to consider the achievements you have made so far. You should now be able to use the emotional intelligence skills that you have already learned to focus on in your personal development. Think about any differences you have been able to make to your personal and professional life since you began reading this book. Make a note of these in the boxes below. Include everything you can think of – however small. Bear in mind that it can sometimes be the small changes which have the most significant effect on your quality of life. For example, you may have found that simply by giving yourself the time to read and consider some of sections in this workbook, you are now able to recognize and label different emotions as they occur. This is a personal competence skill. Refer back to the previous sections if it helps and see how many you can list.

Future competence activity 1 – emotional intelligence achievement record

I have achieved the following in each of the three areas covered so far:

Personal competence

Relationship competence

Leadership competence

Hopefully you were able to think of examples which gave some evidence in each of the competencies already covered. Don't worry too much if you haven't; you can come back and/or add to this page when you feel ready.

It is likely that you will, however, have recorded some entries and may be pleasantly surprised with what you've achieved so far. Now, building on what you've written in your achievement record, use the following Emotional Intelligence wheel to self-assess how far you are towards gaining the EI Advantage.

Future competence activity 2 – emotional intelligence wheel

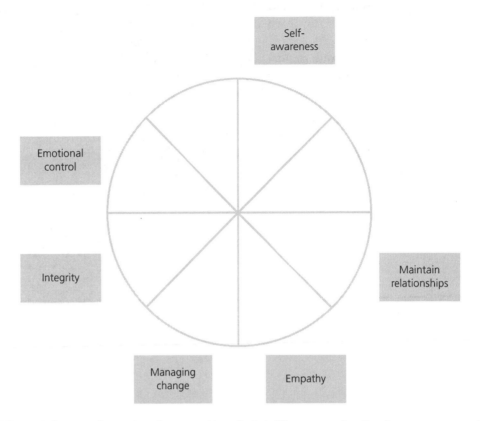

The eight sections in the emotional intelligence wheel above represent emotional equilibrium. Six EI competencies have been identified. Add two more which you feel should be included.

Using the centre of the wheel as 0 (representing nothing) and the outside edge as 10 (representing excellent), grade your level of competence for each EI skill by drawing a line to create a new outer edge. It might look something like this:

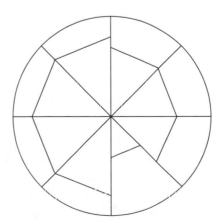

Look at the perimeter of the emotional intelligence wheel that you have created. How balanced is it? Take note of the segments in which you feel you need to improve competency, and discuss with someone you trust how you might achieve this. Try to keep perspective though by thinking back to what your emotional response levels were when you started this workbook. Congratulate yourself on the milestones already reached! (This diagram is adapted from *Mindstore* by Jack Black, HarperCollins, 1994.)

Let's now move into this final section of the workbook and look at the ways you can harness your natural emotional intelligence strengths to achieve maximum personal development. We begin with a life style audit.

Chapter 22

Future competence advantage 1
Lifestyle appraisal

I can teach anybody how to get what they want out of life. The problem is I can't find anybody who can tell me what they want.

(Mark Twain)

What is a lifestyle appraisal? It is simply taking a good hard look at what is currently going on in our lives and then making an assessment of which elements we want more or less of. It's also about making some choices in respect of long-term goals and how these might be achieved. You will have to decide what needs to be done now to start working towards these goals.

Let's start by looking at the relationships that you currently have in your life and how happy you are with them. Remember that a key measure of emotional intelligence is relationship competence. This does not mean that you will always only have good relationships. It does, however, mean that you will be able to identify the unsatisfactory ones, and then consider how to improve them. Perhaps you already have a range of very good relationships. Here, the emotionally intelligent approach would involve the measures you are going to take to maintain that level of contentment.

Lifestyle appraisal activity 1 – relationship balance

The questionnaire below will help you determine what sort of balance you have in terms of relationships within your life. To complete it, read the items on the left and circle on the dotted line where you feel you sit on the continuum between the scale of feelings quoted. If you feel this relationship is generally unsatisfactory circle closer to the left where it is marked 'non-existent'. If the relationship is on the whole fulfilling, circle nearer to the right, closer to where it is marked 'perfect'.

1. My relationship with my partner is: Non-existent 1..2..3..4..5..6 perfect

2. My relationship with my children is: Non-existent 1..2..3..4..5..6 perfect

3. My relationship with work colleagues is: Non-existent 1..2..3..4..5..6 perfect

4. My relationship with my parents is: Non-existent 1..2..3..4..5..6 perfect

5. My relationship with my friends is: Non-existent 1..2..3..4..5..6 perfect

6. My relationship with my neighbours is: Non-existent 1..2..3..4..5..6 perfect

7. My relationship with other members of my family is: Non-existent 1..2..3..4..5..6 perfect

Look at how you've scored and, either working alone, or with your buddy, discuss the results. Consider what it tells you about the balance across your personal and professional relationships. Perhaps one area is impacting upon another? Discuss what you could do to improve any areas that you marked as 1–3. If you have marked 'non-existent' in any areas, consider whether you feel you'd like to change this. If so, how might you begin?

If you've marked 6s or 'perfect' that's wonderful, and you will undoubtedly want to maintain this. How will you do it? Again, talk this through with your buddy, if you have one.

Perfect relationships

Fran Johnstone

We have dipped back into Relationship competence a little here, but in order to move forward successfully, it is important to consider the balance of relationships which make up your life. You need to know where you have strong bonds and where these are less satisfactory.

Lifestyle appraisal activity 2 – life goals

Now you can start thinking about what else is going on in your life and how content you are with the component parts of it. Which parts are satisfying? Which parts could be improved? Where do you see yourself in say six months, then a year and in five years? Can you start to picture the things that you want to achieve? Do you have a vision for yourself? Thinking about all these aspects can be daunting. If this seems a little overwhelming, bear in mind that the emotionally intelligent approach is to be creative and proactive about your life. The steps involved can be small ones. The exercises in this section will help you build up an image of where you are now, where you want to be and how you can get there.

Let's move on and think about what you want from your life. If you are one of the many people unaccustomed to asking for something for yourself, or even just acknowledging to yourself what these things are, then you are in good company. Research has shown that when people are asked what they have to live for, an overwhelming proportion admit to having no significant purpose for their lives. Taking this sort of generalized finding at face value could be quite depressing! The thought of so many people with little real direction or purpose to their lives is certainly disturbing – so much wasted and unidentified potential.

You could start by thinking about what you don't want. This is just as important, and can be a good way to begin tackling any areas which are having a negative effect on you. Being unhappy with something has an emotional base. Typically, your emotions and instincts will begin feeding messages into your subconscious long before your logical conscious picks it up. It is only at this stage that you switch into practical mode and start thinking about making plans to change. Consider Jeremy's experience.

JEREMY'S STORY

Jeremy had worked in a company for four years. He had enjoyed much of his time there and this was reflected in his approach and motivation in the workplace. As a result, Jeremy had been promoted several times, eventually to a senior management post. A little while into his new role, Jeremy began to feel less happy about his job. He'd always enjoyed problem-solving but now it felt that all he did was sort out petty issues for other people! He went home every night still feeling angry about certain events of his day. Jeremy's family noticed that he was always tense around the house and had an uncharacteristic weariness about him.

During this time Jeremy attended a training course where he fell into discussion with another delegate, Irene. Having detailed his situation at work to Irene, Jeremy was quite shaken by her response. 'You're looking for other jobs, aren't you?' she asked. 'In fact, though you are there in body, you've already left.' She was perfectly correct! Jeremy had been applying for new vacancies. He was worried that though he had not talked about leaving his job, he had given an impression of being uncommitted or unprofessional. Irene assured him that this was not the case. She recognized the symptoms, having recently been in a very similar situation. Irene explained how she'd known on an instinctive level that she needed to leave her job. She felt irritable and tired all the time and kept having stomach upsets. It was almost as though her logical mind was a little way behind her emotions, but fairly soon she came to realize where the problem was. That was when she started job-hunting, quickly moving into new employment.

And very soon after his conversation with Irene, Jeremy too successfully applied for a new job.

Do Jeremy or Irene's experiences ring any bells with you? The issue you need to be sensitive to from this example is: pay attention to what your emotions are telling you!

Lifestyle appraisal activity 3 – wants and not wants

Now use the following box to make a list of six things that you *don't* want in your life right now.

Things I don't want in my life
1.
2.
3.
4.
5.
6.

Did you find it fairly easy to come up with some points for the list? It is likely that you did – people are often much more aware of the things that they could do without in their lives! Let's follow this list up by thinking about what you want in their place. Transfer all the things you don't want in your life to the following table. Alongside these write what you would prefer to have instead. The first line, for example, gives you an idea of how to use this activity.

I don't want	I do want
The job I have	A more interesting job
1.	
2.	
3.	
4.	
5.	
6.	

These lifestyle appraisal exercises should be helping you to decide how you can best move from the things you don't want, to the things you want in their place. You will also need to be clear about what these things will look like. Coming back to the example above: what would an interesting job look like? What makes a job interesting to you? How will you feel when you get it? Look at what you've included as 'do wants' on your list and explore the following questions:

■ What will it look like?
■ How will I know when I have it?
■ How will I feel when I have it?
■ What difference will it make to my life?

You now need to change the answers to these questions into tangible, clearly defined outcomes. You can start by setting yourself some SMART objectives.

Lifestyle appraisal activity 4 – SMART goals

Many of you will be familiar with the SMART acronym but just to recap, these are objectives which must be:

- **S**pecific
- **M**easurable
- **A**chievable
- **R**esults-oriented
- **T**ime-limited.

People with high levels of emotional intelligence have powerful goal-setting abilities. They have the motivation to carry through their objectives and don't simply leave them gathering dust. So, how does this skill break down into practicalities? You have already done some of the work through the previous exercises in this section. You already know at least one thing that you want to achieve. All you are going to do now is to bring everything together in a format you can easily refer to and use.

You may remember using SMART goals for confidence-building in the Personal competence section (p. 53)? You are using the same technique here, and although the format is slightly different, the aim of the exercise is again to help you break down a personal goal into practical steps.

We need to go back for a moment to the Lifestyle appraisal activity 3 example above. Remember we talked about what a new job might look like? Let's use the same example to illustrate how you'd set SMART goals if one of your 'do wants' is a new job. Your overview SMART goal might read something like 'I want to have a new job as a restaurant manager within the next six months'. You can also use the SMART criteria to further develop your goal:

Goal: a new job	
Specific	Restaurant manager
Measurable	Acceptable salary range £20–30,000, based within 15 miles of my home
Achievable	Building on skills and experience already held. Need to take up-to-date qualification.
Results oriented	Start visiting and writing to potential restaurants. Contact relevant agencies.
Timely	Within six months.

Your SMART objectives need to give you results which can be measured in terms of cost, quantity, quality, behaviour and time. Make your own SMART objectives to support at least one of the things on your 'do want' list using the table below. If you have a buddy you can support each other in this activity. Refer back to the previous section on how to coach (p. 254). This is an excellent opportunity to practise!

SMART goal
Specific
Measurable
Achievable
Results oriented
Timely

Lifestyle appraisal activity 5 – future goals

You've looked at what's currently going on in your life, so now it's time to focus on future goals. Try making a list of things you want to achieve in your life, using the table below. Some examples are included – you don't have to use them, they are simply ideas to get you started.

What I want to achieve	
To live a happy life and enjoy a healthy old age	To bring up my children to be healthy, happy adults
To become very wealthy	To make my hobby my profession
To help others	To be successful in my career
To be a famous singer	To make a difference

Lifestyle appraisal activity 6 – personal aspirations

Naturally, many things do happen to us which are outside our control. Similarly, we all need to be realistic; if you have a terrible singing voice you are unlikely to perform at The Royal Opera House. In this sort of situation you need to channel your emotional energy into finding out what it is that so appeals to you about becoming a famous singer. Is it the celebrity status? Maybe you need to prove a point? What would being this famous singer give you? Analyse your motives. Then use your conclusions to come up with an alternative route to accomplishing the same outcome. Enter the things you live for, from the previous table on to the following one to help you pick out the emotions behind your personal drivers. The first line is an example – try to write in three of your own.

Personal aspirations		
Purpose	*What would this give me?*	*How else could I get this?*
To be a famous singer	Respect Admiration Wealth	By setting up my own music-based business

Bear in mind that you probably have more control than you are aware of. The key factor here is to take charge. If *you* don't plan your life, someone else will do it for you! As the old saying goes, if you don't know where you're going, you could end up somewhere you don't want to be.

So, by now you should have a good idea of the things that you do and don't want in your life. Maybe you have reflected on the reasons why you are reticent in being up-front about what you do want. Congratulate yourself on the progress you've made already. Now that you have an idea of the things that you do not want in your life, let's go on to assess the personal and professional aspects of your life – the work/life balance.

Lifestyle appraisal activity 7 – work/life balance

This heading requires you to determine which parts of your life are in harmony and which parts are in disharmony. Do you live to work or work to live? The life balance wheel should help you gain a holistic view of what currently makes up your life.

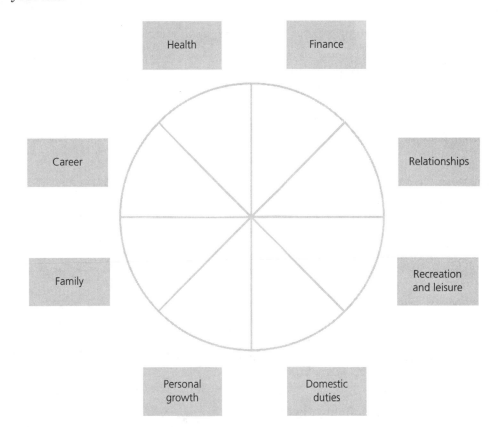

FIGURE 22.1

Life balance wheel (adapted from Mindstore *by Jack Black, HarperCollins, 1994)*

The life balance wheel is similar in structure to the emotional intelligence Wheel which you completed on p. 265. It also comprises eight sections, but this time the circle should represent all the elements that make up your life. As before, use the centre of the wheel as 0 and the outside edge as 10, to grade your level of satisfaction across each sector. This will create a new perimeter and illustrate how balanced your life is. As you did before, look at the inner perimeter you have created within the life balance wheel and imagine this as a real wheel. Would it give a smooth or a bumpy ride?

Let's consider what measures you can take to realign your Wheel of Life, if necessary. If you are happy with the balance you currently have – excellent, but don't be complacent – think about what you need to do to maintain this balance. Use the following box to list your findings. There are two extra boxes if you want to add or replace any of the areas from the life balance wheel. Once you have logged your current situation, talk through with your buddy or someone close to you the steps you can take to either improve or maintain the balance you want.

Life balance area	Current satisfaction level	Steps to improve or maintain the balance I want
Health		
Recreation and leisure		
Career		
Finance		
Domestic duties		
Personal growth		
Relationships		

By this stage you should be well aware of how you would like your life to be shaped. Perhaps you will be conscious of the parts that need most attention. An acceptable life/work balance should be starting to form in your mind. So, how can you begin to make your dreams become reality? You obviously need to be highly focused to achieve these aspirations, so let's think about ways to stimulate your motivational levels.

Chapter 23
Future competence advantage 2
Motivation

Motivation is the key to achievement. Much has been written and spoken about this subject, lots from within the sporting world. For example, Roger Black, the UK Olympic medallist, gives inspirational talks on what motivation means to sports men and women. He comments that it is no coincidence that the Olympic Games open with the lighting of the Olympic torch. Haven't we all heard successful people speak of their 'burning desire' to achieve? No doubt we've also experienced being with highly motivated, energized people and witnessed how they appear to 'light up' a room.

> *Ability is what you're capable of doing. Motivation determines what you do. Attitude determines how well you do it.*
> (Lou Holtz, US football coach, author of *The Fighting Spirit*)

Not surprising then that motivation is a key emotional intelligence competence. Goleman, in *Working with Emotional Intelligence*, draws attention to the fact that the words 'emotion' and 'motivate' both originate from the Latin 'motere', which means 'to move'. Our emotions continually 'move' us towards our ambitions, feeding our motivation. This then dictates what we do and how we pursue our goals.

In emotional intelligence, the state of mind described as 'flow' underpins motivation. This describes the mindset you have when you move effortlessly through your work, whatever it is. 'Flow' moves you to take action because it feels good, critically because you enjoy what you are doing. Research into flow levels indicate that people are more likely to experience flow when involved in complex rather than routine activities. It is also more common to those with some degree of control or flexibility in their work. This suggests that during flow, the brain becomes more efficient and focused with an overall lowering of cortical arousal, despite a person being involved in a complex task.

So, how can we ensure that we optimize our own state of flow? We need to come back to what motivates us – what will bring about this feeling of flow.

If you have already read the previous section, Leadership competence, you may remember the motivation activity on p. 219 about pleasure and pain as motivators. In case you've not yet read this yet, a quick resumé would be that most people use a mixture of pleasure and pain drivers, but some people are primarily motivated by one or the other. You might want to refer back to that activity now to establish whether you are a towards (pleasure) or an away from (pain) person. To give you an example, consider these two case studies:

CASE STUDIES

Meena would often find herself working late into the night before a deadline. It didn't matter how much time she'd had to prepare, it was always a frenetic rush at the eleventh hour. Each time she resolved that she would never get herself into this situation again. Until the next one came around . . .

Richard was always well prepared. His reports were ready days before they were needed. Everything was planned, organized and meticulous in presentation. Richard delighted in the feelings of satisfaction he had from knowing a task was completed.

Meena and Richard were equally able to carry out their tasks, the difference was in the way each of their personal motivators worked. Meena needed the fear of not delivering to motivate her into action. She was motivated by pain, an 'away-from' person. Richard on the other hand, was a 'towards' person. His motivation was how it was going to feel for him when the task was completed.

Are you a 'towards' or an 'away-from' person? Using the two basic questions below, think about your own motivational drivers.

1. Do you prepare well in advance of a task?   Yes   No

2. Do you put off doing things as long as you can?   Yes   No

This is a simple way to identify if you are an 'away-from' or a 'towards' person. In fact we are usually quite well aware of this, but perhaps had not used these labels.

If you are naturally a 'towards' person, you have a head start. The issue for the 'away from' people is to see the benefit of becoming more positively motivated. You are draining your emotional energy by allowing fear to force you into action. The good news of course is that you can learn an alternative strategy!

Motivation activity 1 – positive motivation

Sometimes we have to do tasks which we don't especially enjoy. It might be cleaning the car, filling in an overly bureaucratic form, or mowing the lawn. We simply do not want to do these things and the more we put them off, the more they sit accusingly in front of us, making us feel miserable. In this type of situation we have little incentive to tackle the chore.

To be positively motivated we need to focus on what it will be like when the task is done. How good will it feel when the lawn is mown, the car is gleaming and the form is filled in and sent off?

Think about the tasks which you typically put off. Make a list of up to five:

1.

2.

3.

4.

5.

Think about these tasks and tune into what you feel. Do you feel a sense of weariness, perhaps dread, maybe just simply boredom? Now think about how you feel when you have finished each of these chores. Is it relief or achievement? Do you feel lighter in yourself? This is the feeling you need to capture. Hang on to it, appreciate it and store it up. Write down three positive feelings that you'll have when these tasks are completed:

1.

2.

3.

Keep this list for the next time you are tempted to put off a chore. Turn your 'away from' into a 'towards' motivation by concentrating on how good it will feel when the task it done. Try to practise this at least once a day to begin with, then less as it starts to be your automatic response. Remember, you're not removing the old pattern; you are simply using a more efficient and creative route.

You can reinforce the power of this technique by visualizing the task completed. Allow yourself to fully picture how it will be when you have finished what you need to do. Make the picture bigger and more colourful. Feel what it will feel like. You'll want to rush off to do the task so that you can get to that great place now . . . .

Motivation activity 2 – personal motivators

Now that you know what your motivational style is, you need to be able to identify your personal motivators. Look at the following list and put a tick alongside any you aspire to achieve:

Motivator	Important?
Wealth	
Good health	
Safety	
Celebrity	
Influence	
Status	
Success	
Being the best in your chosen field	
Doing right by others	
Your family	
Your future	
Previous success or failures	
Personal satisfaction	
Approval of others	
To get even	
Justice	
To feel valued	
To impress others	
To control others or situations	

This list is not exhaustive – you may well have thought of other motivators. If so, excellent – add them to the list in the table opposite, or write yourself a separate list if you prefer. The important thing is that you are able to identify your personal drivers. You need to be very aware that in order to achieve, you have to have the necessary drive. You have to want it with a passion.

To support your positive motivation, you need to think about your personal demotivators. These can be anything, a person, or a circumstance that influences you to exhibit negative behavior. Demotivators come in all shapes and sizes. They can be something which only you are aware of, or they may be workplace or family values which foster apathetic attitudes. Apathy is one of the most destructive human emotions when it comes to overall functioning, and specifically in terms of productivity, contentment, success, and of course, motivation. What demotivators are hampering your personal growth? For example you might be inhibited by:

- fear of the unknown
- complacency
- change
- apathy.

Think a while about what disheartens you. If, for example, it is the thought of change, try to uncover what it is specifically that switches you off. If you are worried that change would upset the equilibrium of your life too much, then this would be something you'd need to consider carefully. An emotionally intelligent approach to this would be to explore all the circumstances and, drawing on the skills learned previously in this workbook, making an informed choice about the costs and benefits involved. Try the following activity to develop this technique.

Motivation activity 3 – personal demotivators

Emotionally intelligent individuals know how to remove these negative influences, or else learn to work around the consequences of having them so that they do not become draining. Try this three-step approach to kick starting your motivation.

STEP 1   Name at least three personal de-motivators:

1.

2.

3.

STEP 2   Now that you have identified them, think about ways to eliminate them. How could you do this, or how could you switch their impact from being negative to positive? For example if apathy is a de-motivator for you, write down two lists, one of positive and one of negative reasons for doing the job.

1.

2.

3.

STEP 3   Surround yourself with highly motivational objects and people. For example, write down some motivational quotes and either pin them to your desk or keep in an index file. Look at them when you feel bored or uninspired. Think of three people and/or objects that would have a motivating influence on you. Remember 'where your attention goes, your energy flows'.

1.

2.

3.

If you are working with a buddy discuss your findings about your personal motivators and de-motivators. See if you share any and if so, compare ideas on ways to utilize your motivation positively. If you are working alone, think about the same issues. Use the chart below to record what you've thought about. Then read the list of 'Techniques to get you up and running' which the chart. This is a list of practical approaches to use when you feel overwhelmed or snowed under.

Positive motivation chart

My personal de-motivators are:

Things I can do to prevent becoming de-motivated:

Whenever I feel de-motivated I will:

Techniques to get you up and running

The worst / easiest first

Faced with a list of jobs, tackle the worst or the easiest first, dependent on your mood. Then choose the worst or easiest of what is left. Eventually the whole list will be worked through.

Swiss cheese method

Another method to tackle large projects is to start with any part of the project that you feel able to cope with. Continue tackling it a bit at a time, making 'holes' in the larger task like a Swiss cheese. Eventually the whole task is completed.

Balance sheet method

This can be very useful for all the projects that you cannot seem to start. Take a sheet of paper, draw a line down the middle and on one side list all the reasons why you have put off starting. On the other side write all the benefits that will flow from completing the task. Make sure you actually write down the reasons – just thinking about them does not seem to have the same motivating effect.

Put your feet up

Put away all your papers and sit with your feet on the desk. You are not allowed to do ANYTHING else. Just sit there. You'll soon get fidgety and start work!
    (Adapted from Dr. Pam Brown, *Managing Your Time*, Daniels Publishing)

This list of tips for sustaining positive self-motivation might also be helpful to refer to:

■ maintain a sense of humour – it's pleasurable and it helps keeps your stress levels down

■ reward yourself for all successes, however small

■ keep sight of your goals and believe in your ability to achieve them

■ use motivational self-statements: 'I will achieve ...... today', 'I can stick with this and accomplish it well.'

■ keep the flame burning!

Finally, you might want to reflect upon the story of a traveller which Charles Handy recounts in *Waiting for the Mountain to Move*. Whilst journeying around the world the traveller comes upon a mountain in the middle of his path. He sits down and waits for the mountain to move out of his way.

You should now be able to see any mountains in your way to achieving the emotional intelligence advantage, but unlike the traveller, you will seek out alternative paths around these obstacles!

Chapter 24
Future competence advantage 3
Inner dialogue

You will remember the exercises on Monitoring self-talk in the Personal Competence Section (p. 50–1). You might just need to look back to refresh your memory as this topic is relevant here again. We talked about the ways in which we continuously hold conversations with ourselves in our heads. We scold or encourage ourselves, make decisions and many other things. For some people this inner dialogue is motivating, whilst to others it is disheartening.

Emotionally intelligent people have more constructive inner dialogue even though they are able to see the difficulties in life. On the occasions when negativity creeps in, the trick is to recognize ways to turn the situation around. It's the old saying: 'Is the glass half full or half empty?' Which is it for you?

For individuals without a strong sense of purpose it's very easy to find fault with things and self-pity comes easily. Remember, your face is a billboard which advertises what has been going on in your mind for years. There is a pithy saying which goes: 'A person has the face they are born with at twenty, the face they deserve at forty'. Take a look around at the people you work with and those you know socially. Think about their attitudes to life and towards others. Chances are that you will see sufficient evidence to support this little epigram!

Keep in mind the personal goals you've already identified and make sure you have regular 'pep talks' with yourself. Use the activity below to help keep the momentum going.

Inner dialogue activity 1 – improving inner dialogue

Thinking about your life goals, what sort of inner dialogue might you have with yourself about how you are going to achieve them? Use the table below to list some. Talk this through with your buddy or mentor if it helps. There are some examples to help you get going:

Negative thought	Positive thought
It's going to be so hard to get out of the rut I'm in	I am going to find ways of bringing things that I enjoy into my life
I never get a break	I'm going to seek out new opportunities
It's typical that I didn't get the promotion I wanted	I will ask for feedback on why my application for promotion wasn't successful this time

People are always blaming their circumstances for what they are. I don't believe in circumstances. The people who get on in the world are the people who get up and look for the circumstances they want, and if they can't find them, make them.

(George Bernard Shaw)

Remember that the most important opinion you have is your opinion of yourself. The most motivating conversation you can have today is the conversation you have with yourself. Make sure you use it wisely!

Chapter 25

Future competence advantage 4 Visualization

Imagination is more powerful than knowledge.

(Albert Einstein)

As you have already seen in previous sections, visualization can be used as a powerful emotional intelligence tool. In Personal competence, for example, you explored how visualization can be used to help your confidence-building (p. 55). Then, in Leadership competence we talked about developing a vision as a starting point for change (p. 202). You are going to use visualization again now as a tool to support your motivation levels and move you further towards achieving your goals.

Let's check first though that you are confident about what you aspire to. This is sometimes difficult for people. Maybe you are one of them? If so, you might want to think about why it is hard for you to visualize what you want from your life. Bear in mind that if this does apply to you, you are not alone.

So why do we find it so difficult to visualize what we want from our lives? There are a number of reasons why this happens. For example, many people truly believe that they don't have control over their lives. This brings with it an acceptance that life 'happens' to them and they are unable to choose the life that they want. In this way, a person can only be reactive to situations. In childhood and as young adults, many of us received the parental message: 'don't get your hopes up'. While this was most often given in our best interests – to 'protect' us – it had the opposite effect, killing off our ability to aspire and imagine greater things for ourselves. By being emotionally intelligent, however, you will use your emotional energy positively. You will be able to recognize your goals, focus clearly upon them, and be innovative in ways to achieve them.

Visualization is an incredibly powerful skill to develop. By using this technique regularly you are sending compelling images to your subconscious. The subconscious will in turn act as a compass directing your conscious thought towards the things to which you aspire. Visualization should also help you uncover your true beliefs, at an instinctive level. For visualization to work, you have to actually 'feel' your vision. This is something that does not always come easy; you may need to practise some visualization techniques daily. If you do find this difficult, it might be helpful to remember that a vision is a thought; no more or less than this. You simply need to practise turning your thoughts into visions!

Visualization activity 1 – self-energize

This is a good exercise to practise as a warm-up to your visualization or at the end. Try it out and discover if it works best for you to start with it, or to finish with it. You may find you want to do both!

Find somewhere peaceful to lie down or sit comfortably. Imagine you are lying somewhere, relaxed and content. It is warm and sunny. Sunlight is streaming over you. Now imagine yourself passing up through a beam of sunlight, towards the sun. You are weightless but can feel the sun's energy going into your body. It might give a pleasant tingling sensation.

Imagine opening up your arms and legs as if to capture as much of this energy as you can. Really feel it surging through your body. Use inner dialogue to talk yourself through how good it feels; how you can feel the energy reaching and energizing every part of you.

When you feel sufficiently energized, visualize yourself coming slowly back down through the sunbeam, returning to where you started from. You should remain feeling energized for a while afterwards, so this is also a good exercise to use if you are feeling a bit down, or simply whenever your energy levels are low.

If you are not a naturally visual person, you might find you need to practise this technique. It may feel strange or awkward to begin with, but you have nothing to lose by trying and much to gain by persevering.

Now that you are hopefully in full visualization mode, you might want to go straight into the magic wand activity below!

Visualization activity 2 – the magic wand

Go back again to your list of 'do wants' (p. 271). Using these as a starting point, imagine you have a magic wand and can have all of these things and more. In fact you can have anything you wish for – material or emotional. Let your imagination have free rein. Bask in the feeling of trying out all the things that you desire. What would these things be? Are you driving around in a new car? Taking a holiday in an exotic location? Who is with you? Have you just recorded a number 1 album?

Maybe you've become a Member of Parliament and are deciding what portfolio you will have. Or perhaps you've run in a marathon. It doesn't matter what images you conjure up, just enjoy them.

Once you have finished, think about the feelings you experienced. Hopefully they were all pleasant. While it's still fresh in your mind, make note of the things you used the magic wand for and think about how it felt to have them. Record your visualization in the following spaces:

I used my magic wand to:

This is what I did:

This is how I felt:

You can support your visualizations with positive affirmations. Again, this was something that you might remember from Personal competence, when we talked about coupling together a specific visualization with an affirmation (p. 74). You can use this approach again here.

Here's a nice example of how empowering visualisation can be:

EMMA'S STORY

Emma's whole sense of self-worth had taken a hammering during the process of separating from her husband. It had taken a long time for her to accept that there was another woman in his life, and what this meant for Emma and her children. She felt at times that her situation was hopeless. She knew she had to accept the reality and start moving on, but it was a slow and painful process.

Eventually, she found another house that she and her children liked, but the thought of financing it all made Emma very anxious. She wasn't sure if she would be able to hold it all together – practically and emotionally.

Emma discovered, however, that whenever she went to look at the new house, she came away each time feeling slightly more encouraged about things generally. She began to spend more time thinking about how it would be to live there, how she would arrange the rooms, what she could do with the garden.

> Whenever she was feeling upset or low, Emma got into the habit of imagining moving into the new house; it would become her sanctuary. She found talking about it and how it could be made it feel even more real and attainable.
>
> Emma took the decision to move. She was surprised at the way all the practicalities were resolved. There were some difficult bits, but she was focused throughout on achieving her goal. If asked today, Emma would tell you that it was one of the best decisions she has ever made.

Have you been in a situation similar to Emma? How did you cope with it? Thinking back, did you use any form of visualization? Sometimes people do, without being aware of how powerful it can be. You may have called it daydreaming. Discuss with your buddy or a close friend any experiences you have had where you think visualization did, or could have helped you. Between you, explore how empowering visualization and affirmation together can help you achieve the goals on your 'do want' list.

Writing in *You'll See It When You Believe It*, Wayne Dyer talks about the way our behaviour is based upon our feelings, which have already been influenced by our thoughts. The trick therefore, is to work on changing your thoughts, not your behaviour. As soon as your thoughts reflect what you truly want to be, the appropriate emotions and subsequent behaviour will automatically follow. It's a case of 'believe it, and you will see it!'

We're almost at the end of the activities which will help you mentally prepare to achieve your life goals. Before moving into the more practical elements of this section you may want to complete the following questionnaire to consolidate the topics covered so far in Future competence.

Future competence consolidation questionnaire

Answer the following questions:

	Yes	No
1. Would you like your life to be other than it is?	......	......
2. Do you think luck or fate plays a large part in your success or failure?	......	......
3. Do you know what would improve your life?	......	......
4. Do you think of yourself as a success?	......	......
5. Do you feel you rarely achieve things as well as others?	......	......

6. Can you 'see' and 'feel' the things you aspire to?   ....

7. Are you confident that you can maintain the balance of   ....
    good things in your life?

Your answers to these questions should give you a view on where you've got to in terms of your future competence. Use this as a benchmark and either working alone, or with your buddy, refer back through this section and make sure that you are either happy with the level of competence you've gained, or that you know where your weaknesses are and are committed to addressing them. And, of course, don't forget to congratulate yourself on the progress that you continue to make!

Chapter 26

Future competence advantage 5 Networking

Some people find the mere mention of having to 'network' off-putting. Other people become enthused at the thought. Whichever you are, you need to recognize that networking is a key emotional intelligence competency. Consider the fact that good business practice is all about relationships with people. Positive professional relationships are built by creating trust, by honouring agreements and maintaining integrity. This of course is very much in keeping with the fundamentals of good friendships.

Remember in the Relationship competence section we talked about how emotionally intelligent people worked hard at maintaining positive relationships. We practised the skills underpinning this, for example, empathy, rapport and conflict management. Now we are building further upon your relationship competence. By developing and using your networks, you will find that you can save valuable time and energy by tapping into the expertise of others in mutually beneficial ways.

It is more than likely that to achieve and to be successful you need to seek the support of others. Goleman, for example in *Working with Emotional Intelligence*, stresses the importance of establishing wide formal and informal networks. He details the advantages of being part of a network of people joined by what he calls a 'psychological proximity'. These people may not be geographically close, but they will be those persons with whom you have established a relationship of mutual trust and respect. Let's look at the scope of your of networks at the moment.

Networking activity 1 – current networks

Have you ever considered how much you already use your existing formal and informal networks? For example, if you need a plumber or a vehicle mechanic, how often do you ask a friend or colleague for recommendations? No doubt you would reciprocate to others seeking your advice in the same way. This is a form of networking and we all probably spend a fair amount of time doing it.

Draw a spidergram using the diagram below to give you an idea of how your current network looks. Write your own name in the middle of the oval and then draw lines off writing the names of people you know reasonably well at the end of each line. Indicate relationships between people by drawing dotted lines joining names.

My current network of friends and colleagues

Now use the information on your spidergram to help you complete Networking activity 2.

Networking activity 2 – range of networks

1. How would you describe your circle of friends and colleagues? (tick any that apply):

    ❒ Wide-ranging

    ❒ Interesting

    ❒ Pleasing

    ❒ Loyal

    ❒ Narrow

2. Are you:

    ❒ Content with the number of friends and colleagues you have?

    ❒ Discontented with the number of friends and colleagues you have?

    ❒ Seeking to widen your circle of friends and colleagues?

3. Are most of people you mix with:

    ❒ Friends?

    ❒ Work or business colleagues?

    ❒ Family?

    ❒ A mixture of all these?

4. How hard do you work at maintaining good relationships with friends and colleagues? (For example by visiting, writing, e-mailing or telephoning.)

❒ Very hard

❒ Quite hard

❒ Not very hard

❒ Not at all

5. How much do you value the time spent with friends or colleagues?

❒ It is very important to me

❒ It is nice but not a priority

❒ I prefer to be on my own

What do your answers tell you? Do they indicate a fairly healthy range of contact with others? Do you think you need to do anything to extend or improve this? Why might you choose to do this – what do feel is missing? If you are comfortable with this aspect of your life, how are you going to make sure it stays this way? Discuss your findings and what you can deduce from them with your buddy or someone close to you. Jot down some issues using these prompts:

1. I think my range of networks could be improved or maintained by:

2. Some of the ways I could achieve this are by:

3. This is what I will gain:

So, now that you've thought a little about what you might gain from your network of relationships, think about what you can offer in return. As with any relationship, the issue is one of mutuality. What support or expertise could you offer to others?

Networking activity 3 – networking grid

In each of the boxes below identify an area of expertise you have that others might like to learn from.

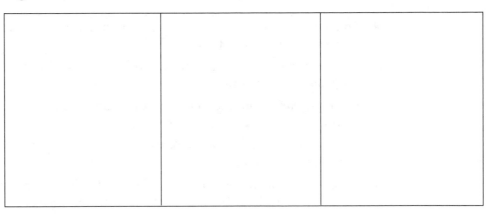

To conclude this activity, you may also like to consider how best you could offer this help.

Networking activity 4 – networking advantages

As we have already detailed, good networks will be very important to your continuing development. If you do not already do so, you will need to invest some time extending these. Without a doubt, it is in your own best interests to do so. For example, here a is short list of some advantages that good networking links will bring:

- hearing about the best jobs before they are advertised
- hearing about new initiatives
- information on best practice
- saving time and effort by having a range of expertise to draw upon
- feedback on your own behaviour and development towards increased emotional wisdom
- the feel-good factor from having a range of positive and rewarding relationships.

Now add three more that you can think of:

1.

2.

3.

So, how will you, as an emotionally intelligent individual, make certain that you develop your scope of networks? Think about the ways that you intend to do this and add them to the next list, which already has a few suggestions to get you going.

- Hold practice conversations with your buddy where you simulate being in a formal networking situation.
- Identify the subjects that you want to know more about, then actively seek out people with this relevant expertise. Cultivate these relationships.
- Practise your communication skills, especially rapport-building. As a good networker your interpersonal techniques need to be first-rate.
- Use your listening and other skills. Be sensitive to non-verbal communication signals.
- If you are stuck for something to talk about ask the other person to tell you something about themselves. This is always a popular subject! Remember too, the PRONES approach in Relationship competence (p. 144).
- Keep up to date with current affairs so that you are confident about speaking generally on a range of topics.
- Become a member of formal network groups. Try to obtain the delegate list before events and decide whom you want to meet. Make sure that you make contact with them.
- Always, always, have to hand a business card or something with your contact details on.

As soon as you feel confident to do so, start building and extending your range of contacts. It will be invaluable as you take control and plan for your future development. Good luck!

Chapter 27

Future competence advantage 6
Career development

Self-development is becoming ever more important. We need to upgrade our skills to maintain our position in the workplace. Closely linked to this is the need to raise our emotional quotient; our sense of self-worth and accomplishment. Consider yourself for a moment as a commodity – what would your market value be? Are you happy with this? If not – what would you like it to be? How can you achieve this? Remember that everything you do to improve yourself is a lifetime investment – it will be with you much longer than a new winter coat and hat!

Thousands of books and training courses have been developed over the past fifty years proposing ways to help people be more successful. Some of these self-development strategies will have worked for some people, maybe not so well for others. Suffice therefore to say that this is a complex arena. Whilst this workbook does not claim to offer a 'six easy steps to success' approach it does provide a framework for planning and achieving your own personal growth. It will help you to:

■ identify abilities and goals
■ see the blocks to your professional development and how to overcome and manage them
■ identify ways to achieve your full potential
■ approach your career development with confidence
■ encourage individual responsibility for personal development in others.

Career development activity 1 – personal commitment

Be aware that knowledge is empowering and we should all be committed to our own ongoing educational process. Answer the questions below to gauge how committed you already are to continuous professional development.

1. What new skills and knowledge have you acquired in the last ten years?
2. What do you do to ensure you bring new, stimulating ideas to your company?

3. What are you doing on a daily basis to assure yourself that you are giving the best you can?

All learning has a emotional base.

(Plato)

Career development activity 2 – identify personal learning and development needs

A good way to approach personal development is not to stack skills on top of those you already have, but rather develop more of your natural talents. You could say that it is about becoming more than the sum of your parts!

Remember the SWOT analysis on your strengths and weaknesses that you completed back in Personal Competence (p. 44). Look back at this now and make sure that you are happy that it still accurately reflects you. Then, take a career goal from your lifestyle appraisal which you completed earlier in this section and, building on your original SWOT analysis of your natural abilities, complete this grid:

Career goal

Strengths (skills that will help me achieve my goal)	*Weaknesses* (skills I need to improve achieve my goal)
Opportunities (to achieve my goal)	*Threats* (what might stop me achieving and how I'll overcome it)

Have you included any emotional intelligence skills?

Continuous feedback

You read about ways to give and receive feedback in the previous section, Leadership competence (Coercive leadership activities 3–5, pp. 227–32). Remember to use these tools for your continuous development. For example, after a job interview *always* ask for feedback. Even if you are successful, it is helpful to know what impressed the interview panel. Alternatively, if there were things that they felt you could improve upon, you will undoubtedly want to know. In your current job, too, it is important to make sure you actively seek feedback on tasks or projects which you complete. It is up to you to convince others that you are serious about wanting their genuine feedback. You are not seeking gratuitous compliments but objective comments on your performance.

Career development activity 3 – career development pathway

With your partner discuss which of the following ideas you will use to help you to continue with your career development:

Method	How I'll achieve this	Time scale
Reading		
Courses		
Web research		
Setting yourself challenges		
Finding a mentor		

Lifelong learning		
Other		
Other		

Did you remember to think about and include your emotional development? We all make investments in our professional knowledge base as well as our external appearance – but how much investment do we commit to our emotional progress? For example, what investment will you make to either improve or maintain positive attitudes? And don't forget that mistakes and set-backs are a necessary part of success. Look upon these as genuine learning experiences.

Health and well-being

This is also probably a good time to mention the importance of good health maintenance. Commitment and motivation both demand energy and you will need to adopt strategies to ensure this is maintained at its optimum level. Much of this is common sense, however, many of us are guilty of being complacent with regard to our health. It is not until something goes wrong that we become aware of the things we've taken for granted.

Answer honestly how many of these health maintenance tactics you regularly follow:

1. Exercise

2. Health checks

3. Stress management

4. Balanced nutrition

5. Moderate alcohol

6. No smoking

7. Regular and adequate amounts of sleep

8. Relaxation breaks.

It is up to you to respect your health and well-being and it is far better to be pro-active in this way. For example, you may want to consider the fact that many elderly people, particularly women, are in care simply because they have no upper body mobility. This prevents them from being able to lead independent lives as they are unable to lift themselves out of bed or open and close curtains. This can easily be avoided by regular, moderate exercise to build muscle tone. Respect your body and do not neglect your health or well-being.

> *There is only one corner of the universe you can be certain of improving . . . and that's your own self.*
>
> (Aldous Huxley)

Career development activity 4 – celebrating success

You have been encouraged to stop at points throughout this workbook and congratulate yourself on achievements reached. This is an important EI technique. Positive thinking brings positive outcomes and you should do this regularly. Think back over the previous three years and jot down here some of your accomplishments and successes. They don't have to be great milestones, just times that left you feeling happy and good about yourself. See if you can think of a time from each element of your life to include, for example, relationships and career. Write down at least three of these memories, more if you can think of them.

1.

2.

3.

4.

5.

What was happening in your environment at that time? What was happening more widely in the world? Go back and re-live these experiences. Be sensitive to what was important to you about these events. Enjoy them again now.

As part of celebrating your success, remember to use inspiring self-statements to reinforce your belief in your ability to achieve. For example you could:

- write down a selection of successfully completed tasks on cards and keep these in a card index box; refer to them if you feel your motivation diminishing
- surround yourself with like-minded, focused people
- reward yourself with occasional treats – a special day out with family or friends, or a special day to yourself
- only seek support from those people whom you know will give it – don't waste your time seeking encouragement from anyone who doesn't give it readily and unconditionally
- above all – be kind to and believe in yourself.

So, you've now come to the end of this section and with it, the complete workbook. You know what your goals are, understand how to use positive motivation and visualize what achievement feels like. You are able to maintain positive relationships with others, know what your personal strengths and weaknesses are and how to harness these. Now capture your 'flow' and go for it. Use the EI Advantage creatively to achieve your ambitions, whatever these may be. Our best wishes go with you.

Recommended reading

Back, K. and Back, K., *Assertiveness at Work*, McGraw Hill, Maidenhead, 1991.
A practical guide to handling awkward situations with confidence.

Bennett-Goleman, T., *Emotional Alchemy: How the Mind Can Heal the Heart*, Rider Press, London, 2001.
Shows how emotional alchemy can be used to address typical habits, such as mistrust, fear of rejection, feeling unlovable.

Black, J., *Mindstore: The Ultimate Mental Fitness Programme*, Thorsons, London, 1995.
Discover how to exceed your limitations and achieve your dreams.

Burley-Allen, M., *Managing Assertively*, Wiley, Toronto, 1995.
A self-teaching guide.

Buzan, T., *The Mind Map Book – How to use Radiant Thinking to Maximise Your Brain's Untapped Potential*, BBC, 1993.

Carnegie, D., *How to Win Friends and Influence People*, Vermilion, London, 1997.
Practical advice on how to get out of a rut and make your life more rewarding

Cava, R., *Dealing with Difficult People*, Piatkus, London, 1990.
Strategies for handing stressful situations and defusing tensions

Childre, D. and Martin, H., *The Heartmath Solution*, Piatkus, London, 1999
EI techniques for reducing stress, making better decisions and living a healthier, happier life.

Collins, B., *Emotional Unavailability*, Contemporary Books, Lincolnwood, IL, 1997.
Recognizing it, understanding it, and avoiding its trap.

Covey, S., *Principle Centered Leadership*, Simon & Schuster, London, 1992.
Working with sound principles.

Covey, S., *The 7 Habits of Highly Successful People*, Simon & Schuster, London, 1999.
Powerful lessons in personal change.

Cox, G., and Dainow, S., *Making the Most of Yourself*, Sheldon Press, London, 1987.
A confidence-building book with practical exercises.

Davidson, J., *The Complete Idiot's Guide to Managing Stress*, Alpha Books, New York, 1997.
Quick and easy techniques for reducing stress.

Downey, M., *Effective Coaching*, Orion, London, 1999.
Tools, models and guidance on how to coach in the workplace.

Field, T., *Bully in Sight*, Success Unlimited, Wantage, 1996.
How to predict, resist, challenge and combat workplace bullying

Goleman, D., *Emotional Intelligence*, Bloomsbury, London, 1996.
Why EQ can matter more than IQ.

Graham, G., *How to Become the Parent You Never Had*, Real Options Press, Blaydon upon Tyne, 1986.
A treatment for extremes of fear, anger and guilt.

Gray, J., *Men are from Mars, Women are from Venus*, Thorsons, London, 1993.
Understand how the opposite sex thinks and improve your communications.

Hillman, C., *Recovery of Your Self Esteem*, Simon & Schuster, New York, 1992.
Techniques for women who want to feel better about themselves.

Horn, S., *Tongue Fu!*, St Martin's Griffin, New York, 1996.
How to deflect, disarm, and defuse any verbal conflict.

Katherine, A., *Boundaries*, Fireside, New York, 1991.
Where you end and others begin.

Laborde, G., *Influencing with Integrity*, Syntony, Palo Alto, CA, 1987.
Using NLP to improve communications and negotiations.

Lewis, L., *Curing Conflict*, Pitman Publishing.

Lindenfield, G., *Managing Anger*, Thorsons, London, 1993.
Explains the effects of anger and offers practical advice on how to prevent it.

Lindenfield, G., *Emotional Confidence*, Thorsons, London, 1997.
How to know your feelings so that you can tame your temperament.

Linkemar, B., *Working with Difficult People*, Marshall Publishing.

Luft, J., *On Human Interaction*, National Press, Palo Alto, CA.
Johari's window explained.

Luft, J., *Group Processes: An Introduction to Group Dynamics*, second edition, National Press, Palo Alto, CA, 1970; third edition, Mayfield Publishing Co,1984.

Murray Parkes, C., *Loss and Bereavement*, Routledge, Harmondsworth, 1991.

Pease, A., *Body Language*, Sheldon Press, London, 1997.
An easy to read book with clear illustrations

Pesuric, A. and Byham, W., The new look in behavior modeling, *Training and Development*, 25–33. In: Consortium for Research on Emotional Intelligence in Organizations, *The Business Case for Emotional Intelligence*, 1996.

Phillips, M., *Emotional Excellence*, Element
A practical guide to self-discovery.

Porras, J. I. and Anderson, B., Improving managerial effectiveness through modeling-based training, Organizational Dynamics, 9, 60–77. In: Consortium for Research on Emotional Intelligence in Organizations, *The Business Case for Emotional Intelligence*, 1981.

Richardson, J., *The Magic of Rapport*, Meta, Capitola, CA, 1987.
How you can gain personal power in any situation using NLP.

Rogers, J., *Influencing Skills*, Video Arts, London, 1999.
A guide to thinking and working smarter.

Savage, E., *Don't Take it Personally: The Art of Dealing with Rejection*, New Harbinger Publications, Oakland, 1997.
A guide to exploring the rejection encountered in family, intimate, office, and social relationships.

Sharpe, R., *Self-Help for Your Anxiety*, Souvenir Press, London, 1990.
How to get an anxiety antidote and stay in control.

Shelton, C., *Achieving Moral Health*, Crossroads, New York, 2000.
An exercise plan for your conscience.

Shoone, R., *Creative Visualisation*, Thorsons, London, 1984.
Visualisations to help you in a range of situations.

Tannen, D., *That's Not What I meant!*, Virago, London, 1992.
How conversational style makes or breaks your relations with others.

Tannen, D., *Talking from 9–5*, Virago, London, 1994.
Women and men at work: language, sex and power

Tannen, D., *You Just Don't Understand*, Virago, London, 1999.
Why we find it difficult to talk to the opposite sex.

Toropov, B., *The Complete Idiot's Guide to Getting Along with Difficult People*, Alpha Books, New York, 1997.
Quick guide for better relationships.

Walther, G. R., *Say What You Mean and Get What You Want*, Piatkus, London, 1993.
A range of techniques on clear communication.

Weisinger, H., *Emotional Intelligence at Work*, Jossey-Bass, San Francisco, CA, 1998.
Using EI to achieve personal ambitions and optimize organizational effectiveness.

Answers to activities

Effective listening activity 7 – Separating viewpoints, p. 126–7

1. (a) SP   (b) SC
2. (a) SC   (b) SP
3. (a) SC   (b) SP
4. (a) SP   (b) SC

Questioning skills activity 1 – Identifying question types, p. 136–7

1. O
2. O
3. C
4. O
5. P, O
6. C
7. S, C
8. O
9. C
10. S, C
11. O
12. P, O
13. O
14. P, O
15. C

Index

Abstract intelligence, 11
Acceptance
   loss and bereavement, 110, 112
Acknowledgement, 218, 219
Active listening, 125, 130, 250
Affiliative leadership, 201, 214–20
Affirmations
   positive, 72, 74, 75, 289, 290
Aggression, 177, 192, 211, 249, 250, 251
   indirect, 88, 249, 171
Amygdala, 18
Anger 32, 85, 102,104, 182,188
   acknowledgement, 84
   in loss and bereavement, 110, 111
   overcoming, 86
Annoyance, 32
Assertiveness, 157–84
   assertive letter, 180
   assertiveness and leadership, 245
   assertive listening, 178
   assertiveness rating, 157
   assertiveness scale, 164
Assumptions, 38, 119, 121, 148
   checking, 148
Authoritative leadership, 201, 202–13
Away from, 220, 278, 279

Behaviour patterns, 22
Beliefs
   and fear, 73
   positive, 74
Belief systems, 84, 164, 182
Bereavement, 109
Berne, Eric, 215
Bitterness, saying goodbye to, 80
Blaming others, 217, 189
Blocked emotions, 23, 24, 25
Body language, 101, 108, 125, 142, 172, 183, 233, 250, 251, 257
   changing, 79

culture and, 169
empathy and, 113
matching, 141, 146, 147
understanding, 168
de Bono, Edward, 207–9
Boundaries, 243
Broken record technique, 167
Buddy, definition of, 5, 6
Bullying, 159, 221, 223

Career development, 297
Change
   handling, 13, 210
   climate for, 211
Checking progress, 130
Choices, 179
Coaching
   leadership style, 254–60
   EI skills, 257
   practical skills, 254
Coercive leadership, 221–34
Concrete intelligence, 11
Confidence, 14, 46
   building, 122
   visualizing confident behaviour, 55
Conflict
   management, 185–93
   skills practice, 189
Conscious competence, 7
Conscious incompetence, 7
Continuous professional development
   261–302
Control
   and trust, 151
   controlling partner, 154
   stop being controlling, 152
Coulds, 69
Counselling, 37, 42, 57, 86, 89, 90, 122
Creative visualization, 287
Creativity, 15, 206, 209, 226

Criticism, 172
   assertive statements for, 176
   giving, 176
   receiving, 172–4

Decision-making, 242
Defensiveness, 170
Delegation, 246
Democratic leadership, 241–53
Demotivators, 281
Denial, 111
Difficult people, 249
Diversity, 232, 233

Emotional hi-jacking, 10, 25
Emotional intelligence
   achievement record, 264
   advantages of, 12–16
   disadvantages of not having, 17
   wheel, 265
Emotional landscape, 24
Emotional unavailability, 21
Emotional landscape, 24
Emotions
   blocking, 24
   controlling, 34
   definitions, 32
   identifying, 39, 41
   labelling, 34
   negative, dealing with, 76
Empathy, 100
   and body language, 113
   and gender, 103
   level, 101
   responding with, 105
   recognising, 103
Excuses, 68

Feedback, 255
   continuous, 299
   encouraging, 227
   learning from, 229
   constructive, 236
Feelings
   reflecting, 113
   recognizing feeling messages, 115
Filters, 116, 142
Flexibility, 206, 209
Forgiveness
   asking for, 149
Four styles of behaviour, 161
Future pace, 78
Fuzzy statements, 134

Generalized
   nouns, 135
   verbs, 135
Giving criticism, 176
Goal setting, 52, 269, 273
Guilt
   overcoming, 89
   pushing aside, 91

Habitual behaviour patterns, 22
Health and well-being, 300
Halo effect, 121

Implied helplessness, 135
Inclusive leader, 232
Indirect aggression, 161, 249
Inner dialogue, 285
Inspiring others, 203
Integrity, 13, 19, 59
   scale, 63
Interest topics, 142

Johari's window, 36

Leader
   inclusive, 232
   inspiring, 197
Learning log, 38
Life goals, 269
Life-Style Appraisal, 267
Limiting beliefs, 73
Listening
   active, 125
   assertive, 178
   effective, 116
   barriers to, 117
   getting people to listen to you, 252
   to the opposite sex, 122
   distractions from, 124
Loss and bereavement, 109
Loss cycle, 110

Maps, own, 24, 43
Martyrdom, banishing, 83
Matching
   body language, 140, 146
   tone of voice, 142, 147
   language, 142
   interest topics, 142
   positive/negative, 143
   towards/away from, 143
   values, 143
Mind maps, 210

Mistakes, learning from, 15
Moaners, 252
Moods, changing, 78
Motivation, 227
Musts, 69

Naming emotions, 9
Needs, unmet, 166
Negotiation skills, 187
Negative beliefs, 72
Negative emotions, dealing with, 76
Neocortex, 18
Networking, 292
Neuro Linguistic Programming, 57
Nimbus effect, 121
No blame culture, 224
Non-verbal leakage, 171

Oughts, 69
Over-controlling behaviour, 151, 152,
    153, 155

Pacesetting leadership style, 235
Parent messages, 48, 161
Passive behaviour, 161, 163, 170, 171
Passive aggressive behaviour, 163
Pause, 134
Personal aspirations, 274
Perspectives, seeing another's, 107
Pleasure and pain, 219
Political support, gaining, 210
Positive beliefs, 71
Positive/negative approach, 143
Positivity log, 43
Praise and acknowledgement, 218
Prejudice
    recognizing, 119
    overcoming, 121
PRONES approach, 144
Put-downs, 162

Questions
    challenging, 134
    closed, 133
    designing effective, 137
    leading, 136
    multiple, 136
    open, 133
    probing, 137
    softeners, 136
    to be avoided, 136
    types, 133
    why, 136

Rapport talk, 123
Reciprocity, 144
Recognizing emotions, 41
Reflecting feelings, 113
Relationship balance, 267
Relaxation technique, 239
Report talk, 122
Respect from others, 13
Responsibility, 67, 189
Re-stimulation, 41
Rewording skills, 127
Risk taking, 209
Role model, 54, 149
Rules, implied, 135
Rules for life, 26

Saying 'no', 182
Self-disclosure, 35
Self-talk
    monitoring, 50
    negative, 50
    positive, 50
Separating viewpoints, 126
Seven characteristics of an
    emotionally intelligent leader,
    198
Six leadership styles, 198
Six Thinking Hats, 207
SMART goals, objectives, 53, 256,
    272
Shoulds, 69
Social intelligence, 11
Soft Skills, 3
Speech, inspiring, 204
Stages of learning, 7
Standards, establishing, 212
Stress, 15
Strokes, 217
    and knowledge of staff, 217
Sulking, 87, 159, 162
Summarizing, 129
Success, celebrating, 301

Three choices, 89, 155
Three steps to personal competence,
    33
Towards/away from, 143, 220
Transactional Analysis, 215
Trust, 151, 156
Two second pause, 87

Unconscious competence, 8
Unconscious incompetence, 7

Values, 143
   and integrity, 61
   conflicting, 186
   discovering, 145
Visualizing confident behaviour, 55
Visualizations, 79, 287

Wants and not-wants, 270

Whingers, 252
Words
   wind up, 270
   that wound, 240
Work/life balance, 275, 276
Vision for change, 210
Voice, matching, 147
Worry, 92

The EI Advantage workshops

Research among high achievers in the workplace shows overwhelmingly that these outstanding people have one thing in common – the skills and attitudes that make them emotionally intelligent. Developing your emotional intelligence brings out the best in yourself and others you interact with, resulting in positivity, motivation, increased performance, and success.

Workshops are designed to support this book and can be tailored for individuals across whole organizations or could be used as a team-building event by training all members of a team together.

The EI Advantage workshops can be run over a period of between one and five days to meet your requirements. A sample outline is shown below.

Leading with Emotional Intelligence

Five-day course programme

Who should attend?

Managers and supervisors who want thorough understanding and development of these vital skills and the ability to pass them on to others.

Key areas covered in this programme

- *What is emotional intelligence?* – recognizing your own emotions, controlling them, and communicating effectively.
- *Demonstrating empathy* – so that you can understand the point of view of your staff, your colleagues and your senior managers.
- *Self-awareness* – understanding yourself, your behaviour and the effects it has on others.
- *Principle-centred leadership* – clarifying your values, transmitting your values to others, coping when values conflict.

- *Emotional control* – how to control feelings of anger, guilt and worry.
- *Self-motivation* – having initiative, being proactive, avoiding constant fire-fighting, overcoming procrastination, improving your ability to focus.
- *Ability to handle change* – feeling comfortable with change, helping others to do the same.
- *Rapport skills* – to give you the best possible choice of successful communication.
- *Listening skills* – making the other person feel valued by giving full attention, reading behind what's said.
- *Conflict management* – using assertion skills to resolve difficult issues.
- *Delegating* – overcoming reluctance to delegate, steps for effective delegation.
- *Flexibility* – developing an approach that looks at all angles before reaching a decision.
- *Valuing and benefiting from diversity* – working with the differences between people to the benefit of all.
- *Bullying* – how to recognize a bully, and how to stop bullying in its tracks.
- *No blame culture* – getting the culture right for creativity and openness.
- *Balancing home / life needs* – to ensure a happy and fulfilled life.
- *Stress management* – using visualization to manage stress as it happens, planning for reduced stress in future. Recognizing and dealing with staff who are stressed.
- *Coaching skills* – a full day on how to coach those problem staff who need to develop their emotional intelligence skills.
- *Action plans* for continuing success.

If you are interested in bringing the EI Advantage to your organization then please contact 01223 890 089 for further information.